Religion and Politics in Europe, the Middle East and North Africa

In the early twenty-first century, it is now clear that religion is increasingly influential in the political realm in ways which call into question the principles and practices of secularism. The Iranian revolution of 1978–9 marked the decisive 'reappearance' of political religion in global politics, highlighting a major development which is the subject of this edited volume.

Addressing a highly salient and timely topic, this book examines the consequences of political interactions involving the state and religious actors in Christian, Muslim and Judaist contexts. Building on research, the basic premise of this text is that religious actors – including Islamist groups, the Roman Catholic and the Orthodox churches – pose various challenges for citizenship, democracy and secularisation in Europe, the Middle East and North Africa (MENA). The key questions on which the book focuses are: Why, how, and when do religious actors seek to influence political outcomes in these regions?

Providing a survey of what is happening in relation to the interaction of religion and politics, both domestically and internationally, this book will be of interest to students and scholars of politics, religion, European and Middle East studies.

Jeffrey Haynes is Associate Head of Department (Research and Postgraduate Studies) and Professor of Politics at London Metropolitan University, UK.

Routledge/ECPR studies in European political science
Edited by Thomas Poguntke
Ruhr University Bochum, Germany on behalf of the European Consortium for Political Research

The Routledge/ECPR Studies in European Political Science series is published in association with the European Consortium for Political Research – the leading organisation concerned with the growth and development of political science in Europe. The series presents high-quality edited volumes on topics at the leading edge of current interest in political science and related fields, with contributions from European scholars and others who have presented work at ECPR workshops or research groups.

Also available from Routledge in association with the ECPR:
Sex Equality Policy in Western Europe, *Edited by Frances Gardiner*; **Democracy and Green Political Thought**, *Edited by Brian Doherty and Marius de Geus*; **The New Politics of Unemployment**, *Edited by Hugh Compston*; **Citizenship, Democracy and Justice in the New Europe** *Edited by Percy B. Lehning and Albert Weale*; **Private Groups and Public Life**, *Edited by Jan W. van Deth*; **The Political Context of Collective Action**, *Edited by Ricca Edmondson*; **Theories of Secession**, *Edited by Percy Lehning*; **Regionalism Across the North/South Divide**, *Edited by Jean Grugel and Wil Hout.*

Religion and Politics in Europe, the Middle East and North Africa

Edited by Jeffrey Haynes

LONDON AND NEW YORK

First published 2010
by Routledge
2 Park Square, Milton Park, Abingdon, Oxon OX14 4RN

Simultaneously published in the USA and Canada
by Routledge
270 Madison Ave, New York, NY 10016

Routledge is an imprint of the Taylor & Francis Group, an informa business

Typeset in Times by Wearset Ltd, Boldon, Tyne and Wear
Printed and bound in Great Britain by TJI Digital, Padstow, Cornwall

British Library Cataloguing in Publication Data
A catalogue record for this book is available from the British Library

Library of Congress Cataloging in Publication Data
Religion and politics in Europe, the Middle East and North Africa / edited by Jeffrey Haynes.
p. cm. – (Routledge/ECPR studies in European political science)
Includes bibliographical references and index.
1. Religion and politics–Europe. 2. Religion and politics–Middle East.
3. Religion and politics–Africa, North. 4. Europe–Politics and government. 5. Middle East–Politics and government. 6. Africa, North–Politics and government. I. Haynes, Jeffrey.
BL65.P7R4279 2009
201'.72--dc22

2009017202

ISBN10: 0-415-47713-1 (hbk)
ISBN10: 0-203-86948-6 (ebk)

ISBN13: 978-0-415-47713-0 (hbk)
ISBN13: 978-0-203-86948-2 (ebk)

Contents

Illustrations

Contributors

Guy Ben-Porat Department of Public Policy and Administration, School of Management, Ben-Gurion University.

Francesco Cavatorta School of Law and Government, Dublin City University.

Luigi Ceccarini LaPolis – Laboratory of Social and Political Studies, University of Urbino 'Carlo Bo'.

Ioannis N. Grigoriadis Department of Political Science, Bilkent University.

Jeffrey Haynes Associate Head of Department (Research and Postgraduate Studies) and Professor of Politics, Department of Law, Governance and International Relations, London Metropolitan University.

Anja Hennig PhD candidate in the field of religion and comparative public policy at the Department of Comparative Politics, Faculty of Cultural Studies, European University Viadrina, Frankfurt/Oder.

Xabier Itçaina Chargé de recherche au CNRS, SPIRIT, Sciences politique, relations internationales, territoire, Sciences Po Bordeaux, Domaine universitaire.

John T. S. Madeley Department of Government, London School of Economics and Political Science.

Michael Minkenberg Max Weber Chair for German and European Studies, Center for European and Mediterranean Studies, New York University.

Işık Özel Sabancı Universitesi, Faculty of Arts and Social Sciences.

Series editor's preface

In the late 1960s and early 1970s, there was a debate in European political science about the political significance of religion or, more precisely, religious orientations. While some scholars argued that it continued to be an important factor in explaining the way people think politically and vote, others maintained that class had become the dominant force. In the wake of the New Left movements, this seemed to be almost self-evident.

However, Europe has changed in many ways since then. First, migration has substantially altered the religious composition of Western European societies, and a significant portion of those who migrated into the affluent Western European states are less secularised than the majority of the citizens of the host countries. Second, with the end of the Cold War, religion reasserted its role as an important factor in some countries of the East–Central Europe, most notably in Poland. And third, religion did not just dwindle away to nothing in the secularised societies of Western Europe. The Christian churches and their collateral organisations remained influential political actors, not least due to the simple fact that their links with the political systems are highly institutionalised in many countries. While the Lutheran Church is virtually a part of the state apparatus in some Scandinavian countries, significant portions of the welfare spending is administered through church-related organisations elsewhere. This institutional anchorage provided the Christian churches with sufficient resilience, and religiously inspired debates and conflicts have remained on the agenda of many European nations.

Furthermore, the debate mentioned above focused exclusively on Western Europe, and the example of migration highlights the fact that the relationship of religion and politics can no longer be fully understood by focusing on one region alone. After all, significant shifts in religious thinking in one region can have far-reaching repercussions elsewhere via its potential impact on groups of migrants.

The current volume is one of the few books that takes a broadly comparative view. By looking at very diverse countries including, among others, Turkey, Morocco, Israel and Spain, attention is drawn to commonalities and differences between very different religious actors and the way they interact with the political system. The book concentrates on three central and interrelated themes, namely citizenship, secularisation and democracy.

While generalisations are very difficult on the basis of such diverse cases, one lesson is obvious: The often bemoaned strong involvement of religious actors in issues of citizenship, secularisation and democracy in the countries of the Middle East and Northern Africa does not constitute a fundamental distinction to European countries. To be sure, the democratic credentials of European religious actors may be less doubtful in most cases than is often true for the Middle East and Northern Africa. Yet the fundamental issue of the boundary between religion and the secular state is by no means fully resolved in European countries. In some countries, there is considerable institutional linkage which guarantees the continued influence of religious actors in state affairs. What is more, such privileges may be extended to the religious organisations of immigrants, as the example of Germany shows, where the state actively promotes the formation of Islamic overarching organisations.

Hence, religious actors have considerable influence in some of the secular European societies and, arguably, the likelihood of conflicts between them and secular states increases with increasing secularisation. As the progress of medical technology is marching on, it gives rise to a range of ethically charged debates where secular states tend to take pragmatic positions which are likely be met with resistance by religious communities. To be sure, issues of the so-called bio-politics, including the regulation of reproductive medicine, stem cell research, euthanasia and cloning, will provide a battleground for ongoing struggles over the boundaries of the secular European state.

Thomas Poguntke, Series Editor
Bochum, May 2009

1 Religion and politics in Europe, the Middle East and North Africa

Jeffrey Haynes

The main premise of this book is that religion has left its assigned place in the private sphere in both Europe and the Middle East and North Africa (MENA), becoming politically active in various ways and with assorted outcomes. The starting point is to note that from the 1980s, 'what was new and became "news" … was the widespread and simultaneous refusal of religions to be restricted to the private sphere' (Casanova 1994: 6). This involves a remodelling and re-assumption of public roles by religious actors – which theories of secularisation had long condemned to social and political marginalisation. This is what the chapters of this book collectively seek to accomplish.

While differing in terms of specific issues that encourage them to act politically, religious entities commonly reject the secular ideals that have long dominated theories of political development in both developed and developing countries, appearing instead as champions of alternative, confessional outlooks, programmes and policies. Seeking to keep faith with what they interpret as divine decree, religious entities[1] typically refuse to render to secular power holders automatic material or moral support. They are concerned with various social, moral and ethical issues, which are nearly always political. They may challenge or undermine both the legitimacy and autonomy of the state's main secular spheres, including government and more widely political society. In addition, many churches and other comparable religious entities no longer restrict themselves to the pastoral care of individual souls. Now, they raise questions about, *inter alia*, interconnections of private and public morality, claims of states and markets to be exempt from extrinsic normative considerations, and modes and concerns of government. What they also have in common is a shared concern for retaining and increasing their social importance. To this end, many religious entities now seek to bypass or elude what they regard as the cumbersome constraints of temporal authority and, as a result, threaten to undermine the latter's constituted political functions. In short, refusing to be condemned to the realm of privatised belief, religion has widely reappeared in the public sphere, thrusting itself into issues of social, moral and ethical – in short, political – contestation.

The aim of this book is to examine the current relationship between selected religious actors and the state in Europe and the MENA. Its title, *Religion and Politics in Europe, the Middle East and North Africa*, seeks to capture what its authors believe are the key analytical issues in this context. Overall, the book is concerned with the outcomes of political interactions involving the state and selected religious entities in various countries in both regions. In Europe, the main religious actors on which we focus are Christian churches, including the Roman Catholic Church, while in the MENA Islamic and Judaist entities are the centre of attention.

The key point, however, is not from which religious tradition individual religious actors come. In both Europe and the MENA, all of the religious entities on which we focus share a desire: to change their societies in directions where what they regard as *religiously acceptable standards of behaviour* are central to public life. Pursuing such objectives, they use a variety of tactics and methods. For example, the Roman Catholic Church in both Italy and Poland and the Jamiat al-Adl wal-Ihsan in Morocco operate at the level of civil society, although their concerns also spill over into the realm of formal politics – that is, political society.

Our examples from Israel and Turkey highlight a different context and form of politics. They focus on what Ben-Porat, following Beck (1994, 1997), describes in his chapter in this collection as 'sub-politics'. This is where struggles over the role of religion in public life are absent from or marginal to the *formal* political arena – that is, political society. Instead of focusing exclusively on formal politics, Beck suggests, scholars need also to pay attention to 'sub-politics'. This is regarded as the 'new' politics, often played out not in the formal political arena but instead promulgated at the level of civil society. Ben-Porat argues that sub-politics rises in prominence when significant numbers of citizens lose all or most of their faith in formal political institutions – including political parties and the state.

In sum, these are the main conclusions of the book:

- In both Europe and the MENA, there is a formal, tripartite division of polities into state, political society and civil society.
- According to (Western) conventional social science wisdom, this arrangement 'should' inevitably lead to religion's permanent privatisation, with a corresponding clear and significant political decline.
- However, in the sphere of religion and politics in both regions, there is widespread 'deprivatisation' of previously privatised religious entities.
- In European and the MENA, religion's deprivatisation is expressed politically in a focus on: citizenship, secularisation and democracy.

Defining religion and politics

Before turning to these issues in detail, it is useful to start by seeking to define two of the key terms used in this book: religion and politics. Defining politics is relatively simple: it is about the pursuit of power, and the struggles involved in trying to wield it authoritatively. Defining religion satisfactorily is notoriously difficult. Sociologists use two main approaches. Religion is either: (1) a system of beliefs and practices related to an ultimate being or beings, or to the supernatural; or (2) that which is sacred in a society, including ultimate inviolate beliefs and practices (Aquaviva 1979). For purposes of wider social science analysis, religion can usefully be approached (1) from the perspective of a body of ideas and outlooks – that is, theology and ethical code; (2) as a type of formal organisation – that is, ecclesiastical 'church' or comparable entity; or (3) as social group – that is, a religious organisation, movement or party. Religion can affect the temporal world in one of two ways: by what it *says* and/or *does*. The former relates to religion's doctrine or theology, the latter to its importance as a social phenomenon and mark of identity, which can function through various modes of institutionalisation, including civil society, political society and religion–state relations.

It is necessary to distinguish between religion expressed at the *individual* and *group* levels: only in the latter is it normally of importance for understanding related political outcomes. From an individualist perspective, we are contemplating religion's *private*, spiritual side, 'a set of symbolic forms and acts which relates man [*sic*] to the ultimate conditions of his existence' (Bellah 1964: 359). But to move into the realm of politics, as we do in this book, is necessarily to be concerned with *group* religiosity, whose claims and pretensions are *always* to some degree political. That is, there is no such thing as a religion without consequences for value systems, including those affecting politics and political outcomes. Group religiosity, like politics, is a matter of collective solidarities and, frequently, of inter-group tension, competition and conflict, with a focus on either shared or disputed images of the sacred, or on cultural and/or class – in short, political – issues. To complicate matters, however, such influences may well operate differently and with 'different temporalities for the same theologically defined religion in different parts of the world' (Moyser 1991: 11).

To try to bring together political and religious spheres in all their varied aspects and then to discern significant patterns and trends is not a simple task. But in attempting it three points are worth emphasising. First, there is something of a distinction to be drawn between looking at the relationship in terms of the impact of religion on politics, and that of politics on religion. At the same time, they are interactive: the effect of one stimulates and is stimulated by the other. In other words, because we are concerned with the ways in which power is exercised in society, and the ways in which religion is involved, the relationship between religion and politics is both dialectical and interactive: each shapes and influences the other. Both causal directions need to be held in view.

Second, religions are creative and constantly changing; consequently their relationships with politics also vary over time. In this book, we are concerned with interactions of religious entities and government over the last few decades.

Finally, as political actors religious entities can only usefully be discussed in terms of specific contexts; in the chapters that comprise this book, it is the relationship with government which forms a common focal point. Yet the model of responses, while derived from and influenced by specific aspects of particular religions, is not necessarily inherent to them. Rather, this is a theoretical construct suggested by much of the literature on state–society relations, built on the understanding that religion's specific role is largely determined by a broader context. The assumption is that there is an essential core element of religion shaping its behaviour in, for example, Christian, Islamic or Judaist societies. The contributions to this book explicitly question this assumption. The focus of many earlier studies was to seek to analyse how existing religious beliefs or affiliations affect political actions. In this book, however, we are equally concerned with the reverse process: how do specific national political contexts affect how and what selected religious entities do politically?

Religion and state in comparative perspective

To understand the political importance of religious actors in Europe and the MENA, it is necessary to comprehend what they say and do in their relationship with the state. I mean something more than 'mere' government when referring to the state. The state is the continuous administrative, legal, bureaucratic and coercive system that attempts not only to manage the various state apparatuses, but in addition to 'structure relations between civil and public power and to structure many crucial relationships within civil and political society' (Stepan 1988: 3). As a result, almost everywhere in the world, apparently regardless of nature of political system and/or level of economic development, states have sought to reduce or at least significantly control religion's political importance – that is, states have wanted to privatise religion, considerably to reduce its political impact. Sometimes, for example in Poland and Italy (Catholicism) and Turkey (Sunni Islam), states will attempt to erect a 'civil religion' arrangement, whereby a certain designated religious format effectively 'functions as the cult of the political community' (Casanova 1994: 58). The declared purpose is to try to create and develop forms of consensual – corporate – religion, claiming to be guided by general, culturally appropriate, specific religious beliefs of intrinsic societal significance (Hallencreutz and Westerlund 1996). In short, to develop 'civil religions' is an attempted strategy to try to avoid social conflicts and promote national coordination and cohesion.

The chapters of this book illustrate that religious actors' relationships with the state in Europe and the MENA are by no means limited to attempts to build civil religions. In fact, in many countries in both regions, relations between religious entities and the state are now not only more visible but also increasingly problematic. Why is this the case? First, it may be that recent increases in religious challenges to the authority of the state are merely transitory reactions in the context of the onward march of secularisation. Second, even if the modern state is particularly vulnerable to legitimation crises, it does not necessarily mean that religion is again becoming *automatically* relevant to state functioning. Third, religion-based challenges to state hegemony have roots in endeavours by the latter to assert a monitoring role vis-à-vis religion, in effect to control it. We can see such a development at three levels: political society, civil society and at the level of the state itself.

Religion and political society

Religion is being liberated from providing slavish legitimacy to secular authority because representatives of religious organisations are now increasingly willing to criticise and challenge the state in various ways in relation to a variety of issues and themes. Yet, even if heightened concern about the state's policies can be held up as evidence of the regeneration of the socio-political power of religion, we still need to ask further questions. The issues are themselves secular and in so far as religious agencies are active in these areas, this is a radical shift of concern from the supernatural, from devotional acts, to what are largely secular goals pursued by secular means. However, a note of caution is in order: we need to bear in mind that when religious interests act as 'pressure groups' – rather than as 'prayer bodies' – they are not necessarily going to be effective. This is because, as Wilson (1992: 202–3) notes, the more secularised a society, the less likely religious organisations will be able to play a politically significant role.

At the level of political society – that is, the arena in which the polity specifically arranges itself for political contestation to gain control over public power and the state apparatus – we can note a range of religious responses that are in part dependent upon the degree of secularisation. These include (1) resistance to the disestablishment and the differentiation of the religious from the secular sphere – the goals of many so-called religious 'fundamentalist' groups; (2) religious groups and confessional political parties' mobilisations and counter-mobilisations against other religions or secular movements and parties; and (3) religious organisations' mobilisation in defence of religious, social and political freedoms – that is, demanding the rule of law and the legal protection of human and civil rights, protecting mobilisation of civil society and/or defending institutionalisation of democratically elected governments. In recent times in pursuit of such goals, we can note Roman Catholic mobilisation in Poland and Spain (Casanova 1994) and activities of Islamic groups in a variety of countries in the MENA, including Morocco and Turkey.

Religion and civil society

Civil society is the arena where various social movements – including, neighbourhood associations, women's groups, religious entities and intellectual currents – join with civic organisations, including, lawyers', journalists', trade unions' and entrepreneurs' associations, to constitute themselves into an ensemble of arrangements to express themselves and seek to advance their collective interests. Sometimes, the concept of *civil* society is used in contrast to *political* society. Unlike the latter, civil society refers to organisations and movements – *not* political parties – formally uninvolved in both the business of government and overt political management. Note, however, that this does not necessarily prevent civil society organisations from sometimes seeking to exert or actually exerting political influence on various matters, including democratic outcomes and the content of national constitutions.

Regarding religion at the level of civil society, one can distinguish between hegemonic civil religions – such as Evangelical Protestantism in nineteenth-century America – and the recent public intervention of religious entities, concerned either with single issues such as anti-abortion or with morally determined views of wider societal development, for example in relation to homosexual rights or appropriate days for shops to open. In trying to influence public policy – without themselves seeking to become political office-holders – religious entities may employ a variety of tactics, including, in no particular order: (1) lobbying the executive apparatus of the state; (2) going to court; (3) building links with political parties; (4) forming alliances with like-minded groups, both secular and/or from other religious traditions; (5) mobilising followers to lobby and/or protest; and (6) working to sensitise public opinion via mass media. The overall point is that religious actors may use a variety of methods to try to achieve their objectives.

Religion and the state

Interactions between the state and religious entities are often referred to as 'church–state' relations. It is useful to point out, however, that one of the difficulties in seeking to survey contemporary church–state relations is that the very concept of *church* is a somewhat parochial, Anglo-American standpoint with relevance only to Christian traditions. It is derived primarily from the context of British establishmentarianism – that is, maintenance of the principle of 'establishment' whereby one church is legally recognised as the only established church. In other words, when we think of church–state relations we may assume a single relationship between two clearly distinct, unitary and solidly but separately institutionalised entities. In this implicit model built into the conceptualisation of the religio-political nexus there is but *one* state and *one* church; both entities' jurisdictional boundaries need to be carefully delineated. Both separation and pluralism must be safeguarded, because it is assumed that the leading church – like the state – will seek institutionalised dominance over rival religious organisations. For its part, the state is expected to respect individual rights even though it is assumed to be inherently disposed towards aggrandisement at the expense of citizens' personal liberty. In sum, the conventional concept of church–state relations is rooted in prevailing Christian conceptions of the power of the state of necessity being constrained by forces in society – including those of religion.

The traditional European-centred Christian perspective is that both church and state have a fair degree of power in relation to each other. Yet when we look at the situation in, for example, Central and Eastern Europe countries under communism from soon after World War II until the early 1990s, there is a different picture. There, states dominated by communist ideology presided over – and rigorously enforced – a monolithic unity, involving institutional interpenetration of political-administrative and religio-ideological orders. In Western Europe, on the other hand, we can see in most countries a declining regional position over time for Christian churches. In France, for example, as a result of the French Revolution, the demographically dominant Catholic Church placed itself on the wrong side of the ideological divide; the church as a result lost a great deal of its power, privilege and moral authority. By the mid-twentieth century, the church in France was greatly lacking in political clout, with declining societal relevance (Martin 1978: 16). The overall point is that in contemporary Europe, state prevails over church, while the political saliency of church–state issues is variable although overall declining in importance as secularisation increases.

Expanding the problem of church–state relations to non-Christian contexts necessitates some preliminary conceptual clarifications – not least because the very idea of a prevailing state–church dichotomy is culture-bound. As already noted, *church* is a Christian institution, while the modern understanding of *state* is deeply rooted in the post-Reformation European political experience. In their specific cultural setting and social significance, the tension and the debate over the church–state relationship are uniquely Western phenomena, present in the ambivalent dialectic of 'render therefore unto Caesar the things which be Caesar's and unto God the things which be God's' (Luke 21: 25). Overloaded with Western cultural history, these two concepts cannot easily be translated into non-Christian terminologies.

The differences between Christian conceptions of state and church and those of other world religions are well illustrated by reference to Islam. In the Muslim tradition, mosque is not church. The closest Islamic approximation to 'state' – *dawa* – means, as a concept, either a ruler's dynasty or his administration (Vatikiotis 1987: 36). Only with the specific Durkheimian stipulation of *church* as the generic concept for *moral community*, *priest* for the *custodians of the sacred law*, and *state* for *political community* can we comfortably use these concepts in Islamic and other non-Christian contexts. On the theological level, the command–obedience nexus that constitutes the Islamic definition of authority is not demarcated by conceptual categories of religion and politics. Life as a physical reality is an expression of divine will and authority (*qudrah'*). There is no validity in separating the matters of piety from those of the polity; both are divinely ordained. Yet although both religious and political authorities are legitimated Islamically, they invariably constitute two independent social institutions. They do, however, regularly interact with each other (Dabashi 1987: 183).

The overall point is that tensions widely exist between secular power and religious organisations in the modern world. It is often the case in both Europe and the MENA that religious entities, regardless of their religious persuasion, work towards reducing the ability of the state to sideline them. They do this by aiming to reverse religious privatisation, a course of action which impacts on a variety of political and social concerns.

Religious deprivatisation and political change

Two phenomena are simultaneously taking place in Europe. First, there is said to be an *increase* in various forms of spirituality and religiosity, although this also implies fragmentation and declining societal clout of hitherto leading churches across the region (Davie 2000). The increase in spirituality and religiosity are manifested primarily in various 'new' religious and spiritual phenomena, including manifestations of 'New Age' spirituality; 'foreign', 'exotic' Eastern religions, including Hare Krishna; 'televangelism'; renewed interest in astrology; and 'new' sects, such as the Scientologists. Note, however, that such religious entities, as Casanova (1994: 5) points out, are 'not particularly relevant for the social sciences or for the self-understanding of modernity', because they do not present 'major problems of interpretation ... They fit within expectations and can be interpreted within the framework of established theories of secularization'. The point is that they are *normal* phenomena. They are examples of *private* religion. They do not individually or collectively question or challenge the extant arrangements of society, including political and social structures. Indeed, such religious phenomena are *apolitical*; and 'all' they really show is that many people are interested in spiritual issues and sometimes they involve new expressions. In addition, in many European Catholic countries – for example, Italy, Poland and Spain – the Catholic Church is losing moral appeal for many people, especially among the young (Hooper 1996; also see the chapters by Ceccarini and Hennig in this collection). In sum, the multiplicity of extant religious phenomena in Europe belies the idea of an inexorable, popular loss of interest in religious meaning – even in apparently highly secular countries. In addition, innovative religious forms appear to be increasing their appeal, often at the expense of traditional religions. But from a *political* perspective new religions are not of importance.

Second, and most importantly for this book, not only Christian churches but also religious entities in Muslim countries in the MENA – our main examples in this book are provided by Cavatorta (Morocco) and Ozel (Turkey), and Judaist entities in Israel (Ben-Porat) – now openly seek to articulate viewpoints on a variety of political and social issues, more readily and openly than in the past. Such religious entities typically resist state attempts to sideline them.

Three questions are central in seeking to account for religion's current political impact. First, *why* should religious organisations seek to become actors with political goals? In this book, contributors contend that this occurs when religious entities feel that change is necessary and that the state is not well equipped to oversee and lead such changes, not least because the solutions it seeks are secular ones and they do not chime well with religious interpretations. Second, how *widespread* is the phenomenon? Our starting assumption is that it is extensive, although the following chapters indicate that it is not uniform in its implications. Third, what are the *political consequences* of religion's intervention? The short answer is that they are variable, as the following chapters indicate. For example, sometimes religion appears to have a pivotal influence on political outcomes – for example, the role of the Roman Catholic Church in Poland in relation to democratisation in the 1980s. Later, however, as Hennig's chapter covering Poland and Ceccarini's focusing on Italy show, such influence can wane. Elsewhere, however, as Cavatorta shows in relation to Islamists in

Morocco, Ozel regarding Islamic movements in Turkey, and Ben-Porat looking at Jewish fundamentalists in Israel, outcomes can be unexpected and variable, sometimes expressed at the level of 'sub-politics'.

Citizenship, secularisation and democracy

Citizenship

What is citizenship? To belong to a state in the modern world is necessarily to engage with nationally defined rules of citizenship. Membership of a state is typically regulated by the notion of citizenship. In addition, in recent years the concept of citizenship has expanded to include various ideas, including: 'multicultural' and 'post-national' citizenship (see Kymlicka 1995; Soysal 1994). Ideas of transnational or group rights of citizenship are understood in some religious traditions: for example, in the Muslim world the concept of the *umma* (transnational Muslim community). In addition, the European Union (EU) has tentatively established its own idea of EU citizenship which, as Madeley shows in his chapter in this volume, has solidly Christian Democratic foundations and credentials. However, as Minkenberg points out in his contribution, despite such developments, neither transnational citizenship (*umma*) nor regional citizenship (EU) nor any other forms of what might be called post-national citizenship have replaced *national* citizenship; nor is there any indication that such a development might occur in the near future. In other words, *individual* rights and *nation*-states are the fundaments of membership rules and citizenship in individual countries in Europe.

Over time, national citizenship has effectively replaced the logic of group rights, involving other forms of membership rules in larger communities, often beyond the territorial state. At least in the West, the very concept of citizenship has religious – actually, Christian – roots. This is because, in the pre-modern past, citizenship was closely connected to the membership of a religious (Christian) community. Modern citizenship can be seen as one of the results of secularisation. On the other hand, up to the present time, national identity and the logic – if not code – of nationality are tied in many European countries to cultural or even in some cases (for example, Poland, Greece and Ireland) to explicitly religious criteria: membership of a particular Christian denomination (see Hennig's and Grigoriadis' chapters in this volume). In his chapter, Minkenberg discusses the argument relating to the role of 'cultural idioms' for citizenship, linked to religious components of cultural and national identities. Finally, the current debates of Muslim integration in Western democracies, examined by Minkenberg in his chapter in this collection, or Turkey's status as a membership candidate for the EU, alluded to by Ozel in her chapter, offer compelling evidence that religious arguments draw distinct dividing lines of access and membership.

On the other hand, in the field of comparative politics very few studies have explicitly asked what role religion plays in the politics of immigration and the functioning of multicultural societies. Those that do often focus on the religious background of migrants rather than that of the host society and polity. For Minkenberg there is a new, post-9/11 era of major conflict, on the one hand focused on debates about religious symbols in public places and, on the other, informed by the question of the compatibility of Islam and democracy in both Europe and the MENA. His chapter commences with an important point: the increased significance of religion in the politics of Western democracies, linked to two simultaneous processes: pluralism and globalisation. Both developments are significantly related to increasing global migration. He focuses on what he calls 'a typology of nationality codes' in 19, mainly European, Western democracies (he also refers to three non-European but Western states in his chapter: Australia, Canada, the United States of America). Minkenberg understands religion in four respects – confessional legacy, individual religiosity, institutional actors and Christian parties. Minkenberg examines what role religion plays in informing citizenship policies in the 19 countries. He argues that the interplay of nation building, religious traditions and church–state relations brings religion back into this highly secular policy domain.

Grigoriadis' chapter addresses what he calls the 'bifurcated' role that the Orthodox Church plays in Greek–Turkish relations, an issue closely related to the significant issue of citizenship in Greece. Greek–Turkish relations have been burdened by long-running political disputes, covering various issues, from Cyprus to the Aegean, involving minority and sovereignty disputes. Through historical factors, which led to the formation of the Greek nation-state and the emergence of the Autocephalous Church of Greece, two religious actors appeared for Orthodox Greeks. The Ecumenical Patriarchate and the Church of Greece often competed against each other and maintained a significant influence on Greek–Turkish relations. Yet their role has become increasingly bifurcated. This became clear during the latest rapprochement effort between Greece and Turkey. While the Church of Greece generally takes positions which do not contribute to the peaceful resolution of Greek–Turkish disputes and embed existing prejudices, the Istanbul-based Ecumenical Patriarchate follows a distinctively different line. Although being itself the victim of Turkish anti-minority policies, it actively promotes Greek–Turkish cooperation and the peaceful resolution of existing disputes and has earned the respect of international political and religious leaders, being a primary example of religious soft power.

Grigoriadis seeks possible explanations for this ambivalence. He investigates the status of state–church relations in Greece, the role of leadership as well as socio-political conditions in both Greece and Turkey. Grigoriadis also explores the links between religion and nationalism, and within this context the religious connotation of citizenship. He argues that nationalism has often instrumentalised religion to achieve mass mobilisation. He investigates under what conditions religious institutions can act at a supranational level, disseminate social values and norms promoting peace, toleration and mutual understanding and thus increase their soft power at the international level.

Secularisation

It was once believed to be axiomatic that modernisation inevitably leads to religious privatisation and secularisation. As a result, there would be a fundamental global decline in religion's social and political importance. This was believed to be the case regardless of religious tradition or form of political power dominant in the context in which religion found itself. The 1979 revolution in Iran posed fundamental questions in relation to this conventional wisdom. Contemporaneously, the Roman Catholic Church began to play an increasingly important role in relation to democratisation in Central and Eastern Europe, Africa, East Asia and Latin America. These two developments collectively emphasised not only that modernisation does not always leads to secularisation but also that religion can sometimes play a fundamental role in issues of political representation and legitimacy. Contrary to the secularisation theory, there has been a widespread – some say global – resurgence of religion, often as a political actor in numerous countries. This has involved various religious traditions. Overall, it emphasises not only that there is more than one relevant interpretation of modernisation but also that religion can and does play a role in political changes, even in parts of the world, including Europe, that have been long regarded as inevitably secularising.

Ben-Porat investigates the relationship between secularisation and politics in Israel. Against the predictions of the secularisation paradigm that forecast the demise of religion and its irrelevance for public life, religion is still highly significant in Israel; for many people it plays a central role in both life and politics. Casanova (1994) describes a process of deprivatisation of religion that refuses to be relegated to the margins of society and emerges instead as a political force to be reckoned with. The consequence is that religious entities may clash with secularising trends to protect their preferred religiously oriented way of life (Haynes 2006). Israel is home to an often tense political arena with a growing schism between two poles separated by values and moving towards an inevitable clash over the boundaries of state and society. However, the question is not primarily in what ways and in what contexts religion and secularism are advancing or declining, but rather in what realms these dynamics operate.

Israel is a highly volatile example of a world trend of a secular–religious clash with, on the one hand, a territorial debate laden with religious sentiments and, on the other hand, a secularising public sphere with a religious resurgence. Two major developments underscore these factors. The first is the overlap between religiosity/secularity and hawkish/dovish perceptions that turns the question of the state of Israel's future borders into a quasi-religious debate. The second development is the erosion of what are referred to as 'status quo' church–state arrangements, which have defined the role of religion in public life since the creation of the state of Israel in 1948. These have included regulation of marriage and the observation of the Sabbath as a day of rest. In addition, the Israeli polity is supposedly aligned across the secular–religious divide with a deep rift in the middle and a growing politicisation of religion. The assassination of Prime

Minister Yitzhak Rabin in 1995 was probably – so far – the high (or low) point of the religious–secular divide in Israel. Rabin's assassination followed a long hate campaign in which his government's decision to offer territory for peace was described by some Israelis as a fundamental betrayal of Jewish values. The assassination, which was carried out by a young religious student, seemed to worsen further deteriorating secular–religion relations.

Ben-Porat argues that the two issues, territoriality and status quo, while related in many respects, actually move in opposite directions. The territorial question (often described as 'peace for land') is where religion and politics became strongly linked from the 1970s. This change involved what Ben-Porat calls the 'religious national camp', previously passive in relation to high politics, which began nevertheless to perceive itself as a leader and standard bearer of 'true' Zionism. Against the desire of the other – mostly secular – camp to compromise occupied territories for peace, this became the central dividing line of Israel politics. Status quo issues, the second concern, were earlier at the centre of political debate and negotiations over the shape and direction of the public sphere. Erosion of these agreements led, however, not to politicised struggles but rather to a de-politicisation and 'alternative' politics or, as Ben-Porat terms it, 'sub-politics'.

Ben-Porat begins his chapter with an examination of theoretical connections between religion and politics. He goes on to describe the Israeli historical secular–religious *modus vivendi* (the 'status quo') and its recent collapse. The third – empirical – part of his chapter describes the simultaneous occurrence of politicisation and de-politicisation in Israel. It examines the strong links that have developed between religion and politics on the issue of the future of the (occupied) territories and, second, investigates other issues of religious–secular debate played out at the level of sub-politics: Sabbath, non-kosher meat, and marriage. He concludes by stating that the religious–secular struggle in Israel is both multi-dimensional and partly de-politicised.

Moving from Israel to the Basque Country of southern France and northern Spain, Itçaina focuses on the Basque conflict and a consequential interaction between nationalism and democracy. He notes that this conflict is one of the last violent ethno-territorial struggles in Western Europe. The political process initiated by the ceasefire announced by ETA in March 2006 raised hopes for a peaceful and permanent solution – but this optimism came to an abrupt end nine months later, with the Madrid bomb attacks on 30 December 2006. Earlier than this, from the late 1980s, pro-peace associations from civil society had joined forces and fought against persistent violence, both in the Spanish and, to a lesser extent, in the French Basque Country. Over time, the Roman Catholic Church has played a prominent role in these new forms of pro-peace action.

Itçaina approaches the church's activism from three complementary perspectives. First, the Catholic Church has specific features that differentiate it from other civil society actors. The church has long buttressed its actions by a theological and ideological principle of subsidiarity conducive to popular mediation and peace-keeping initiatives. Even in the secularised Basque society, or perhaps *thanks to* this secularisation, the Catholic Church is still favourably thought of by a large majority of the population, who see it as both deeply immersed in local reality and uninvolved in the political debate. From an empirical perspective, the church acts as a mediator, in both meanings of the word. As a generalist (*médiateur généraliste*) the mediator tries to bring together institutional milieus which do not share the same knowledge or the same representations (the cognitive dimension of mediation). As a broker (*médiateur courtier*) the mediator is looking for acceptable solutions between very different groups which have to find an interest in cooperating while pursuing different aims and defending different interests (the strategic dimension of mediation). The Catholic Church has played this double role in the Basque Country until now, achieving better results in terms of cognitive mediation than in strategic mediation.

The Catholic Church has also revealed its own internal pluralism. First, as a religious organisation, the Catholic Church has maintained a double relation with the public authorities, acting both as a *cause group*, rallying around general causes, and a *sectional group* mobilised for its own interests. The church has thus been perceived by the public authorities both as an actor for the defence of peace and dialogue, and as a negotiator on issues such as education, social services, public regulation of religion, and so on. The church in the Basque Country has also been fraught with internal fragmentation – opposition between the Basque bishops and the rest of the Spanish Episcopal Conference, and internal cleavage within the Basque–Navarre clergy. In that respect, the various positions of the Spanish Episcopal Conference on the Basque question have to be carefully analysed, since they have evolved according to changing equilibriums within the church. Some sectors of the church have assumed this impossible neutrality by tentatively reducing the scope of the conflict.

Finally, the empirical analysis of the role played by the Catholic Church raises more general questions about the interaction between Catholicism, the public sphere and democracy in an increasingly secular region: Southern Europe. The political involvement of the church is also somewhat linked to its relativist approach to the majority-based, constitutionalist conception of democracy, as it advocates a deliberative conception of democracy that would seek to better defend the rights of the minority. This suggests that, for the church, the very nature of a norm may, under certain circumstances, be more important than the way it has been adopted. The point is that a legal norm will lack legitimacy when or if there is no societal consensus on its values even if the law is endorsed by the majority. Such a conception may lead either to a depoliticised conception of collective identities or, conversely, to highly politicised commitments and to new forms of religious regulation of politics. In the Basque Country such issues are played out in the context of a swiftly secularising public realm.

In his chapter, Madeley turns attention to the topic of European integration, and the role of secularisation in its realisation. He argues that since the end of the Second World War, the politics surrounding the project of European integration has provided a context in which various religious entities – including, individuals, groups and institutions – have all played important roles. During this time, Madeley argues that Europe has experienced not so much a rise in the influence exerted by religious forces in politics as a rise in the salience of religious or religion-related issues, regardless of outcome. This indicates not so much a clear-cut resurgence of the religious factor in the region as a heightened incidence of controversies in which religious groups and individuals have become involved – a level of incidence which has only been amplified by a growing resistance to religious influence of secular liberals. In short, increased salience of religion-related issues might as much reflect struggles to neutralise as to maximise religious influences in politics.

Madeley illustrates this contention in relation to secularisation in the context of European integration. He examines the involvement of religious–political actors (both individual and collective) in the launching of the political project of European integration after the Second World War. He also focuses on the post-1992 period, during which the European Union's range extended both northwards and eastwards, increasing from fifteen to twenty-seven members. He argues that the impact of religious–political actors, in particular political parties of religious inspiration which ranged themselves in support or opposition to the project, varied markedly between those two time periods in both degree and direction. In attempting to understand these variations, three explanatory hypotheses are briefly reviewed which suggest that one of the reasons for the hypothesised rise in secular(ist) resistance to religious influences of recent years is associated with the revival of intra- as well as inter-confessional differences among the religious themselves. In short, it would appear that, instead of religious voices having greater impact in Europe recently than they had in the 1945 to 1965 period, the issue is now more and more whether religious voices – themselves progressively seen as discordant and conflicting – should have a significant role in public affairs at all.

Democracy

There are many examples of religion's recent significant impact on democratic outcomes. For example, there was the leading role of the Roman Catholic Church in the 'third wave of democracy' from the mid-1970s until the late 1990s. This had a fundamental political effect in Southern and Eastern Europe, Latin America and Africa. There was also the contemporaneous rise of the Christian Right in the United States of America, and its considerable impact on the electoral fortunes of both the Republican Party and the Democratic Party. Add to this the widespread growth of Islamist movements across the Muslim world, with significant ramifications for electoral outcomes in various countries, including Algeria, Egypt, Morocco, electoral successes for the Bharatiya Janata Party in India, and substantial political influence over time for various 'Jewish fundamentalist' political parties in Israel, and we have clear evidence of religion's recent democratic importance.

Ozel identifies and examines the rise of political Islam in Turkey, which occurred in the context of the country's post-1983 democratisation. She is particularly interested in a linked phenomenon in Turkey which has attracted relatively little scholarly attention: connections between political Islam, so-called 'Islamic economics' and transnational Islamist business networks. She explains that transnational networks in many ways symbolise the process of globalisation and its pervasive forces that foster sometimes puzzling linkages across a broad range of actors and spheres. Religion-based networks are no exceptions in this overarching trend.

She begins by highlighting the re-invention of what she calls *homo Islamicus* within the realm of Islamic economics that epitomises an ideational legitimacy in line with dominant discourses of neoliberalism. Islamic finance institutions, on the other hand, facilitate the workings of Islamic economics through legitimate instruments appropriate for Islam's interest-opposing principles. In her study, she focuses on Islamic business in Turkey and its linkages with the recent upsurge of political Islam. Examining transnational and national Islamic business networks; expansion of Islamic finance and the ideational factors such as the so-called 'quiet Islamic Reformation' or 'Islamic Calvinism' said to be taking place in Turkey, her chapter sheds significant light on the recent revival of entrepreneurship, usually explained by 'green capital' and so-called 'Islamic Calvinism'.

Ozel analyses the expansion of Islamic capital beginning from the 1980s, and examines connections between such expansion and the unprecedented recent rise of political Islam in Turkey. Overall, her study focuses on understanding intertwined processes: the rise of transnational Islamist networks of business which facilitate the spread of new ideas; and connections between these networks and political Islam in Turkey. She seeks to identify and examine the bases of the alleged connections between Islamist networks and revival of entrepreneurship, along with the role of the alleged ideational reformation, referred to as 'Islamic Calvinism'. To this end, she examines not only the political outcomes of the activities of religious networks, but also the economic ones. She contends that these are the locales where such networks have recently expanded, helping to explain an otherwise puzzling economic revival. Exploring such linkages, Ozel's study is a major contribution to the analysis of Turkey's recent revival in 'Islamic' entrepreneurship and political Islam.

Cavatorta's chapter focuses on politics and political change in Morocco, in the context of that country's hesitant democratisation process. He notes that, in general, the issue of Islamist parties in the MENA region is very controversial. On the one hand, Islamist movements that attempt to play a full role in political society are typically treated with considerable suspicion by both domestic governments and international actors, including the European Union and the government of the USA. On the other hand, there is also often recognition on the part of such actors that *without* inclusion of Islamists in a regenerated political system democratisation is very unlikely to occur. In short, some politicians and policymakers see political Islam as a potential pro-democracy resource, while others see it as the unequivocal enemy of democracy.

However, as Cavatorta emphasises, Islamist groups can differ considerably from each other in terms of ideological differences and methods of action.

Broadly speaking, Cavatorta notes three types of radical Islamist groups in the MENA. First, there are movements such as Hamas (Palestine) and Hezbullah (Lebanon) which are in equal part social movement, political party and national liberation movement. Second, there are the *salafi* movements, willing to use violent means in order to achieve their political objectives. Examples include: the Algerian Al-Qaeda in the Maghreb. The third group comprises all Islamist movements that do not employ violence, while combining political party activities with provision of social services, in line with the ethos of the Muslim Brotherhood. While examinations of movements belonging to the first two categories have been carried out, much greater attention has been paid to the third category: mainstream Islamist parties, with involvement in both political and institutional changes in individual countries. Such actors, *rhetorically* committed to peaceful democratisation, have attracted scholarly attention not least because they are seen alternatively as potential pro-democracy actors or as prospective spoilers of democratisation.

Cavatorta rejects the analytical approach whereby it is thought possible to determine a priori the true ethos of a political actor by analysing their documents, statements, organisational structure and past behaviour. The problem is that, if interpreted in isolation from the surrounding institutional setting and in a political vacuum, a scholar's preconceptions will inform interpretations of what political actors do and seek to accomplish. Cavatorta's chapter examines, in its institutional and political environment, the Jamiat al-Adl wal-Ihsan in Morocco. He sets out to explain why al-Adl refuses both to participate in Morocco's political system *and* to undertake radical – that is, violent – actions in pursuit of regime change. Cavatorta contends that it is only by looking at the dynamic interactions that such a movement has with the other relevant actors in the system and the institutions of the Moroccan political system that it is possible to grasp fully not only the popular appeal of the movement, but also the strategic choices it makes over time. The case of al-Adl is particularly interesting because it allows the possibility of examining how a prominent Islamist movement manages the balance between revolution and participation in an authoritarian context while retaining considerable popularity among ordinary Moroccans.

Moving from Morocco to Italy, Ceccarini is concerned with the democratic involvement of the Roman Catholic Church, specifically its involvement in the emergent issue of *biopolitics*. The church now plays a different role in Italian politics compared to the past. From the 1940s until the early 1990s, the church was represented politically by the Christian Democratic party (DC). Delegation and collateralism characterised this phase. In the early 1990s, following the demise of the First Republic and the collapse of the DC, the church embarked on a new public presence, with a revised political representation strategy. The church moved beyond the collateralism strategy and became an 'extra-parliamentarian' actor (Magister 2001). Since then, the church has followed a strategy of *neutrality* from political parties and from political alliances, by means of the Italian Episcopal Conference (CEI), led by Cardinal Ruini. It has functioned instead as a lobby group, without any intermediary. In other words,

Ceccarini argues, the church's political representation has moved 'from the party to the pulpit'.

Over the last few years, however, in a shift reminiscent of what Ben-Porat notes in relation to Israel and Hennig notes regarding Poland, the political scene in Italy has been complicated by the public emergence of ethical and moral issues. In Italy, what is known as *biopolitics* – that is, 'life as moral value' – is now at the core of the political agenda, a new frontier in relation to social and political questions. Various issues – including, stem cell research, medically assisted fertilisation, abortion, the RU486 pill, 'biological will', euthanasia, cloning, and various other social issues concerning the family – have become politically significant, with various, especially Catholic, legislators seeking to influence debate and outcomes. The result is that both ethical bipolarism and political bipolarism have become interwoven in public debate. The ensuing confrontation among political and religious actors has become very heated. Over the last few years, Ceccarini explains, the Catholic Church has played a direct role in this area, not only taking a public stand but also trying to influence political decision-making and outcomes. In other words, it has sought to act as a *political entrepreneur*, mobilising resources and taking advantage of Italy's (open) windows of political opportunity.

Hennig focuses in her chapter on the political activities of the Catholic Church in Poland, a country where around 95 per cent of the population regard themselves as Catholic. Like Ceccarini, she is concerned with the church's political position in relation to moral and ethical issues; in Poland, the issues are heavily contextualised and influenced by recent democratisation. She notes that Poland – like Italy – is one of many European societies that are now affected by moral conflicts. As in Israel, this is a context where secular and religious worldviews collide. This implies that, in Poland, despite continuing processes of individual detachment from traditional religion, both the secular state and parts of the society have to accept the prevalence of religious communities and the consequential emergence of religion-based arguments on political and democratic agendas.

She observes that, more generally, under conditions of global biotechnological development and European efforts to harmonise policy regulations, national policies not only in Poland but in Europe more generally are now significantly influenced by moral questions. While concerns about the legalisation of genetic engineering or euthanasia pose ethical problems to all liberal democracies, as already noted in the case of Italy, the quest for a liberal abortion regime or a legal status for homosexual partnerships is particularly salient in a predominantly Catholic, still democratising society, such as Poland.

Hennig explains that a political voice for the church is not a new phenomenon in Poland. The Catholic Church has consistently sought to defend its interests publicly, especially in the nearly two decades since the collapse of communism. However, as she notes, the Catholic landscape in Poland is not monolithic. Poles no longer unthinkingly accept the church's public and political role; half of Poles think that the Catholic Church should in general be less influential on life in

Poland. However, while Hennig examines the church's overall relationship with society, public religion and politics in Poland, she also goes beyond this issue to analyse the country's wider interaction between societal actors, religion and public policy in the course of a 'moral conflict'. This is the context within which gay, lesbian and feminist interest groups have become increasingly high profile in recent years, demanding equal rights while opposing the position of the Catholic Church and its value-based political position. This conflict focuses on the public appearance of gays and lesbians in Poland and their campaign for equal rights.

Finally, Hennig traces the political engagement of homosexual and left-wing liberal actors and the church's response since the early 2000s. She seeks to give an insight into the dynamics of this issue, in terms of agenda-setting, policy implementation and policy output.

Note

1 A religious entity is any actor encouraged to action by religious faith. Such actors include: churches and comparable religious organisations; social movements whose main motivating factor is religious belief; and political parties, whose ideology is identifiably religious.

Bibliography

Aquaviva, S. (1979) *The Decline of the Sacred in Industrial Society*, Oxford: Blackwell.

Beck, U. (1994) 'The Reinvention of Politics', in U. Beck, S. Lash and A. Giddens, *Reflexive Modernization: Politics, Tradition and Aesthetics in the Modern Social Order*, Stanford, CA: Stanford University Press, pp. 1–26.

Beck, U. (1997) 'Subpolitics', *Organization & Environment*, 10, 1, pp. 52–65.

Bellah, R. (1964) 'Religious Evolution', *American Sociological Review*, 29, pp. 358–74.

Casanova, J. (1994) *Public Religions in the Modern World*, Chicago and London: University of Chicago Press.

Dabashi, H. (1987) 'Symbiosis of Religious and Political Authorities in Islam', in T. Robbins and R. Robertson (eds), *Church–State Relations*, New Brunswick, NJ, and London: Transaction Books, pp. 183–203.

Davie, G. (2000) *Religions in Modern Europe*, Oxford: Oxford University Press.

Hallencreutz, C. and Westerlund, D. (1996) 'Anti-secularist Policies of Religion', in D. Westerlund (ed.), *Questioning the Secular State. The Worldwide Resurgence of Religion in Politics*, London: Hurst, pp. 1–23.

Haynes, J. (ed.) (2006) *The Politics of Religion: A Survey*, London: Routledge.

Hooper, J. (1996) 'John Paul's Critical Mass', *Observer* (London), 6 April.

Kymlicka, W. (1995) *Multicultural Citizenship*, Oxford: Oxford University Press.

Magister, S. (2001) *Chiesa extraparlamentare*, Naples: L'ancora del mediterraneo.

Martin, D. (1978) *A General Theory of Secularization*, Oxford: Basil Blackwell.

Moyser, G. (1991) 'Politics and Religion in the Modern World: An Overview', in G. Moyser (ed.), *Politics and Religion in the Modern World*, London: Routledge, pp. 1–27.

Soysal, Y. (1994) *Limits of Citizenship. Migrants and Postnational Membership in Europe*, Chicago and London: University of Chicago Press.

Stepan, A. (1988) *Rethinking Military Politics. Brazil and the Southern Cone*, Princeton, NJ: Princeton University Press.

Vatikiotis, P. J. (1987) *Islam and the State*, London: Routledge.

Wilson, B. (1982) *Religion in Sociological Perspective*, Oxford: Oxford University Press.

Part I
Citizenship

2 Church, state and the politics of citizenship

A comparative study of 19 Western democracies

Michael Minkenberg

Introduction

In the modern world, membership in a territorial state is usually regulated by nationally defined rules of citizenship. In some of the literature on citizenship, a trend is detected towards – or a concept is prescribed in terms of – some version of 'multicultural' or 'post-national' citizenship (see Kymlicka 1995; Soysal 1994). But while layers of transnational or group rights of citizenship are introduced and the European Union (EU) established its own Union citizenship, the fact remains that individual rights and nation-states are still the cornerstones of membership rules in nation-states – neither group rights nor EU or other forms of trans- or post-national citizenship are in the process of – or meant to be – replacing *national* citizenship (see Joppke 1999; Koslowski 2000; Thränhardt 2003).

However, national citizenship itself has effectively replaced other forms of membership rules in larger communities or the territorial state which were tied to the logic of group rights. As Tomas Hammar reminds us, the very concept of citizenship has religious roots, as in the pre-modern past it was closely connected to religion, i.e. membership in a religious community (Hammar 1990: 49–51). Hence, modern citizenship can be seen as one of the results of secularisation.[1] But until today, in many countries national identity and the logic – if not code – of nationality are tied to cultural and in some cases (e.g. Poland, Ireland, Greece) explicitly religious criteria (see Bruce 2003; Mavrogordatos 2003). The well-known argument by Rogers Brubaker (1992) about the role of 'cultural idioms' for citizenship can be linked to religious components of cultural and national identities. Finally, the current debates of Muslim integration in Western democracies or Turkey's status as a membership candidate for the EU most vividly illustrate how religious arguments draw distinct dividing lines of access and membership. Yet very few studies in the field of comparative politics ask what role religion plays in the politics of immigration and the functioning of multicultural societies, and if they do, they tend to focus on the religious background of migrants rather than that of the host society and polity.

This chapter attempts a more systematic analysis of the relationship between religious legacies of receiving countries of immigration and the politics of citizenship. Citizenship here is defined not in the general sense of certain rights enjoyed by the status of a 'citizen', along with more universal rights, but in a stricter sense of formal membership rules which determine who is a member of a nation-state, i.e. nationality. In general we should expect religious legacies to somehow inform these modern concepts of membership in political communities. Hence, one of the central questions of this chapter is: does variation in the politics of citizenship correlate with cultural and religious variations, and to what extent can it be attributed to these differences within the world of Western democracies? One might hypothesise that cultural heritage in Western democracies (i.e. Catholicism versus Protestantism) is a significant predictor for variation in these policies, as has been found for other policy areas as well (Castles 1998; see also below). This, however, needs to be tested in comparison with other dimensions of the religious factor, in particular the institutional arrangement of church–state relationship and official recognition of organised religion, the degree of secularisation and also the existence and importance of religiously oriented political parties. For example, one recent study on state accommodation of Muslim religious practices in three Western European countries (the UK, France, Germany) argues that the inherited particularities of church–state relations can better explain a nation's approach to Islam and the type of religious demands that Muslims have made than can the political resources of the Muslim communities, the political opportunity structures available to them or ideological factors such as a nation's ideas on citizenship and nationality (Fetzer/Soper 2005). Other studies emphasise the importance of a Christian Democratic model of politics and policies (van Kersbergen 1995) which, by implication, means that a vigorous role of Christian Democratic parties in a nation's politics should also affect the politics of citizenship.

In light of this, the chapter tries to 'map' the patterns of religion with regard to the politics of citizenship and, having established the general patterns, asks which role particular religious factors play in shaping them. The chapter is built on the conceptual framework developed elsewhere with regard to 19 Western democracies, a group of countries characterised by a certain size (i.e. certain levels of internal variation), high levels of socio-economic development, stable democratic systems and a (Latin) Christian religious legacy (Minkenberg 2002, 2004).

Processes of pluralisation and globalisation: new challenges to the political regulation of religion and the functioning of democracies

For a long time, the so-called 'Western world' has been interpreted as undergoing a long-term process of secularisation or decline of religion, the replacement of religious values by secular values. However, there is sufficient empirical evidence to demonstrate that religion, even in the Western world, is a power that does not want to vanish and that assumes a new significance in an ever more complex and pluralistic world (see Willems/Minkenberg 2003). In Europe, more than anywhere else, many signs have pointed at a receding political impact of organised religion since the 1960s, such as church attendance rates, the number of priests per population, the participation of the young, the knowledge of the faiths (see Bruce 2002; Davie 2000). But also here, the pluralisation and increasing heterogeneity of the religious map leads to a growing number and intensity of conflicts at the intersection of politics and religion. Let us consider a few examples. First, one of the most visible examples is the immigration and growth of non-Christian minorities, in particular Muslims. They are at the centre of current controversies about multiculturalism, integration of ethnic and religious minorities, and transnational identities (see Addi *et al.* 2003; Escudier 2003; Heitmeyer/Dollase 1996; Kastoryano 2002; Nielsen 1995, 2001). Second, we must not overlook those immigrant minorities which have a Christian background but of a rather different theological orientation of Eastern European Orthodoxy or Christianity in the developing countries. Nor should we, third, forget the increasing number of atheists or unaffiliated. For example, in Germany, with the accession of the GDR to the Federal Republic in 1990, the percentage of officially counted non-religious, or those not affiliated with any church, jumped from a few in the old Federal Republic to about a third today. They prompt new public debates on the regulation of the relationship between religion and politics, not always with results in their favour. Finally, it is the European integration process itself which triggers new and heated discussions, such as the issue of religious references in the preamble of the future constitution of the EU, or even more vividly the debate whether Turkey, for religious and cultural reasons, belongs to Europe and should be an EU member or not (see Robbers 2003). An overview of the current – and growing – religious complexity of Western societies is given in Table 2.1.

Several trends stand out. Most importantly, in fourteen out of nineteen Western democracies Islam is now the third or even second largest religious community (countries in shaded cells). The countries where Islam is second are among those which are traditionally very homogenous in denominational terms, two Lutheran cases in Scandinavia (DK, N) and two Catholic cases (B, F) located in the west of Europe. In Spain, as in Austria, Muslims are on the verge of leaving Protestants behind. Somewhat mirroring this pattern, it is in particular the group of Protestant immigrant countries, Australia, Canada and the United States, plus Finland, in which the Orthodox Church takes third or second place.

Moreover, from around 1980 until around 2000, religious pluralism has increased in all Western democracies, except for Sweden and the United States. In traditional immigration countries such as Australia, Canada and New Zealand – along with the Netherlands – religious pluralism has increased from an already high level. In other countries like Austria, France, Italy and Spain – all Catholic – the jump started from a much lower level and has been particularly pronounced, thus challenging the dominant religion and its actor, the Catholic Church, as well as the established mechanisms in the relationship between the church and the state in a fundamental way. If it is true, as some argue (e.g. Castles 1993, 1998; Martin 1978; van Kersbergen 1995), that within Western democracies religious traditions, in particular Catholicism, assume a particular

Table 2.1 Trends in religious pluralism in 19 Western democracies, *c.*1980–*c.*2000 (letters in parenthesis indicate sources)

	Catholics	Protestants		Orthodox	Jews	Muslims	Other/ none	Pluralism index, c. 1980*	Pluralism index, c. 2000*
		Anglicans	Other Protestants						
Australia	27.7 (a)	20.7 (a)	16.8 (a)	2.8 (a)	0.45 (a)	1.5 (a)	30.0	0.74	0.82
Austria	73.6 (b)	0.0 (b)	4.7 (b)	1.9 (b)	0.1 (c)	4.2 (c)	15.5	0.15	0.41
Belgium	80.9 (b)	0.1 (b)	1.6 (b)	0.5 (b)	0.35 (c)	3.8 (d)	12.8	0.05	0.21
Canada	41.8 (b)	2.6 (b)	22.6 (b)	4.7 (e)	1.2 (c)	2.0 (c)	25.1	0.66	0.70
Denmark	0.6 (b)	0.1 (b)	88.4 (b)	0.0 (b)	0.06 (c)	2.8 (d)	8.0	0.07	0.23
Finland	0.1 (b)	0.0 (b)	91.0 (b)	1.1 (b)	n.d	0.4 (d)	7.4	0.09	0.25
France	78.8 (c)	0.0 (c)	1.6 (c)	0.3 (c)	1.1 (c)	8.5 (c)	9.7	0.08	0.40
Germany	32.1 (c)	0.0 (c)	31.8 (c)	1.1 (c)	0.12 (c)	3.7 (c)	30.3	0.54	0.66
Great Britain	11.0 (c)	29.0 (c)	14.0 (c)	0.6 (c)	0.48 (c)	2.7 (d)	42.2	0.59	0.69
Ireland	77.0 (c)	9.1 (c)	7.4 (c)	0.0 (c)	0.8 (c)	0.2 (d)	5.5	0.09	0.15
Italy	97.2 (b)	0.0 (b)	1.5 (b)	0.2 (b)	0.05 (c)	1.0 (d)	0.1	0.03	0.30
Netherlands	34.5 (b)	0.1 (b)	30.0 (b)	0.0 (b)	0.19 (c)	5.7 (c)	29.9	0.62	0.72
New Zealand	12.8 (b)	21.4 (b)	37.3 (b)	0.2 (b)	n.d.	0.6 (f)	27.7	0.76	0.81
Norway	1.0 (b)	0.0 (b)	97.1 (b)	0.0 (b)	n.d	1.4 (c)	0.5	0.15	0.20
Portugal	90.8 (b)	0.0 (b)	4.2 (b)	0.0 (b)	0.02 (c)	0.3 (d)	1.3	n.d.	0.14
Spain	96.1 (b)	0.0 (b)	1.1 (b)	0.0 (b)	0.04 (c)	0.7 (d)	2.1	0.02	0.45
Sweden	2.0 (b)	0.0 (b)	95.2 (b)	1.3 (b)	0.2 (c)	1.1 (c)	0.2	0.29	0.23
Switzerland	41.8 (c)	0.2 (b)	35.3 (c)	1.8 (c)	0.2 (c)	4.3 (c)	16.4	0.55	0.61
USA	20.8 (b)	0.9 (b)	51.4 (b)	2.1 (b)	2.1 (c)	1.4 (c)	21.2	0.88	0.82

Notes
a Australian census of 2001 in Cahill *et al.* (2004: 46).
b Bowden (2005: 32, 94, 404) on the basis of Barrett *et al.* (2001). The Protestant group includes independent Christian groups which do not belong to an organised denomination. In some countries such as Australia, Great Britain and Canada, but also Norway and the Netherlands, the size of this group varies between 3 and 4 per cent. In the USA this groups counts c.28 per cent, more than 80 per cent of whom are Evangelical Christians, according to survey data (see Wald 2003: 161).
c Census data and other government statistics around 2000 in Fischer Weltalmanach (2004). Estimates by Maréchal und Dassetto (2003: Tables 1 and 2) for Muslims in various European countries diverge somewhat from Census data, in some countries even significantly (Muslims in France: 7.0 per cent, in Norway 0.5 per cent, in Austria 2.6 per cent, in Switzerland 3.0 per cent).
d Estimate by Maréchal and Dassetto (2003: Tables 1 and 2) for the late 1990s (census data, corrected by expert opinion).
e For the year 2000 according to Noll (2002: 282f.).
f According to New Zealand census of 2001 (www.stats.govt.nz/people/default.htm, accessed 7 February 2006).
* These values indicate the degree of religious fragmentation, measured by 1 − H (Value of the Herfindahl Index): the smaller H, the higher the degree of pluralism. H is defined as the probability that two randomly drawn persons belong to the same religious denomination (vgl. Iannaccone 1991: 166). Data for c.1980 from Chaves and Cann (1992: 278), data for *c.*2000 from Alesina *et al.* (2003).

   Countries in which Islam constitutes the third or second largest religious community are shaded in grey. Here, all Protestants are counted as one religious community.

role in shaping politics and policies, hence constituting distinct 'families of nations' (Castles), we should expect that in these nations the growth of religious pluralism and the increasing weight of Islam will provoke distinct responses by political and religious actors in the field of immigration and multiculturalism.

All these developments push in the same direction: the established institutional and political arrangements to regulate the relationship between religion and politics in the framework of liberal democracies, long seen to have been solved, are challenged fundamentally and require new justifications. Even without 9/11 the multicultural facts of modern Western society raise new (and very old) questions about the political regulation of religion – and about issues of citizenship. Accordingly, we see some major shifts in the debate in two groups of Western democracies, the ones with a more or less established church structure, and those with a more or less clear separation between church and state (see Minkenberg 2003a, 2003b).

In the first group (Great Britain, the Federal Republic of Germany as well as some Scandinavian countries) we witness increasingly conflictual processes of realigning religion in the public sphere, for example with regard to the role of religious education (an increasingly controversial topic in Germany), the presence of headscarves and Christian symbols in the public, the fight for religious freedom for non-Christian churches (e.g. the debate in Great Britain regarding the recognition of Muslim communities and the torn position of the established Church of England, the controversies around mosque-building in Denmark, or the steps towards disestablishment of the state church in Sweden in 2000; see Gustafsson 2003; Modood 1997). But also in the 'separationist group' (the US and France, but Turkey as well), the governance of religion is experiencing increasing pressures from actors who interpret the neutrality and indifference of the state in religious matters as an adoption of particular political positions at the expense of religion. Secularism is seen not as a guarantee for state neutrality and a balance between all religious forces, but as a political programme equivalent to a secularist state religion (see Kymlicka/Norman 2000; Wald 2003).

Conceptualising the politics of citizenship

So far, only a few medium-to-large-N comparative projects have attempted to collect in a systematic manner data on issues of citizenship and nationality policies, which are useful for such comparisons. Among these, the 'Comparative Citizen Project' deserves special mention because here, over a number of years, a large group of scholars have collaborated in systematically categorising and collecting data on citizenship (Aleinikoff/Klusmeyer 2000, 2001, 2002; Weil 2001). For analyses such as this, this data collection provides an excellent resource. Another source of data can be found in the study by Koopmans *et al.* (2005; see also Koopmans and Statham 2000a) which includes a variety of measures and indicators for the comparative analysis of the politics of citizenship and ethnic relations – however, this study covers only five of the nineteen countries under consideration here (France, Germany, the Netherlands, Switzerland, the United Kingdom).

In order to manage the complexities of the issues at hand, the analysis of citizenship will focus on one key aspect: the degree of restrictiveness or openness of the nationality code, i.e. the logic of the rules which determine membership in the nation-state.[2] The time frame for the analysis comprises the period after World War II with regard to many factors such as constitutional and institutional provisions, the role of political parties, etc. But the dependent variable of citizenship policies has been specified and analysed more narrowly for the years before the turn of the century, i.e. prior to 2000. While it is too complex to include issues of policy change from the 1970s to the 1990s and beyond 9/11 in all countries studied here, it is assumed that the policies of the late 1990s reflect longer-lasting policy patterns in each country which preceded the end of the Cold War and, to a considerable extent, survived the shock waves of 9/11 which altered significant portions of immigration-related policies in the West, especially by their increasing securitisation (see Chebel d'Appollonia/Reich 2008).

The concept of citizenship politics borrows heavily from the work of other experts in the field (e.g. Kastoryano 2002, contributions to Koopmans/Statham 2000a). In particular, the conceptual framework developed by Ruud Koopmans and Paul Statham (2000b, 2005) seems fruitful for such a comparison. In this, they distinguish two dimensions of integration, one based on individual rights, such as access to citizenship and benefits, voting rights, and another based on cultural group rights such as the recognition of religious communities, education, political representation. Following this distinction, the comparison in this chapter addresses measures of (political) inclusion in terms of the access to citizenship by non-citizens as regulated by the respective nationality code. Here, individual rights are important, as measured by two principles: the existence of a *ius soli* (territorial principle) in addition to the traditional *ius sanguinis* (blood relation principle), and the openness of the requirements for naturalisation. For each principle, points are given for the existing rule, ranging from 0 (restricted) to 2 (open). The classification of countries is based on a survey of expert literature and the countries are presented in Table 2.2 (for details, see Appendix):

Table 2.2 A scale of nationality codes: access to citizenship in nineteen Western democracies (before 2000)

Restricted (0–1 point)	*Medium (1.5–2.5 points)*	*Open (3–4 points)*
Austria	Belgium	Australia
Denmark	Great Britain	Canada
Finland	Spain	France
Germany	Sweden	Ireland
Italy		Netherlands
Norway		New Zealand
Portugal		USA
Switzerland		

The distribution of countries in Table 2.2 shows some familiar patterns, with the 'ethnic nations' of Germany and Austria, along with Switzerland and Italy and the Scandinavian countries, exhibiting rather restrictive nationality codes, while the family of 'classical immigration countries' (post-colonial democracies) along with traditionally open France and the Netherlands appear on the opposite end. Surprisingly, Ireland also entered this group, a country more known for its history as an emigration country.

It could be argued that citizenship policies are a function of a country's immigration policy. After all, if a country pursues an open immigration policy it could be expected to make an effort easily to include the various new migrants in the workings of their politics. An overview of these two policy areas is presented in Table 2.3.

The pattern in Table 2.3 demonstrates indeed that there is a clear relationship between a country's immigration policy and its nationality code. There are five countries with 'consistent' positions at the restrictive end of these two scales, and six countries at the open end. The relationship is, however, not perfect because the group of moderate immigration policies spreads across the continuum of nationality codes. In order to explain some of this variation, a closer look at the most relevant cultural and political factors follows.

As shown earlier (Minkenberg 2004), standard explanatory models of comparative policy research have not yielded clear results with regard to immigration policies, although some patterns could be identified. In the following, the religious dimension will be introduced and it will be discussed whether Castles' model of 'family of nations' is more appropriate than the others in analysing variations in immigration policy. Unlike with Castles, however, religion will not

Table 2.3 A typology of immigration and citizenship policies (before 2000)

		Nationality code		
		Restricted	*Medium*	*Open*
Immigration policies	Restrictive	Austria Denmark Germany Norway Switzerland		
	Moderate	Finland Italy Portugal	Belgium Great Britain Spain	Ireland
	Open		Sweden	Australia Canada France Netherlands New Zealand USA

Sources: see Appendix and Minkenberg (2008b).

be reduced to the confessional heritage or role of Catholic parties. Instead, following earlier analyses the religious factor is decomposed into a historico-cultural dimension, i.e. the role of confessional patterns, and a socio-cultural dimension of religiosity, as measured in church-going rates, further an institutional dimension of patterns of church–state relations (see Minkenberg 2002, 2003a, 2003b). Moreover, a more political dimension is introduced by looking at religious parties.

Confessional patterns and secularisation

The first step in the analysis involves the cultural legacy of religion. In order to measure this legacy, two dimensions are considered: the confessional composition of a country which, if at all, is the standard variable of religion's input in comparative public policy research, and the level of religiosity as a measure of a country's 'embeddedness' in religious practice (see Bruce 2000: 3). In terms of the secularisation argument, the first might be seen as an indicator of a country's cultural differentiation, or cultural pluralism, whereas the second points to the country's path of secularisation as disenchantment. Most texts that emphasise the role of confessions in a nation's history classify countries as Catholic, Protestant or confessionally mixed, and most of them, as well as some of the public policy literature (see above), assert a long-lasting influence of these cultural patterns on current policy and politics (see Martin 1978; Bruce 1996; Inglehart 1997; Inglehart/Baker 2000). Following David Martin and his distinction between 'crucial events' (such as the success or failure of the Reformation and the outcome of civil wars and revolutions) on the one hand, and 'resultant patterns' on the other (for example, the British, American, Russian, Calvinist and Lutheran patterns), three categories will be used for the countries under consideration: (1) cultures with a Protestant dominance, resulting either from a lack of Catholics (the Scandinavian countries) or because Catholic minorities arrived after the pattern had been set (England, the United States); (2) cultures with a Protestant majority and substantial Catholic minorities according to the historic ratio of 60:40 (the Netherlands, Germany, Switzerland)[3] where a cultural rather than a mere political bipolarity has emerged along with subcultural segregation; (3) cultures with a Catholic dominance and democratic or democratising regimes (France, Italy, Belgium, Austria, Ireland) that are characterised by large political and social fissures, organic opposition and secularist dogmas (Martin 1978: 119).[4]

The second component of the cultural legacy is the actual degree of individual attachment to established religion. This is important because high levels of religiosity assure churches high legitimacy as political actors. Moreover, religiosity may be a better predictor for public policy than confessional composition alone if the question whether a country is Catholic or Protestant is held to be less important than whether Catholics or Protestants actually attend church or believe the teachings of the church. In this analysis, religiosity is measured by frequency of church-going rather than by religious beliefs because it ties religiosity to existing institutions instead of more abstract religious concepts and values. Data on church-going in the 19 countries analysed here are taken from the 1980s and 1990s waves of the World Values Survey (see Inglehart/Baker 2000; Inglehart/ Minkenberg 2000). The data for the 1980s and 1990s are then averaged and the countries are grouped according to the frequency of church-going, ranging from low (less than 20 per cent who go at least once a month), to medium (20–40 per cent), to high (above 40 per cent) (see Minkenberg 2002: 238).

The relationship between the religious legacies of the 19 countries and their nationality codes are shown in Table 2.4.

The overall picture is far from clear. Neither confessions nor church-going rates correlate with the degree of openness of the countries' citizenship rules. While concerning immigration policies, a certain 'Catholic effect' could be shown in that none of the Catholic countries had implemented an open immigration policy (see Minkenberg 2008b), this does not reappear with regard to citizenship. The suggestion to identify a special Southern or 'Mediterranean' type of countries with regard to their public policies (see Castles 1998: 8f.; Baldwin-Edwards 1992) is not supported by the distribution in Table 2.4 because the group of Mediterranean countries (France and Italy, Portugal and Spain) do not cluster but spread along the entire scale.

Some other patterns stand out in Table 2.4, as well. With the exception of Great Britain and Sweden, the two Protestant groups divide up into opposite camps of citizenship policies. As the Scandinavian group demonstrates (again with the exception of Sweden), secularisation does not translate into an open nationality code, although a declining significance of established churches might facilitate a country's departure from its exclusionist traditions and its dealing with increasing cultural diversity. Generally, church-going rates seem less telling than confessional legacies when it comes to citizenship policies. In the welfare state debate it has been argued that Protestant countries need to be distinguished

Table 2.4 Religious legacy: confessions, religiosity, and nationality codes

	Restricted	*Medium*	*Open*
Predominantly Protestant	*Denmark* *Finland* *Norway*	*Sweden* Great Britain	Australia New Zealand **USA**
Mixed Protestant	Germany Switzerland		Netherlands **Canada**
Catholic	Austria **Italy** **Portugal**	Belgium **Spain**	*France* **Ireland**

Sources: see Appendix.

Note

Countries in **bold** are those with **high religiosity**; countries in *italics* with *low religiosity*.

according to the type of Protestantism which dominates: Lutheran or Reformed/ free church Protestantism. The more encompassing and egalitarian welfare regimes have been introduced in Lutheran Protestant countries, whereas in those where Reformed Protestantism or Calvinism dominated, welfare systems were introduced later and emphasised individualism and a restrained role of the state (see Manow 2002). This distinction can help explain that the Lutheran Protestant countries share a restricted nationality code (and immigration policy, see Table 2.3) despite diverging rates of immigration flows in Denmark and Norway/ Finland, although it does not explain why Sweden has strayed from the camp, as it does not explain why Calvinist Switzerland and the Netherlands diverge with regard to nationality codes and immigration policies. Yet the general confessional pattern is that, among Protestant countries, Lutheran nations exhibit a restrictive nationality code, while Reformed Protestantism seems to result in more open concepts of citizenship – but this finding is mitigated by the fact that most countries in which Reformed Protestantism dominates are classical immigration countries. In contrast to Protestantism, there is no pattern with or within the Catholic group. The nationality code today seems more or less completely separated from its confessional beginnings in the transition to the modern age (see Rokkan 1970; Madeley 2003) – a clear sign of 'secularisation'.

Institutional patterns and citizenship policies

Hence, when looking for a common religious denominator for the group with an open nationality code, one must go beyond confessional legacies and church-going rates. As some analyses suggest (see Minkenberg 2002, 2003a; Monsma/ Soper 1997; Fetzer/Soper 2005), the regime of church–state relations can also claim a certain explanatory power for variations in particular public policies. This institutional dimension of religious legacies is measured by the degree of deregulation of churches in financial, political and legal respects, and builds on a scale developed by Chaves and Cann (1992). In a critique of the supply-siders' market-based argumentation, they argue with de Tocqueville that the theoretical focus of state–church relations needs to be adjusted towards political aspects:

> Like Smith, [de Tocqueville] focused on the separation of church and state, but he highlighted the *political* rather than the *economic* aspect of that separation: the advantage that religion enjoys when it is not identified with a particular set of political interests.
>
> (Chaves and Cann 1992: 275; emphasis in original)

Moreover, regardless of the official relationship between church and state, Catholic societies are almost by definition much less pluralistic in religious terms than Protestant societies. But as the data in Table 2.1 demonstrate, this historical inequality is already in the process of revision.

For the purpose of the analysis here, the church–state scale is summarised into a three-fold typology: countries with full establishment (such as the

Scandinavian countries), countries with partial establishment (such as Germany but also Italy and Great Britain), and countries with a clear separation of church and state (such as the US and France) (for details, see Minkenberg 2002, 2003b).

Table 2.5 shows that, contrary to confessional legacies and secularisation (as disenchantment), institutional differentiation of church and state corresponds clearly with the type of nationality code. That is, the more state and church are separated, the more open the code. All countries with church–state separation exhibit an open nationality code, and this includes the classical immigration countries (former members of the British empire) as well as European cases. On the other hand, the Scandinavian group with established state churches falls into the opposite camp, except for Sweden. Here, a disestablishment process has set in in the late 1990s in part as a response to increasing immigration and pressures from a growing cultural pluralism (see Gustafsson 2003).

There exists a close relationship between the histories of nation-building, democratisation and the respective religious (confessional) histories and church–state regimes. The patterns in Tables 2.4 and 2.5 indicate a close link between processes of nation-building and secularisation on the one hand, and the respective dominance of Lutheranism, Calvinism, Anglicanism and Catholicism on the other. With the exception of laicist and Republican France and the Netherlands with its particular Calvinist trajectory, all countries in the upper right field are former British colonies and countries of immigration. (Ireland only very recently became a country of immigration but can be considered a former British colony.) As such, this group except for Ireland is characterised by an early plurality of religions and a separationist model of church–state relations in distinct opposition to their former 'mother country', Great Britain, and its traditional Anglican

Table 2.5 Church-state relations and nationality codes

	Restricted	*Medium*	*Open*
Separation			*Australia* *New Zealand* *USA* Canada Netherlands **France** **Ireland**
Partial establishment	Germany Switzerland **Austria** **Italy** **Portugal**	*Great Britain* **Belgium** **Spain**	
Full establishment	*Denmark* *Finland* *Norway*	*Sweden*	

Note
Countries in bold are **Catholic**, countries in italics are *predominantly Protestant* countries.

state church. The Australian history is a case in point. When the country was faced with an increasing denominational pluralisation, the initial adoption of the British model of establishment gave way to the American model of separation. This had already taken place during colonial times, initiated by the New South Wales Church Act of 1836 and was completed, by and large, at the end of the nineteenth century (see Bouma 2006; Breward 2001). Put differently: in the course of the process of these countries' separation from Great Britain, nation-building was intertwined with the process of separating church and state while keeping the Westminster model of parliamentary democracy. In contrast to this pattern, the Scandinavian countries experienced nation-building along with parliamentarisation and maintenance of the Lutheran state church model (see von Beyme 1999: Ch. 2).

Again, this finding points at the necessity to modify the 'family of nations' concept proposed by Castles. In terms of citizenship policies even more so than of immigration policies (Minkenberg 2008b), there is some support for the existence of a Scandinavian family and English family – *sauf* Great Britain itself which underwent a growing restrictiveness in its nationality code during the Thatcher years (see Joppke 1999). But the Continental group falls apart. With regard to this policy area, the Catholic family splits up and falls into different categories, as do the bi-confessional countries Germany, Switzerland and Netherlands. Policy-wise, these countries plus Austria constitute a type of democracy – labelled 'consensus democracies' by Lijphart (1999) as opposed to the Westminster or majoritarian model – in which early historical conflicts between confessions resulted in a particular emphasis on consensus in decision-making in order to integrate different groups, mostly religious or lingual, into the political process. As the cases of Switzerland and the Netherlands show, doctrinal similarities – here the historical dominance of Reformed Protestantism and Calvinism – recede in the face of divergent processes of nation-building and post-colonialism; they do not play the same role as in the area of social policies (see above).

Christian parties: a Catholic political effect?

The final step in the analysis of religious factors in variation of citizenship policies concerns the role of religiously oriented parties. In analogy to the studies of strong left-wing parties and generous welfare states, one might expect a relationship between the presence of these parties and a restrictive output in this policy domain. In fact, the most direct link between religion and politics at the intersection of the electoral and policy-making levels exists where explicitly religious parties, most notably Christian Democratic ones, play a role in the party system. Moreover, the relevance of religious cleavages in the contemporary Western world has been demonstrated by a variety of election studies. While the class cleavage has undergone a steady decline in significance, the religious cleavage in terms of the relationship between religiosity (as measured by church attendance) and voting behaviour has stayed rather stable. In the US, there was even a slight but steady increase of religious voting in the United States, which can be attributed to the growing mobilisation efforts of the Christian Right (see Dalton 1996: 176–85; see also Inglehart 1997; Minkenberg 1990).

Instead of focusing on classical Christian Democratic parties alone, the chapter recognises the variety of the confessional party landscape with at least four versions of Christian parties in Western democracies after the Second World War: political Catholicism in homogenously Catholic countries with a high level of system support (Austria, Belgium); political Catholicism in mixed confessional countries representing Catholic minorities and exhibiting – initially – low levels of system support (Germany, the Netherlands, Switzerland); the special case of Italy where 99 per cent of the population is Catholic, yet where Catholics feel suppressed; Protestant Christian parties in predominantly Lutheran Scandinavia (Denmark, Finland, Norway, Sweden). In the four non-European democracies, specifically Christian parties did not emerge (see von Beyme 1984: 121–7; see also Hanley 2003; Whyte 1981). In order to arrive at a measure that captures a Christian party impact, the 19 countries are classified according to the role of religion in these parties' identity and platforms, their relationship to religious groups, the salience of the religious cleavage in voting behaviour and the length of these parties' participation in national governments (for details see Minkenberg 2002). The resulting six-point-scale was summarised in three categories, ranging from low to medium to high religious impact (see Table 2.6). This categorisation shows a striking similarity between the ranking of these nations and the ranking of the salience of religious voting, with the Netherlands, Belgium and Denmark at the top, the UK, Canada and the US at the bottom of the scale. There is an obvious relationship between the cleavage factor on the voters' side (see Dalton 1996: 185) and these parties' orientation at the party system and government side. It also shows that with regard to the partisan variable, these countries cannot be ranked according to their confessional composition.[5]

Table 2.6 depicts an interesting role of these parties. With regard to other social policies, it has been shown that a strong Christian Democracy corresponds with moderate – instead of restrictive or radical – abortion rulings and family policies and reflects a particular policy profile of Christian Democracy in association with a larger and distinct vision of society (see van Kersbergen 1995; Minkenberg 2003b). This effect disappears somewhat. Regarding citizenship, a more general correlation occurs: the higher the religious partisan impact, the more restrictive the nationality code.

Interestingly, the group with strong Christian Democratic parties clusters at the more restrictive end of the nationality code (unlike the case of immigration policies where it spreads, see Table 2.3 and Minkenberg 2008b). This indicates that the conjunction of traditional concepts of nationhood and a strong (conservative) Christian Democracy have contributed to a restrictive status quo. Only the Netherlands deviates sharply from this pattern, which again must be seen in light of the post-colonial history of the country – a fate that none of the other countries in the Christian Democratic group share. Unlike their eastern neighbour, the Dutch subscribed to a view of their culture which was less determined

Table 2.6 Religious partisan impact and nationality codes

	Restricted	*Medium*	*Open*
Low religious partisan impact			*Australia* *New Zealand* Canada **France**
Medium religious partisan impact	**Portugal** Switzerland	**Spain** *Great Britain* *Sweden*	**Ireland** *USA*
High religious partisan impact	<u>**Austria**</u> <u>**Italy**</u> Germany *Denmark* *Finland* *Norway*	<u>**Belgium**</u>	Netherlands

Note
Countries in **bold** are **Catholic** countries; countries in *italics* are *Protestant*. Countries that are <u>under-lined</u> are those with <u>strong Christian Democratic</u> elements in the party system.

by notions of ethnicity and closedness (see van Amersfoort and van Niekerk 2003; Koopmans *et al.* 2005). At the other end of the spectrum, all countries with low religious partisan impact share an open nationality code. Finally, the Scandinavian group (without Sweden) again stands out as a distinct type of country also with regard to religious partisan impact. In these countries, as in Germany, Italy and Austria, the traditional concept of a homogenous nation seemed to have informed also party politics, especially on the political right.

Conclusions

Against the backdrop of cultural and religious pluralism Western democracies, this chapter's findings point at the necessity to modify the 'family of nations' concept as developed by Francis Castles (1993, 1998). While there is sufficient evidence for the existence of a Scandinavian family in the domain of citizenship policies (as in many others), the other groups break up and mix anew. The Catholic family spreads across the various categories; it is reduced to a core group which excludes the traditional bi-confessional countries (Germany, Switzerland, the Netherlands). The group of settler or immigration countries (former British colonies) is joined by continental France and the Netherlands, as well as another former British colony, Ireland, in their open approach in citizenship policies. The so-called 'consensus democracies' (Lijphart 1999) in which deep-seated confessional conflicts resulted in a consensual mode of decision-making in order to prevent the exclusion of different, mostly religious groups (Germany, the Netherlands, Switzerland and Austria) show little enthusiasm for an open citizenship policy, with the notable Dutch exception. As the cases of Switzerland and the Netherlands show with their nationality codes at opposite ends of the spectrum, doctrinal similarities (Reformed Protestantism) recede in the face of divergent processes of nation-building and post-colonialism; in contrast to their parallel effects in the establishment of social policies (see Manow 2002).

Contrary to these factors and in line with the logic of nation-building and the role of nation-builders (in the post-war era), state–church relations and the role of Christian Democracy play a significant role in the diverging paths of citizenship policies. Strong religious input into the party system, together with some or full church establishment, result in more restrictive approaches to migrants' political inclusion. And church–state separation, where churches as actors are free to develop their policy input and do not rival with strong religious parties, seems to pave the way towards more open citizenship policies. These findings suggest that a more process-oriented analysis of the role of Christian parties and churches in Western democracies could shed more light on the evolution of citizenship policies and determine the range of variability across time and space. Such an analysis, however, must remain the topic of another study. A preliminary study of churches' role in immigration policies in selected countries demonstrates that in recent times they have often acted in deviation from their political allies, i.e. Christian parties, but that their effects on the policy output are modest (Minkenberg 2008b).

Appendix: a scale of citizenship requirements in nineteen democracies (before 2000)

Criteria for citizenship scale

(Lower end: closed, upper end: open)
1   Existence of *ius soli*
    a   non-existent   0 points
    b   conditional   1 point
    c   unconditional   2 points
2   Naturalisation requirements
    a   restrictive   0 points
    b   medium, or option of purchase   1 point
    c   easy/fast   2 points

Australia

1   Existence of *ius soli*
    c   unconditional   2 points
    Indirect evidence in Price (1993: 20), Betts (1995: 61)
2   Naturalisation requirements
    c   easy/fast   2 points
    After two years' residence, dual nationality (Betts 1995: 66; Price 1993: 13), from assimilationism to multiculturalism (Castles 1998: 180–4)
3   'Concessional family' (Betts 1995: 73; Price 1993: 13f.)
    Total number of points   4

Austria

1   Existence of *ius soli*
    a   non-existent   0 points
    (Bauböck and Çinar 2001; Weil 2001: 96)
2   Naturalisation requirements
    a   restrictive   0 points
    Discretionary, at least ten years of uninterrupted residence, no dual nationality ((Bauböck and Çinar 2001: 261–4)
    Total number of points   *0*

Belgium

1   Existence of *ius soli*
    b   conditional   0.5 points
    Severe restrictions on *ius soli* (parents' declaration for child, at state's discretion) (Liénard-Ligny 2001: 203; Weil 2001: 95)
2   Naturalisation requirements
    c   easy/fast   2 points
    Three years' waiting period, dual nationality (Liénard-Ligny 2001: 204–7; Weil 2001: 96)
    Total number of points   *2.5*

Canada

1   Existence of *ius soli*
    c   unconditional   2 points

> *Could I be a Canadian citizen and not know it?* In general, if you were born in Canada you are a Canadian citizen. You are also a Canadian if you were born in another country after 15 February 1977 and one of your parents was a Canadian citizen before your birth.
>
> (Citizenship and Immigration Canada 2004)

2   Naturalisation requirements
    c   easy/fast   2 points
    (Schmidtke 2003: 212, 214; Weil 2001: 96)
    Total number of points   *4*

Denmark

1   Existence of *ius soli*
    a   non-existent   0 points
    (Ersbøll 2001: 236; Weil 2001: 95)
2   Naturalisation requirements
    a   restrictive   0 points
    Seven years' waiting period, no dual nationality (Ersbøll 2001: 240–4; Weil 2001: 96)
    Total number of points   *0*

Finland
1   Existence of *ius soli*
   a   non-existent   0 points
   Ius soli only if a child born in Finland does not acquire nationality of another state (Ersbøll 2001: 236; Weil 2001: 95)
2   Naturalisation requirements
   a   medium   1 point
   Five-year residence requirement, no dual nationality (Ersbøll 2001: 241; Weil 2001: 96)
   Total number of points   *1*

France
1   Existence of *ius soli*
   c   unconditional   2 points
   (Weil 2002: 249)
2   Naturalisation requirements
   b   medium, or option of purchase   1.5 points
   Five-year residence requirement, with waiver for Francophone countries, but administrative hurdles, dual nationality (Bauböck and Çinar 1994: 193; Weil 2001: 96, 2002: 249–51, 256)
   Total number of points   *3.5*

Germany
1   Existence of *ius soli*
   c   non-existent (prior to 2000)   0 points
2   Naturalisation requirements
   a   restrictive (and loosened)   0.5 points
   Ten-year residence requirement for second generation, (early 1990s), no dual nationality (Bauböck and Çinar 1994: 193); mid-1990s: assimilation requirement loosened, as-of-rule for first generation after 15 years, for second and third generation after eight years (Joppke 1999: 202–4)
   Total number of points   *0.5*

Great Britan
1   Existence of *ius soli*
   b   conditional   1 point
   British Nationality Act of 1981: 'partial abolishment of *ius soli*', 'partial introduction of *ius sanguinis*' (Joppke 1999: 112f., 144)
2   Naturalisation requirements
   b   medium, or option of purchase   1 point
   Five-year residence requirement, dual nationality (Bauböck and Çinar 1994: 193; Weil 2001: 96)
   Total number of points   *2*

Ireland

1 Existence of *ius soli*

    c   unconditional   2 points

    According to 1935 and 1956 Act (Symmons 2001: 279f.)

2 Naturalisation requirements

    b   medium   1 point

    Five-year residence requirement according to 1956 Act, three-year waiting period for spouses, dual nationality (Symmons 2001: 284f.)

    Total number of points   *3*

Italy

1 Existence of *ius soli*

    a   non-existent   0 points

    The 1992 Nationality Law allows *ius soli* only for children of unknown parents, at the same time ethnocultural definition of nationhood (extension of nationality to descendents of Italian emigrants) (Sciortino 2003: 272)

2 Naturalisation requirements

    a   restrictive   0.5 points

    Ten years of uninterrupted residence (1992 law, before: five years) (Sciortino 2003: 271; Weil 2001: 96), dual nationality after 1992 (Koslowski 2000: 145)

    Total number of points   *0.5*

Netherlands

1 Existence of *ius soli*

    b   conditional   1.5 points

    Since 1953 *ius soli* for all immigrant children of third generation, (Böcker and Thränhardt 2003: 125), mixture of *ius soli* and *ius domicilis*

2 Naturalisation requirements

    c   easy/fast   2 points

    Very liberal dual nationality rule, option for Dutch nationality in second generation (1985 law), very high naturalisation levels (Böcker and Thränhardt 2003: 126f.)

    Total number of points   *3.5*

New Zealand

1 Existence of *ius soli*

    c   unconditional   2 points

    Indirect inference from analogy to Australia in Winkelmann (2001)

2 Naturalisation requirements

    c   easy/fast   2 points

    Citizenship Act of 1977: a single citizenship-granting procedure instead of registration and naturalisation, three years of residence (Elliott 1993: 57; Winkelmann 2001: 18, n. 6)

    Total number of points   *4*

Norway

1   Existence of *ius soli*
    a   non-existent   0 points
    (inference from Denmark and literature)
2   Naturalisation requirements
    a   restrictive   0 points
    Seven-year residence requirement, no dual nationality (Ornbrant/Peura 1993: 222)
    Total number of points   *0*

Portugal

1   Existence of *ius soli*
    a   non-existent   0 points
    'In 1981, a new nationality law was passed (Lei 37/81, 3 October 1981) which completely abandoned the *ius soli* principle, with children of non-Portuguese nationals born in Portugal being considered foreigners from 1981' (Morén-Alegret: 2002: 97)
2   Naturalisation requirements
    a   restrictive   0 points

> In 1994 an amendment was passed [to the nationality law Lei 37/81], but the only remarkable change was that the new law established tougher criteria for nationals of non-Portuguese speaking countries to naturalise (Lei 25/94, 19 August 1995): until 1994, six years of legal residence were necessary to naturalise as a Portuguese citizen for all foreigners; from 1994 onwards, six years are required for those from Angola, Brazil, Cape Verde, Guinea Bissau, Mozambique and Sao Tomé e Principe, but ten years of residence are needed for nationals from other countries.
>
> (Morén-Alegret 2002: 97)

Apart from that, Portuguese knowledge is also required
By marriage: three years of legal union (Mendoza 2003: 77)
Children of foreign parents who are born in Portugal need either six (PALOP countries) or ten years of legal residence to naturalise (Mendoza 2003: 77)
Total number of points   *0*

Spain

1   Existence of *ius soli*
   b   conditional   1 point
Art. 17 (Civil Code)
Spaniards are:
   a   those born of a Spanish father or mother
   b   those born in Spain of foreign parents if at least one of them was also born in Spain
   c   those born in Spain of foreign parents if neither of them have a nationality or if the legislation of none of their countries of origin gives the child a nationality
   d   those born in Spain whose filiation is undetermined
(Moreno Fuentes 2001: 131f.)

2   Naturalisation requirements
   a   restrictive   0.5 points

'Spanish law provides for naturalisation of legal immigrants after a term of two years for citizens of former Spanish colonies,[6] excepting the protectorate of Morocco, and after ten years of legal residence of nationals from the rest of the world' (Huntoon 1998: 429)

Also: only one year for those born in Spanish territory and those married to a Spanish citizen (after one year of marriage) (Civil Code, Art. 22)

Spain has signed treaties of double nationality with Bolivia, Chile, Colombia, Costa Rica, Ecuador, Guatemala, Honduras, Nicaragua, Paraguay, Peru, Argentina and the Dominican Republic (Moreno Fuentes 2001: 132)

Total number of points   *1.5*

Sweden

1   Existence of *ius soli*
   b   conditional   1.5 points
Mixture of *ius soli* and *ius domicilis* (Hammar 2003: 237)
2   Naturalisation requirements
   c   easy/fast   2 points
Five-year residence requirement, dual nationality, high levels of naturalisation (Bauböck/Çinar 1994: 193; Hammar 2003: 247)
Total number of points   *2.5 points*

Switzerland

1   Existence of *ius soli*
    a   non-existent   0 points
    Inference from Efionayi-Mäder *et al.* (2003: 26): reform project to introduce *ius soli* for third generation
2   Naturalisation requirements
    a   restrictive   0 points
    Twelve years' residence and cultural assimilation requirements (Hoffman-Nowotny and Killias 1993: 240; Wimmer 1998: 216)
    Total number of points   *0*

USA

1   Existence of *ius soli*
    c   unconditional   2 points
    (Joppke 1999)
2   Naturalisation requirements
    b   medium, or option of purchase   1.5 points
    Several assimilation requirements, 'however minimal and ritual' (Joppke 1999: 275), no financial requirements (Weil 2001: 96)
    Total number of points   *3.5*

Notes

1   It is telling about the comparatively low level of secularisation of the United States that even as late as in the late twentieth century, religious sociologists have pointed out that full membership in the American nation, i.e. citizenship in an encompassing sense, was governed by the principle of being a member of a religious denomination (see e.g. Greeley 1972).
2   For an analysis of another, more broadly defined concept of citizenship, in terms of group rights and multiculturalism, see Minkenberg 2008a.
3   The emphasis is on the 'historic weight' of the Protestant majority, not the current proportion such as, for example, that in the Netherlands of the early 1990s where Catholics (36 per cent) outweigh Protestants (26 per cent) and are rivalled by an equally large group of those with no church affiliation at all. The same applies to Canada, where today Catholics outnumber Protestants (see Table 2.1).
4   Historically, countries with a Catholic dominance and a sizable Protestant minority (a reverse of the 60:40 ratio in Category 2) have not materialised – a very clear illustration of 'limited diversity' of religious patterns,
5   Despite the small vote share of the Christian parties in Scandinavia, the relatively strong religious cleavage in these countries and these parties' comparatively long participation in the national governments place them into the category of 'high impact' (see Hanley 2003: 244; Minkenberg 2002).
6   Includes the states of Iberoamerica, Andorra, the Philippines, Equatorial Guinea and Portugal, and the Sephardic Jews.

Bibliography

Addi, L., Kepel, G. and Roy, O. (2003) *Islam et démocratie*, Special Issue of *Pouvoirs*, 104, Paris: Seuil.

Aleinikoff, T. A. and Klusmeyer, D. (eds) (2000) *From Migrants to Citizens: Membership in a Changing World*, Washington, DC: Carnegie Endowment for International Peace.

Aleinikoff, T. A. and Klusmeyer, D. (eds) (2001) *Citizenship Today: Global Perspectives and Practices*, Washington, DC: Carnegie Endowment for International Peace.

Aleinikoff, T. A. and Klusmeyer, D. (eds) (2002) *Citizenship Policies for an Age of Migration*, Washington, DC: Carnegie Endowment for International Peace.

Alesina, A., Devleeschauwer, A., Easterly, W., Kurlat, S. and Wacziarg, R. (2003) 'Fractionalization', *Journal of Economic Growth*, 82, pp. 219–58.

Almond, G. and Powell, B., Jr (1978) *Comparative Politics. System, Process, and Policy*, second rev. edn, Boston and Toronto: Little, Brown.

Baldwin-Edwards, M. (1992) 'Immigration after 1992', *Policy and Politics*, 19, 3, pp. 199–211.

Barrett, D., Kurian, G. and Johnson, T. (eds) (2001) *World Christian Encyclopedia: A Comparative Survey of Churches and Religion*, second edn, Oxford and New York: Oxford University Press.

Bauböck, R. and Çinar, D. (1994) 'Briefing Paper: Naturalisation Policies in Western Europe', in M. Baldwin-Edwards and M. Schain (eds) *The Politics of Immigration in Western Europe*, London: Frank Cass, pp. 192–6.

Bauböck, R. and Çinar, D. (2001) 'Nationality Law and Naturalization in Austria', in R Hansen and P. Weil (eds), *Toward a European Nationality. Citizenship, Immigration and Nationality Law in the European Union*, New York: Palgrave, pp. 255–72.

Betts, K. (1995) 'Immigration to Australia: A New Focus for the 1990s?' in F. Heckmann and W. Bosswick (eds), *Migration Policies: A Comparative Perspective*. Stuttgart: Ferdinand Enke Verlag, pp. 59–93.

Böcker, A. and Thränhardt, D. (2003) 'Einbürgerung und Mehrstaatigkeit in Deutschland und den Niederlanden', in D. Thränhardt and U. Hunger (eds), *Migration im Spannungsfeld von Globalisierung und Nationalstaat*, Leviathan Special Issue no. 22, Wiesbaden: Westdeutscher Verlag, pp. 117–34.

Bouma, G. (2006) *Australian Soul. Religion and Spirituality in the Twenty-first Century*, Cambridge: Cambridge University Press.

Bowden, J. (ed.) (2005) *Encyclopedia of Christianity*, Oxford: Oxford University Press.

Breward, I. (2001) *A History of the Churches in Australasia*, Oxford: Oxford University Press.

Brubaker, R. (1992) *Citizenship and Nationhood in France and Germany*, Cambridge: Cambridge University Press.

Bruce, S. (1996) *Religion in the Modern World. From Cathedrals to Cults*, Oxford: Oxford University Press.

Bruce, S. (2000) *Fundamentalism*, Oxford: Polity Press.

Bruce, S. (2002) *God Is Dead. Secularization in the West*, Oxford: Blackwell.

Bruce, S. (2003) *Politics and Religion*, Oxford: Polity Press.

Cahill, D., Bouma, G., Dellal, H. and Leahy, M. (2004) *Religion, Cultural Diversity and Safeguarding Australia*, Canberra: Commonwealth of Australia.

Casanova, J. (1994) *Public Religions in the Modern World*, Chicago: University of Chicago Press.

Castles, F. (ed.) (1993) *Families of Nations. Patterns of Public Policy in Western Democracies*, Aldershot: Dartmouth.

Castles, F. (1998). *Patterns of Public Policy. Patterns of Post-war Transformation*, Cheltenham: Edward Elgar.

Chaves, M. and Cann, D. (1992) 'Regulation, Pluralism, and Religious Market Structure', *Rationality and Society*, 4, 3, pp. 272–90.

Chebel d'Appollonia, A. and Reich, S. (eds) (2008) *Immigration, Integration and Security. America and Europe in Comparative Perspective*, Pittsburgh: University of Pittsburgh Press.

Citizenship and Immigration Canada (2004) *Citizenship and Immigration*, 29 February 2004, available at http://www.cic.gc.ca/english/citizen/howto-e.html

Dalton, R. (1996) *Citizen Politics*, second rev. edn, London: Chatham House.

Davie, G. (2000) *Religion in Modern Europe: A Memory Mutates*, Oxford: Oxford University Press.

Efionayi-Mäder, D. *et al.* (2003) *Swiss Country Report in Immigration Management*, Bruxelles: Migration Policy Group; available at http://migpolgroup.com/publications (March 2004).

Elliott, J. (1993) 'New Zealand: The Coming of Age of Multiracial Islands', in D. Kubat (ed.), *The Politics of Migration Policies. Settlement and Integration: The First World into the 1990s*, New York: Center for Migration Studies, pp. 45–59.

Ersbøll, E. (2001) 'Nationality Law in Denmark, Finland and Sweden', in R. Hansen and P. Weil (eds), *Toward a European Nationality. Citizenship, Immigration and Nationality Law in the EU*, New York: Palgrave, pp. 230–4.

Escudier, A. (ed.) (2003) *Der Islam in Europa. Der Umgang mit dem Islam in Frankreich und Deutschland*, Göttingen: Wallstein Verlag.

Fetzer, J. and Soper, C. (2005) *Muslims and the State in Britain, France, and Germany*, Cambridge: Cambridge University Press.

Fischer Weltalmanach (2004) *Der Fischer Weltalmanach 2005*, Frankfurt/Main: Fischer Verlag.

Greeley, A. (1972) *The Denominational Society. A Sociological Approach to Religion in America*, Glenview, IL: Scott, Foresman.

Gustafsson, G. (2003) 'Church–State Separation – Swedish Style', in J. Madeley and Z. Enyedi (eds), *Church and State in Contemporary Europe: The Chimera of Neutrality* (Special Issue of *West European Politics*), London: Frank Cass, pp. 51–72.

Hammar, T. (ed.) (1985) *European Immigration Policy. A Comparative Study*, Cambridge: Cambridge University Press.

Hammar, T. (1990) *Democracy and the Nation State. Aliens, Denizens, and Citizens in a World of International Migration*, Aldershot: Avebury.

Hammar, T. (2003) 'Einwanderung in einen skandinavischen Wohlfahrtsstaat: die schwedische Erfahrung', in D. Thränhardt and U. Hunger (eds), *Migration im Spannungsfeld von Globalisierung und Nationalstaat*, Leviathan Special Issue no. 22, Wiesbaden: Westdeutscher Verlag, pp. 227–52.

Hanley, D. (2003) 'Die Zukunft der europäischen Christdemokratie', in M. Minkenberg and U. Willems (eds), *Politik und Religion*, PVS Special Issue no. 33/2002, Wiesbaden: Westdeutscher Verlag, pp. 231–55.

Hansen, R. and Weil, P. (eds) (2001) *Toward a European Nationality. Citizenship, Immigration and Nationality Law in the European Union*, New York: Palgrave.

Haynes, J. (1998) *Religion in Global Politics*, London: Longman.

Heitmeyer, W. and Dollase, R. (eds) (1996) *Die bedrängte Toleranz. Ethnisch-kulturelle*

Konflikte, religiöse Differenzen, und die Gefahren politisierter Gewal, Frankfurt/Main: Suhrkamp.

Hoffmann-Nowotny, H.-J. and Killias, M. (1993) 'Switzerland: Remaining Swiss', in D. Kubat (ed.), *The Politics of Migration Policies. Settlement and Integration: The First World into the 1990s*, New York: Center for Migration Studies, pp. 231–45.

Huntoon, Lisa (1998) 'Immigration to Spain. Implications for a Unified European Union Immigration Policy', *International Migration Review*, 32, 2 (Summer), pp. 423–50.

Iannaccone, L. (1991) 'The Consequences of Religious Market Structure. Adam Smith and the Economics of Religion', *Rationality and Society*, 3, 2, pp. 156–77.

Inglehart, R. (1997) *Modernization and Postmodernization*, Princeton, NJ: Princeton University Press.

Inglehart, R. and Baker, W. (2000) 'Modernization, Cultural Change, and the Persistence of Traditional Values', *American Sociological Review*, 65, pp. 19–51.

Inglehart, R. and Minkenberg, M. (2000) 'Die Transformation religiöser Werte in entwickelten Industriegesellschaften', in Heinz-Dieter Meyer, Michael Minkenberg and Ilona Ostner (eds), *Religion und Politik – zwischen Universalismus und Partikularismus, Jahrbuch für Europa- und Nordamerika-Studien, Vol. 2*, Opladen: Leske and Budrich, pp. 115–30.

Joppke, C. (1999) *Immigration and the Nation-State*, Oxford: Oxford University Press.

Kastoryano, R. (2002) *Negotiating Identities. States and Immigrants in France and Germany*, Princeton, NJ: Princeton University Press.

Koopmans, R. and Statham, P. (eds) (2000a) *Challenging Immigration and Ethnic Relations Politics. Comparative European Perspectives*, Oxford: Oxford University Press.

Koopmans, R. and Statham, P. (2000b) 'Migration and Ethnic Relations as a Field of Political Contention: An Opportunity Structure Approach', in R. Koopmans and P. Statham (eds), *Challenging Immigration and Ethnic Relations Politics. Comparative European Perspectives*, Oxford: Oxford University Press, pp. 13–56.

Koopmans, R., Statham, P., Giugni, M. and Passy, F. (2005) *Contested Citizenship. Immigration and Cultural Diversity in Europe*, Minneapolis: University of Minnesota Press.

Koslowski, R. (2000) *Migrants and Citizens. Demographic Change in the European State System*, Ithaca: Cornell University Press.

Kubat, D. (ed.) (1993) *The Politics of Migration Policies. Settlement and Integration: The First World into the 1990s*, New York: Center for Migration Studies.

Kymlicka, W. (1995) *Multicultural Citizenship*, Oxford: Oxford University Press.

Kymlicka, W. and Norman, W. (eds) (2000) *Citizenship in Diverse Societies*, Oxford: Oxford University Press.

Liénard-Ligny, Monique (2001) 'Nationality Law in Belgium', in Randall Hansen and Patrick Weil (eds) *Towards a European Nationality*, New York: Palgrave, pp. 193–213.

Lijphart, A. (1999) *Patterns of Democracy. Government Forms and Performance in Thirty-six Countries*, New Haven: Yale University Press.

Madeley, J. (2003) 'European Liberal Democracy and the Principle of State Religious Neutrality', in J. Madeley and Z. Enyedi (eds), *Church and State in Contemporary Europe. The Chimera of Neutrality*, London: Frank Cass, pp. 1–22.

Madeley, J. and Enyedi, Z. (eds) (2003) *Church and State in Contemporary Europe. The Chimera of Neutrality*, London: Frank Cass.

Manow, P. (2002) ' "The Good, the Bad, and the Ugly": Esping-Andersens Sozialstaats-Typologie und die konfessionellen Wurzeln des westliches Wohlfahrtsstaats', *Kölner Zeitschrift für Soziologie und Sozialpsychologie*, 54, 2, pp. 203–25.

Maréchal, B. and Dassetto, F. (2003) 'Introduction: From Past to Present', in B. Maréchal, S. Allievi, F. Dassetto and J. Nielsen (eds), *Muslims in the Enlarged Europe. Religion and Society*, Leiden: Brill, pp. xvii–xxvii.

Martin, D. (1978) *A General Theory of Secularisation*, London: Blackwell.

Mavrogordatos, G. (2003) 'Orthodoxy and Nationalism in the Greek Case', in J. Madeley and Z. Enyedi (eds), *Church and State in Contemporary Europe. The Chimera of Neutrality*, London: Frank Cass, pp. 117–36.

Mendoza, C. (2003) *Labour Immigration in Southern Europe. African Employment in Iberian Labour Markets*, Research in Migration and Ethnic Relations Series, Aldershot: Ashgate.

Minkenberg, M. (1990) *Neokonservatismus und Neue Rechte in den USA*, Baden-Baden: Nomos.

Minkenberg, M. (2002) 'Religion and Public Policy. Institutional, Cultural, and Political Impact on the Shaping of Abortion Policies in Western Democracies', *Comparative Political Studies*, 35, 2 (March), pp. 221–47.

Minkenberg, M. (2003a) 'The Policy Impact of Church–State Relations: Family Policy and Abortion in Britain, France and Germany', in J. Madeley and Z. Enyedi (eds), *Church and State in Contemporary Europe. The Chimera of Neutrality*, London: Frank Cass, pp. 195–217.

Minkenberg, M. (2003b) 'Staat und Kirche in westlichen Demokratien', in M. Minkenberg and U. Willems (eds), *Politik und Religion*, PVS Special Issue 33/2002, Wiesbaden: Westdeutscher Verlag, pp. 115–38.

Minkenberg, M. (2004) 'Religious Effects on the Shaping of Immigration Policy in Western Democracies', paper presented at the ECPR 32nd Joint Session of Workshops, Uppsala, 13–18 April.

Minkenberg, M. (2008a) 'Religious Legacies and the Politics of Multiculturalism: A Comparative Analysis of Integration Policies in Western Democracies', in A. Chebel d'Appollonia and S. Reich (eds) *Immigration, Integration and Security. America and Europe in Comparative Perspective*, Pittsburgh: University of Pittsburgh Press, pp. 44–66.

Minkenberg, M. (2008b) 'Religious Legacies, Churches and the Shaping of Immigration Policies in the Age of Religious Diversity', *Politics and Religion*, 1, 3, pp. 349–83.

Minkenberg, M. and Willems, U. (eds) (2003) *Politik und Religion*, PVS Special Issue 33/2002, Wiesbaden: Westdeutscher Verlag.

Modood, T. (ed.) (1997) *Church, State, and Religious Minorities*, London: Policy Studies Institute.

Monsma, S. and Soper, C. (1997) *The Challenge of Pluralism. Church and State in Five Democracies*, Lanham: Rowman and Littlefield.

Mooney, M. (2006) 'The Catholic Bishops' Conferences of the US and France: Engaging Immigration as a Public Issues', *American Behavioral Scientist*, 49, 11, pp. 1455–70.

Morén-Alegret, R. (2002) *Integration and Resistance. The Relation of Social Organisations, Global Capital, Governments and International Immigration in Spain and Portugal*, Research in Migration and Ethnic Relations Series, Aldershot: Ashgate.

Moreno Fuentes, Francisco Javier (2001) 'Migration and Spanish Nationality Law', in R. Hansen and P. Weil (eds) *Towards a European Nationality*, New York: Palgrave, pp. 118–42.

Nielsen, J. (1995) *Muslims in Western Europe*, Edinburgh: Edinburgh University Press.

Nielsen, J. (2001) 'Muslims, the State and the Public Domain in Britain', in R. Bonney,

F. Bosbach and T. Brockmann (eds), *Religion und Politik in Deutschland und Großbritannien*, München: Saur, pp. 145–54.

Noll, M. (2002) *The Old Religion in a New World: The History of North American Christianity*, Grand Rapids, MI: Eerdmans.

Ornbrant, B. and Peura, M. (1993) 'The Nordic Pact. An Experiment in Controlled Stability', in D. Kubat (ed.), *The Politics of Migration Policies. Settlement and Integration: The First World into the 1990s*, New York: Center for Migration Studies, pp. 202–30.

Price, Charles (1993) 'Australia: A New Multicultural Country?' in D. Kubat (ed.), *The Politics of Migration Policies. Settlement and Integration: The First World into the 1990s*, New York: Center for Migration Studies, pp. 3–22.

Robbers, G. (2003) 'Status und Stellung von Religionsgemeinschaften in der Europäischen Union', in M. Minkenberg and U. Willems (eds), *Politik und Religion*, pp. 88–112.

Rokkan, S. (1970) *Citizens, Elections, Parties: Approaches to the Comparative Study of Processes of Development*, Oslo: Universitetsforlaget.

Schmidtke, O. (2003) 'Das kanadische Einwanderungsmodell: Wohlverstandenes Eigeninteresse und multikulturelles Erbe', in D. Thränhardt and U. Hunger (eds), *Migration im Spannungsfeld von Globalisierung und Nationalstaat*, Leviathan Special Issue no. 22, Wiesbaden: Westdeutscher Verlag, pp. 205–26.

Sciortino, G. (2003) 'Einwanderung in einen mediterranen Wohlfahrtsstaat: die italienische Erfahrung', in D. Thränhardt and U. Hunger (eds), *Migration im Spannungsfeld von Globalisierung und Nationalstaat*, Leviathan Special Issue no. 22, Wiesbaden: Westdeutscher Verlag, pp. 253–73.

Soysal, Y. (1994) *Limits of Citizenship. Migrants and Postnational Membership in Europe*, Chicago and London: University of Chicago Press.

Symmons, Clive R. (2001) 'Irish Nationality Law', in R. Hansen and P. Weil (eds), *Towards a European Nationality*, New York: Palgrave, pp. 273–300.

Thränhardt, D. (2003) 'Der Nationalstaat als migrationspolitischer Akteur', in D. Thränhardt and U. Hunger (eds), *Migration im Spannungsfeld von Globalisierung und Nationalstaat*, Leviathan Special Issue no. 22, Wiesbaden: Westdeutscher Verlag, pp. 8–31.

Thränhardt, D. and Hunger, U. (eds) (2003) *Migration im Spannungsfeld von Globalisierung und Nationalstaat*, Leviathan Special Issue no. 22, Wiesbaden: Westdeutscher Verlag.

Van Amersfoort, Hans and van Niekerk, Mies (2003) 'Einwanderung als koloniales Erbe: Akzeptanz, Nichtakzeptanz und Integration in den Niederlanden', in D. Thränhardt and U. Hunger (eds), *Migration im Spannungsfeld von Globalisierung und Nationalstaat*, Leviathan Special Issue no. 22, Wiesbaden: Westdeutscher Verlag, pp. 135–60.

Van Kersbergen, K. (1995) *Social Capitalism. A Study of Christian Democracy and the Welfare State*, London: Routledge.

Von Beyme, K. (1984) *Parteien in westlichen Demokratien*, München: Piper.

Von Beyme, K. (1999) *Die parlamentarische Demokratie. Entstehung und Funktionsweise 1789–1999*, Opladen/Wiesbaden: Westdeutscher Verlag.

Wald, K. (2003) *Religion and Politics in the United States*, Washington, DC: CQ Press.

Weil, P. (2001) 'Zugang zur Staatsbürgerschaft. Ein Vergleich von 25 Staatsangehörigkeitsgesetzen', in C. Conradand and J. Kocka (eds), *Staatsbürgerschaft in Europa. Historische Erfahrungen und aktuelle Debatten*, Hamburg: Edition Körber Stiftung, pp. 92–111.

Weil, P. (2002) *Qu'est-ce qu'un Français? Histoire de la nationalité française depuis la Révolution*. Paris: Grasset.

Whyte, J. (1981) *Catholics in Western Democracies. A Study in Political Behavior*, New York: St Martin's Press.

Willems, U. and Minkenberg, M. (2003) 'Politik und Religion im Übergang–Tendenzen und Forschungsfragen am Beginn des 21. Jahrhunderts', in M. Minkenberg and U. Willems (eds), *Politik und Religion*, PVS Special Issue, Wiesbaden. Westdeutscher Verlag, pp. 13–41.

Wimmer, A. (1998) 'Binnenintegration und Außenabschließung. Zur Beziehung zwischen Wohlfahrtsstaat und Migrationssteuerung in der Schweiz des 20. Jahrhunderts', in M. Bommesand and J. Halfmann (eds), *Migration in nationalen Wohlfahrtsstaaten: theoretische und vergleichende Untersuchungen*, Osnabrück: Universitätsverlag Rasch, pp. 199–221.

Winkelmann, R. (2001) 'Immigration Policies and Their Impact: The Case of New Zealand and Australia', in S. Djajić (ed.), *International Migration: Trends, Policies and Economic Impact*, London: Routledge, pp. 1–20.

Zapata-Barrero, R. (2003) 'Spanish Country Report in Immigration Management', Bruxelles: Migration Policy Group; available at http://migpolgroup.com/publications.

3   The Orthodox Church and Greek–Turkish relations

Religion as source of rivalry or conciliation?

Ioannis N. Grigoriadis

Introduction

Greece is a successor state of the Ottoman Empire with a predominantly Christian Orthodox population, a member of the Western bloc in the Cold War, and a full member of all European political institutions. The country has intimate historical, political and cultural links with three regions: Western Europe, the Balkans and the Middle East. Since independence in 1830, a combination of Ottoman political traditions and Enlightenment ideas has formed the key framework for state–religion relations.

Greece is an exception in the context of the secularisation process which has characterised much of Western Europe in recent years. In Greece, many people do not accept that 'modernisation' inevitably means a reduction or denial of a significant political role for the Orthodox Church. Under these circumstances, what is widely agreed to be a growing political role for religion since the end of the Cold War in many parts of the world implies in Greece even greater influence for certain religious actors. This claim is made not only in relation to domestic issues but also in relation to the country's foreign policy, especially in relation to Turkey.

Over the years, Greek–Turkish relations have been burdened by long-lasting political problems, including territorial disputes, such as Cyprus and the Aegean, and sovereignty disputes involving minority peoples. Because of historical factors, which led to the formation of the Greek nation-state and the emergence of the Autocephalous Church of Greece, two religious institutions vie for influence among Orthodox Greeks. These two – the Ecumenical Patriarchate and the Church of Greece – have long competed against each other, with a significant influence on Greek–Turkish relations. Over time, however, their positions have become increasingly bifurcated, especially in the context of the post-1999 rapprochement efforts between the two countries. While the Church of Greece, under the leadership of Archbishop Christodoulos, generally took a position which did not obviously contribute to peaceful resolution of Greek–Turkish disputes and arguably helped embed further existing prejudices, the Istanbul-based Ecumenical Patriarchate, led by Ecumenical Patriarch Bartholomew, followed a distinctively different line. Although the church was itself a victim of Turkish anti-minority policies, it nevertheless actively promoted Greek–Turkish cooperation, including peaceful resolution of existing disputes. As a result, it managed to earn the respect of both international political and religious leaders (Williams 2008).

The contention of this chapter is that the church was able to do this through the ability of its leader to wield, what Joseph Nye calls 'soft power'. In this chapter, following Nye, soft power is regarded as:

> the ability to get what you want through attraction rather than coercion or payments. It arises from the attractiveness of a country's culture, political ideals, and policies. When our policies are seen as legitimate in the eyes of others, our soft power is enhanced.
>
> (Nye 2004: ix)

Religious soft power is exercised when religious leaders are able to convince their followers through persuasion to adopt certain positions – not only religious, but also political and social. Religious soft power may or may not serve religious moral values, such as peace, tolerance and conciliation, and may or may not contribute towards conflict resolution and mutual respect. However, it is argued in this chapter that religious soft power can be sustainable in the long run only if its exercise contributes to the reinforcement of religious moral values. In particular, international conflict, which is often underlined by religious difference, appears to be a primary policy area where religious soft power could be applied.

This chapter focuses on the role that the Orthodox Church plays in Greek–Turkish relations. As already noted, Greece has departed from the European secularisation trend. This is due to two main factors: first, the residual effect of the legacy of the Ottoman *millet* system, and second, the important position of religion in the formation, embedding and continuity of Greek nationalism. As a result, Greece has followed a distinct modernisation path in which the church has played a significant social and political role. Its significance appeared to increase after the Cold War. In this chapter we examine Greek–Turkish relations in two main contexts: first, the role over time of Orthodoxy in the dispute and, second, how the church is able to affect – and sometimes help mould – feelings of identity among many Greeks, thanks to the soft power of its leader.

The rise of a bifurcated religious order

Greeks and Turks co-inhabited parts of Southeastern Europe, Anatolia and the Eastern Mediterranean for many centuries. Following independence, the Greek nation-state turned Orthodoxy into its primary badge of identity. Greece won its independence fighting against the Ottoman Empire, and the Ottoman Turk became the 'other', against which 'Greekness' was conceptualised and measured. However, fully to subordinate Orthodoxy to the interests of the Greek nation-state it was necessary to gain clear control over its institutionalised representative: the Autocephalous Church of Greece, cut adrift from the Istanbul-based Ecumenical Patriarchate in 1834. It then became the 'national church' which espoused the 'Megali Idea', that is, a nationalist vision aiming to replace the Ottoman entity with a Greek Empire, a resuscitation of the Byzantine Empire. Meanwhile, the Ecumenical Patriarchate, based in Istanbul, became more circumspect. This was not only because of its sensitive position under Ottoman jurisdiction, but also because of its unease with the idea of nationalism which threatened to undermine the cohesion of its multi-ethnic, multilingual followers. As it was, the Ecumenical Patriarchate barely survived the demise of the Ottoman Empire and its subsequent replacement by individual nation-states, including Turkey. Yet despite its temporal weakness, it managed to maintain a strong symbolic role as the spiritual centre of world Orthodoxy and as a custodian of Orthodox cultural heritage. In addition, the ecumenical character of the Patriarchate influenced the definition of Greekness. In contrast to the more exclusive character of the Greek national identity espoused by the Church of Greece, the Patriarchate favoured a more inclusive and tolerant definition of Greekness based on culture, not ethnicity. This informed the respective positions of both institutions regarding Greek–Turkish relations and later Turkey's European Union membership bid.

This study aims to uncover possible explanations for this ambivalence. In addition, it aims to examine state–religion relations in Greece in the context of secularisation pressures, as well as the role of religious leadership over time. In short, it explores links between religion and nationalism in Greece over time. Given that nationalism has often used religion as a tool to try to increase cohesion and achieve mass mobilisation, I examine under what conditions religious institutions can influence political developments and exercise soft power. In addition, I attempt to establish a link between the sustainability of this power and the compatibility of policy objectives with Orthodox religious values, including peace, toleration and mutual understanding.

Citizenship and religion in Greece

The legacy of the *millet*[1] system which divided the Ottoman society along religious lines has long been influential in Greece. Religious affiliation became the basis of identity formation during the Greek struggle for independence, and Orthodoxy was the cornerstone upon which modern Greek national identity was built. Ethnic descent and language were much less significant than religion in the drawing of dividing lines between Ottoman populations. This was demonstrated in the Compulsory Population Exchange Agreement between Greece and Turkey, signed in Lausanne on 30 January 1923. In this agreement, both states agreed to a mandatory exchange of their minority populations.[2] In this exchange, the defining criterion of 'Greekness' and 'Turkishness' was religion. As a result, Greek-speaking Muslims from Crete were exchanged with Turkish-speaking Orthodox Christians from inner Anatolia. The population exchange was the first major step towards the religious homogenisation of the population of Greece. The hitherto sizable presence of Muslims was reduced to the province of

Western Thrace on the boundary with Turkey and Bulgaria. Soon after, Greece's Jewry was among the worst hit by the Holocaust, with most of the survivors emigrating to Israel after the Second World War. This meant that by 1950 Greece had a population where around 97 per cent professed Orthodoxy, according to official censuses. For many Greeks, this rise in the proportion of Orthodox Christians further strengthened the links between Orthodoxy and Greekness. Later, however, the end of the Cold War and globalisation opened Greece to the influence of new social and economic trends, turning the country from a net exporter to a net importer of immigrants. In a similar development to that which occurred in Israel at about the same time (see Ben-Porat's chapter in this collection), this contributed to a radical change in Greece's social fabric. Since then, Greece has become a multicultural, multi-ethnic society with an immigrant population of approximately one million out of a total population of about twelve million. Most immigrants originate from Eastern and Southeastern Europe, the Middle East and South Asia and do not profess Orthodoxy. Accustomed to a mono-ethnic, monoreligious environment, Greek society has had to adapt to this new reality, rather in the same way that Israelis have had to adapt to mass immigration from the former Soviet Union (see Ben-Porat's chapter in this collection).

Under these circumstances, addressing issues of citizenship became very important. In addition, debate about the role of religion in Greek politics became more pronounced from the late 1990s, as the leadership of the Church of Greece argued for a more influential role in both politics and society. During his tenure from 1998 to 2008 Archbishop Christodoulos attempted to expand the public role of the church on a large range of issues – including citizenship – and to prevent secularisation. He also aimed to expand his authority in relation to the most important institution of Orthodoxy, the Ecumenical Patriarchate. Despite the decimation of Istanbul's Orthodox community and the serious problems which hampered its operation,[3] the Ecumenical Patriarchate has maintained ecclesiastical jurisdiction in parts of the Greek territory as well as a strong appeal to the Greek faithful.

The legal basis of state–church relations in Greece

As already noted, religion was a key element in the formation of modern Greek national identity. More specifically, Christianity became a de facto condition of Greek citizenship. Shortly after the outbreak of the Greek War of Independence, Article 2§2 of the First Constitution promulgated on 1 January 1822 at the First Revolutionary National Assembly in Epidaurus, stated: 'The autochthonous residents of the Greek Territory who believe in Jesus Christ are Greeks and enjoy all the civil rights without any limitation and difference.'[4] Later ethnic criteria were added to the religious ones; nevertheless Greek nationalism used Orthodoxy as the primary marker of Greek national identity. As a result of this, a special relationship between the state and the Orthodox Church was instituted. This was reflected not only in the country's Constitution and in many of its laws but also in the informal yet strong political position of the church. According to Article 3 of the Constitution,

1   The prevailing religion in Greece is that of the Eastern Orthodox Church of Christ. The Orthodox Church of Greece, acknowledging our Lord Jesus Christ as its head, is inseparably united in doctrine with the Great Church of Christ in Constantinople and with every other Church of Christ of the same doctrine, observing unwaveringly, as they do, the holy apostolic and synodal canons and sacred traditions. It is autocephalous and is administered by the Holy Synod of serving Bishops and the Permanent Holy Synod originating thereof and assembled as specified by the Statutory Charter of the Church in compliance with the provisions of the Patriarchal Tome of June 29, 1850 and the Synodal Act of September 4, 1928.

2   The ecclesiastical regime existing in certain districts of the State shall not be deemed contrary to the provisions of the preceding paragraph.

3   The text of the Holy Scripture shall be maintained unaltered. Official translation of the text into any other form of language, without prior sanction by the Autocephalous Church of Greece and the Great Church of Christ in Constantinople, is prohibited.

(Hellenic Parliament 2001: 18)

Article 13 of the Constitution, which regulates religious freedom, is meant to balance the prerogatives of the Orthodox Church, acknowledged in Article 3. However, religious freedom is guaranteed for all 'known religions' in the following terms:

1   Freedom of religious conscience is inviolable. The enjoyment of civil rights and liberties does not depend on the individual's religious beliefs.

2   All known religions shall be free and their rites of worship shall be performed unhindered and under the protection of the law. The practice of rites of worship is not allowed to offend public order or the good usages. Proselytism is prohibited.

3   The ministers of all known religions shall be subject to the same supervision by the State and to the same obligations toward it as those of the prevailing religion.

4   No person shall be exempt from discharging his obligations to the State or may refuse to comply with the laws because of his religious convictions.

5   No oath shall be imposed or administered except as specified by law and in the form determined by law.

(Hellenic Parliament 2001: 26)

Also of major significance is the reference to religion in Article 16, which deals with education affairs. According to Article 16§2:

Education constitutes a basic mission for the State and shall aim at the moral, intellectual, professional and physical training of Greeks, the development of national and religious consciousness and at their formation as free and responsible citizens.

(Hellenic Parliament 2001: 30)

The closeness between the Greek state and the Orthodox Church of Greece, reaffirmed by this Article, means a privileged position in relation both to other Christian confessions and to non-Christian religions. The church was often perceived by state officials and public opinion as part of the state apparatus, while bishops have often exceeded their strictly religious duties by making political statements on issues such as human rights, education, family policy and foreign policy. Church prelates frequently claim to represent the opinion of their flock, while often adopting both a nationalistic and an isolationist discourse concerning various issues, including: globalisation, European integration, conflict resolution and immigration. This trend peaked with the election of Archbishop Christodoulos in 1998, a figure who attempted to consistently expand the church's involvement in public affairs.

The 'identity card' crisis was a prime example of his new conceptualisation of the greater public role of the Church of Greece (Molokotos-Liederman 2003: 296–7). Christodoulos opposed the governmental decision to eliminate any reference to religion in the notion of Greek identity. He organised two major demonstrations against the government's decision, and about three million Greek citizens signed a petition drafted by the church, which demanded a referendum on the issue. Although the government did not succumb to these demands, Christodoulos maintained his claim for a major public role for the church, underpinned by his great personal popularity, manifested in several opinion polls of the time (Mavrogordatos 2003: 130–1). Only a major corruption scandal in the Church of Greece in 2005 limited Christodoulos' popularity, as well as his claim to play a major role in Greek politics.

Before delving into the Church of Greece's position on Greek–Turkish relations, it is necessary to provide some information about the history of the relationship between the Ecumenical Patriarchate and the Church of Greece.

The historical background

The Ecumenical Patriarchate became the only Eastern Roman (or 'Byzantine') institution which survived the collapse of the Empire and the fall of Constantinople in 1453. As the Byzantine aristocracy was annihilated, converted to Islam or fled to Western Europe, the Patriarchate remained as the sole institutional point of reference for the subject Ottoman Christians. The Ecumenical Patriarch became the representative of the Ottoman Orthodox Christians in the eyes of the Ottoman authorities.[5] While the Ecumenical Patriarchate's jurisdiction in the late Byzantine era was sharply contested by the rise of Bulgarian and Serbian medieval kingdoms, in the Ottoman era it managed to expand its jurisdiction in the central and western Balkans with the consent of Ottoman authorities. This allowed for the accumulation of considerable political power in the hands of the incumbent Patriarch and familiarised the Ottoman Orthodox subjects with the idea of clerical rule and the convergence of political and religious authority.[6] As a result, the Patriarch and his bishops were seen as *ex officio* political leaders of the Ottoman Orthodox Christians. This status was only challenged with the advent of the Enlightenment era and the repercussions it caused among the Ottoman Orthodox elites, who became exposed to nationalism and secularism. The French Revolution inspired a Greek merchant bourgeoisie which mainly lived in Ottoman and European cities. Many among such people played an active role both in the leadership of the Ottoman Orthodox population and in the organisation of a nationalist republican uprising in the nineteenth century against Ottoman rule, whose aim was to establish a secular republican nation-state. Most of them adopted nationalism and sought to establish a modern Greek nation-state whose primary identity reference point would not be the Orthodox Byzantine Empire but Greek classical antiquity.[7]

The establishment of the Kingdom of Greece in 1830 did not provide good omens for the continuation of the status quo.[8] The government of the new nation-state wanted to bring domestic religious expressions under sole control. Religious control and authority by an institution which was an integral part of the Ottoman imperial realm was deemed unacceptable, and the establishment of a 'national' state church became one of the first government priorities. The Regent Triumvirate, which was established until the juvenile Bavarian Prince Otto von Wittelsbach came of age, proceeded swiftly to sever the ties of the local church with the Patriarchate. Headed by the intellectual and priest Theoklitos Farmakidis, the Autocephalous Church of Greece was proclaimed in 1834. This comprised the first nationalist schism within the Orthodox realm, dealing a grave blow to the Ecumenical Patriarchate. Relations between the Patriarchate and the Church of Greece were restored only with the Patriarchal Tome of 29 June 1850, yet the repercussions of the event were felt throughout the nineteenth century. The Bulgarian Schism of 1870, the creation of a Bulgarian National Church – which appealed to Bulgarian-speaking Orthodox Christians – and the direct challenge of the Patriarchate's authority even within Ottoman territories, led in 1872 to the declaration that nationalism was a heresy (Matalas 2002).

However, a new status quo emerged following decisive wars between 1912 and 1922 which caused the collapse of the Ottoman Empire, resulting in the inclusion of former Ottoman provinces and Patriarchal dioceses into Greece. A new question then emerged: Would the Patriarchate cede jurisdiction over the dioceses of the provinces the Ottoman Empire ceded to Greece? The issue was resolved with the Synodal Act of 1928, which acknowledged the tutelary rights of the Patriarchate over these dioceses but transferred their administration to the Church of Greece. While this arrangement worked for decades, it was challenged by Archbishop Christodoulos in the early 2000s. He claimed that the jurisdiction of the Church of Greece should coincide with the territory of Greece. This was a direct challenge to the 1928 compromise. A serious crisis in the relations of the Ecumenical Patriarchate and the Church of Greece erupted, only resolved in 2003 when the Church of Greece withdrew its claims. However, various problems continued to affect their relationship, including: Greek–Turkish relations, where their positions differed greatly.

The political background

Greek–Turkish relations have long been problematic, for various historical and political reasons. Greece gained its independence from the Ottoman Empire, the predecessor state of the Republic of Turkey, in 1830. Greece and the Ottoman Empire fought wars in 1897 and 1912, while Greece also confronted Turkish nationalist forces who later established the Republic of Turkey between 1919 and 1922. Greek and Turkish forces clashed most recently over Cyprus in 1974. Additionally, the formation of Greek and Turkish national identities developed in relation to the Muslim Turk or Orthodox *Rum*-Greek[9] identity, which served as the quintessential 'other'. From the time of the 1912 and 1922 wars, the Cyprus issue was a source of considerable tension in Greek–Turkish relations, especially from the 1950s. The Greek-instigated coup and subsequent Turkish invasion of 1974 led to a new status quo deemed unacceptable by the international community. Persistent efforts to reunify the divided island on the basis of a bizonal, bicommunal federation have, however, so far failed.

Regarding the Aegean disputes, Greece and Turkey disagree on the extent of their territorial waters, continental shelf, airspace, flight information region (FIR) and the militarisation of some Greek Aegean islands, while Turkey has recently disputed the sovereignty of Greece over several islets and rocks of the Aegean. The status of the Ecumenical Patriarchate and the Greek Orthodox minority in Istanbul and the two Aegean islands and the Muslim minority of Western Thrace have also caused considerable tension. Overall, these factors have led to a very confrontational environment, with each state perceiving the other as a major security threat, leading to a very expensive arms race which served to militarise Greek–Turkish land and maritime borders. During the Cold War, Greece prioritised the 'Eastern threat' (Turkey) over the 'Northern threat' (the Soviet bloc) in its strategic planning. Greece's membership of the European Economic Community (EEC; later European Union, EU) in 1981 provided Greek foreign policy with additional leverage against Turkey. Thanks to the unanimity rule in EU decision-making, any improvement of EEC–Turkey relations became conditional upon Greek consent. This was not given because of the stalemate on the Cyprus question and Greek–Turkish bilateral disputes.

In the 1990s, there were two major crises. In January 1996, Greece and Turkey came to the brink of war over the sovereignty of the Imia/Kardak islet in the eastern Aegean. In February 1999, the leader of the Kurdistan Workers' Party (Partiya Karkaren Kurdistan, PKK) and Turkey's then most wanted person, Abdullah Öcalan, was captured by Turkey after having found refuge at the Greek Embassy in Nairobi. These two events marked the lowest point in Greek–Turkish relations since 1974. Yet things were soon to improve. Through close cooperation between Foreign Ministers George Papandreou and Ismail Cem, a new era of Greek–Turkish relations began (Evin 2004: 8–10, 2005: 396–8). The tragic coincidence of two earthquakes, which hit Istanbul and Athens within a month of each other in August and September 1999, and the spontaneous support of both peoples to the plight of the earthquake victims, suggested that rapprochement efforts might not meet with grassroots opposition. In December 1999, in Helsinki, the Council of the European Union named Turkey as a candidate state for EU membership (Grigoriadis 2006: 138–45). Greece, which had since its EEC membership been the fiercest opponent of an upgrade in EU–Turkey relations before Greek–Turkish disputes were resolved, became one of the most vocal supporters of Turkey's EU membership. An exponential rise of trade and investment between the two countries further strengthened the improved climate in Greek–Turkish relations. The initiation of an unprecedented political reform process in Turkey aiming at the fulfilment of the Copenhagen Criteria for EU membership raised hope among many Greeks that more conciliatory views would increasingly prevail on all bilateral issues.

Nonetheless, Greek–Turkish disputes in the Aegean remained unresolved, while no breakthrough was achieved on the issue of the rights of Turkey's Greek minority. Much effort was put into attempts to resolve the Cyprus question, a key element in popular perceptions of continued Greek–Turkish conflict (Çarkoğlu and Kirişçi 2004: 138–45). In late 2002 a comprehensive United Nations plan was offered to both sides on the eve of the island republic's membership of the European Union. Yet in the 24 April 2004 referendum, Greek Cypriots rejected the proposed solution of the Cyprus question, which left the Cyprus issue unresolved after Cyprus joined the Union in 2004. The change of government in Greece in 2004 did not change the official discourse regarding Turkey's EU aspirations. However, as in other EU member states, the debate on Turkey's European or Asian identity and its ability to adapt to European political principles has persisted. This debate was also informed by Turkey's record on protecting the rights of its Greek minority and the Ecumenical Patriarchate. Soon two lines appeared on the issue. The first maintained that efforts to bring Turkey into the European Union were in vain and that Turkey was a cultural misfit for the European family. The second insisted that Turkey was eligible for EU membership if it fulfilled the Copenhagen Criteria like any other member state. In other words, It was in Greece's interest to promote Turkey's transformation into a fully consolidated democracy, in which minority rights would be fully respected and which would help resolve its disputes with its neighbours, such as Greece and Cyprus, following negotiations on the basis of international law. Turkey's EU accession process provided a suitable framework for the promotion of greater democracy and the resolution of Greek–Turkish disputes. Religious actors also positioned themselves on this issue. This was no surprise for the Church of Greece, as Archbishop Christodoulos had repeatedly stated that he reserved the right to intervene in the public debate on issues of 'national significance' and to speak on behalf of the church or 'the Greek Orthodox nation'. In the case of the Ecumenical Patriarchate, which normally avoided any intervention in Greek political affairs, this issue was of the utmost significance, as the very existence of itself and the Greek minority also depended on the course of EU–Turkey relations.

The position of the Church of Greece on Turkey's accession to the EU

The Church of Greece under Christodoulos questioned the Greek–Turkish rapprochement and opposed Turkey's membership of the European Union. The line followed was essentially a hard-line Greek nationalist one, in which Turkey was represented as a quintessentially non-European country which still represented an existential threat to both European civilisation and Christianity. Based on these assumptions, efforts to promote a Greek–Turkish rapprochement, before the resolution of the Cyprus and Aegean disputes according to Greek views were treated with suspicion, if not outright hostility, by some bishops. Efforts to achieve compromise solutions were deemed to be either naïve or treacherous, as Turkey would thus be rewarded for its expansionist agenda and encouraged to advance it further. In these talks, Turks were often portrayed as barbaric infidels, unable to behave properly, or at best powerless pawns in the hands of an evil state. Selective use of history was also made in attempts to corroborate such claims. In 2003, Archbishop Christodoulos launched an even more vitriolic attack against the Turkish nation during a service in memory of an Orthodox saint executed in the Ottoman era:

> That is why they [the Turks] impaled him. And now these people want to enter the European Union. Barbarians cannot enter the family of Christians. We cannot live together. This is not out of malevolence. This is consistency, and we should keep it in order not to lose everything in the name of diplomacy. Diplomacy is good, but we cannot forget our history ... Those who disagree with us do so because they know no history ... We cannot forget everything and betray the struggles of our fathers.
>
> (Bailis 2003)

Traumatic events in Greek history were repeatedly used to promote a view of an unchangeably barbaric Turkey. In numerous cases, Christodoulos referred to the killings of Pontic Greeks by Turkish forces in the early twentieth century, accusing foreign powers for their lack of redemption of the victims and reassuring the victims that in the end they would be vindicated, adding: 'We will never forget the inextinguishable stigma of the perpetrators.' Later he also stated: 'The Turkish people is induced by its fanatical leadership and shows baseness and villainy ... Let us not believe that Turks can become Europeanised. I am afraid that Europe will become Turkified' (Bailis 2005).

Such positions were too far-fetched even for the right of the Greek political spectrum. Coming under pressure for his openly racialist views in the new political environment created by the Greek–Turkish rapprochement efforts, Christodoulos followed a more circumspect line in his opposition to Turkey's EU accession. Despite himself opposing European integration, he subscribed to the line of leading European federalists who saw Turkey's potential EU membership as a stumbling block to the process of European integration. In that view, the accession of Turkey threatened the very feasibility of the European project, because of its relative poverty, size and allegedly 'non-European' culture. In late 2005, when asked in an interview whether he still thought that Turkey should not enter the European Union despite the EU decision to start accession negotiations, Christodoulos responded:

> I think what is more important than the opinions of religious leaders is the clearly negative position on this issue [Turkey's EU membership] of paramount and historical figures of the European community such as Giscard d'Estaing and Jacques Delors. Even more important is the opinion of the European – as well as the Greek – citizens, who in recent polls have overwhelmingly opposed Turkey's EU membership. We should also not forget that the rejection of the European Constitution in big countries such as France and Holland is said to have occurred to express the opposition of the European public opinion to that possibility. Nowadays, many political analysts and intellectuals express the concern that instead of Europeanising Turkey, we may end up Turkifying Europe. There is no need to add anything else.
>
> (Christodoulos 2005)

His rhetoric and opinions could not go unaddressed in Turkey. Columnists fiercely reacted to his harsh attacks against Turkey and Turks, calling him a 'psychopath', contrasting his intemperate comments with the new era of Greek–Turkish relations at both political and social levels. In the words of Oktay Ekşi, a major columnist on the popular Turkish daily *Hürriyet*:

> The Turkish and the Greek people want to forget the bad memories of the past. And they actually did. But the church cannot accept that. To tell the truth, we cannot understand this. Does the church exist as religious institution to spread love or hate and animosity?
>
> (Ekşi 2004)

Addressing a significant political audience in Greece, Christodoulos did not defend Christian principles but Greek nationalist stereotypes against Turkey. He used his persuasive powers – arguably a form of religious 'soft power' – in order to try to rekindle old animosities and instil fear and animosity in relation to continuing rapprochement efforts. This served to relegate him to the level of a fringe political figure, who enjoyed strong sympathy from a few but also strong criticism from many others. This had the effect of severely limiting his soft power potential, not least because his forcefully expressed opinions appeared to many to be in direct contrast to what were widely understood to be universal religious principles, such as peace, toleration and reconciliation.

The position of the Ecumenical Patriarchate

The position of the Ecumenical Patriarchate on Greek–Turkish relations was diametrically different. Following a line of reconciliation, it defended the need for dialogue and cooperation between Greece and Turkey. This position also fitted the Christian virtues of toleration and peace-building. In an interview in the Greek daily newspaper *Eleftherotypia* in 1999, Ecumenical Patriarch Bartholomew stated:

> This is our principle, peace and brotherhood of humans and peoples. This principle also refers to Greek–Turkish relations. We have repeatedly taken a position on Greek–Turkish relations ... We have always supported the need for good neighbourly relations, friendship and cooperation between the two peoples ... Because of that position we have been criticised by a part of the Greek press. Nonetheless, we will not cease to fervently support the good neighbourly relations and cooperation of Greece and Turkey for the benefit of both peoples.
>
> (Ecumenical Patriarch Bartholomew I 1999)

This statement was not well received by Greek nationalists inside and outside the Church of Greece, as it appeared that one of the foremost victims of Turkish nationalist policies, the Ecumenical Patriarchate, was taking both a conciliatory and a moderate position on Greek–Turkish relations. As a result, Bartholomew was accused of 'supporting Turkish and not Greek interests', while some columnists suggested the transfer of the seat of the Ecumenical Patriarchate from Istanbul to Greece. Thessaloniki, Mount Athos and the island of Patmos were – at times – suggested as possible seats (Giannaras 1999). On this issue, Greek and Turkish nationalist circles were in harmony, as several Turkish nationalist groups demanded the expulsion of the Patriarchate from Turkey (Kerinçsiz 2006). They were especially annoyed by the Patriarch organising Masses in abandoned churches throughout Anatolia (Yıldırım and Tuna 2006).

Bartholomew's attempt to propose a new approach for Greek minority questions was of major significance in this context. The Patriarchate did not ignore the persistent violations of its rights and the rights of the Greek minority. Turkey's European perspective was thus perceived as the only realistic hope for improvement in the field of minority rights, which could benefit not only the dwindling Greek minority of Istanbul but also the Ecumenical Patriarchate itself. Being a victim of Turkish minority discrimination policies, the Patriarchate was naturally interested in the democratic reform process, which would, it was expected, include provisions for the protection of minority rights and the restitution of past injustices. This entailed careful screening of the reform process and criticism in the cases where insufficient progress was made. Closure of the religious seminary in Heybeliada (Chalki) became one of the key issues in the reform process. Turkey's refusal to allow the reopening of the seminary was one of the clearest manifestations that the reform process still faced serious shortcomings (Grigoriadis 2008: 36). However, positive steps were also recognised, including Turkey's bid to join the European Union, which would necessarily involve complete resolution of all minority problems, including those related to the Greek minority. Addressing the Parliamentary Assembly of the Council of Europe in early 2007, Bartholomew explained:

> At this point, we must mention that the Ecumenical Patriarchate and the surrounding Greek-Orthodox minority in Turkey feel that they still do not enjoy full rights, such as the refusal to acknowledge and recognise a legal status to the Ecumenical Patriarchate, the prohibition of the operation of the Theological School of Chalki, property issues and many more. We do recognise, however, that many reforms have been made and some remarkable steps have been taken for the accession of the internal law towards the European standard. Therefore, we have always supported the European perspective of Turkey in anticipation of the remaining steps to be taken according to the standards of the European Union.
>
> (Ecumenical Patriarch Bartholomew I 2007)

Turkey's convergence with EU standards on minority rights was presented not as a concession but as something essentially beneficial for the country. Recognising the rights of the Patriarchate and the Greek minority would not only pose no threat for Turkey, it would also benefit it, as this would comprise a clear manifestation of the maturity of its democracy. Referring to the issue of the Chalki Seminary in 1999, Bartholomew argued:

> We will not cease to wish that Turkey realises that the reopening of the Chalki Religious Seminary not only does not harm its interests, but will be on the contrary to its benefit. Orthodox and non-Orthodox youth will come to study here … When they return to their home countries and take over responsible positions, they will boast of having studied at the Ecumenical Patriarchate and the historic Chalki School, in modern Turkey, in which religious freedom is so protected that it allows for the operation of such a Christian Seminary, although the vast majority of its population is Muslim.
>
> (Ecumenical Patriarch Bartholomew I 1999)

On this issue, Bartholomew sided with many among the Turkish liberal intelligentsia who fervently supported the EU reform process and did not see it as antithetical to Turkish national security interests (Birand 2007). In fact, many reformist intellectuals in Turkey suggested a new definition of Turkish national interest, with acknowledgment of minority rights henceforward not perceived as a major threat to Turkish security. On the contrary, such a development might actually improve Turkish security, as minority members would eventually feel themselves to be respected as citizens of the Republic of Turkey (Grigoriadis 2007: 431–2).

Nonetheless, perhaps the most impressive statement made in that interview referred to the issue of nationalism. Bartholomew reminded the interviewer of the 1872 synodal decision which had declared 'nationalism' as heresy and pointed to what he regarded as the fundamentally anti-Christian nature of nationalist ideologies:

> We would like to remind [you] that nationalism has been condemned by the Church as 'heresy' … The revival of nationalism is a burning contemporary question, as it is directed against Orthodoxy and Christianity in general, even when the Christian and in general the religious element is presented as a means to further nationalist goals. Nationalism isolates the peoples, directs them against each other, while the quintessence of Christianity is love and brotherhood of peoples. The unity of humankind is one of the basic messages of Apostle Paul and the whole Church, as well as the finding of true philosophical and biological thought. From that perspective, racism has been worldwide condemned and is related to nationalism, from which, though, one should differentiate laudable patriotism.
>
> (Ecumenical Patriarch Bartholomew I 1999)

This position was an explicit condemnation of Greek and Turkish nationalism from a theological vantage point, which clearly dissonated with the stance of the Church of Greece on the same issue. Bartholomew chastised divisive and intolerant elements apparently inherent to all nationalisms. This could only cause major surprise in large parts of Greek public opinion, which had been familiarised with the identification of Orthodoxy and Greek nationalism and the depiction of Orthodoxy as Greece's 'national religion'. In response to the divisive effects of nationalism, Bartholomew suggested interreligious dialogue as the means to bring about convergence, reconciliation and peaceful coexistence.

> That however which is accomplished fluently through interreligious dialogues is the cultivation of a spirit of tolerance, reconciliation and peaceful coexistence of the faithful of the various religions, free from fanaticism and phobias. Contrary to political positions that many times foster the spirit of conflict and confrontation, catching thus within it both victims and victimisers, we try and pursue sowing the spirit of equal rights and responsibilities for all and for their peaceful cooperation, independently of their religion. For only through the opening of hearts and minds and the acceptance of one's difference as an equal value to our own is it possible to build peace in this world.
>
> There is one more accomplishment and goal of the interreligious dialogues that is not of any less importance. This is the enrichment of the mind and perception of each faithful by considering things through the religion of somebody else. This enrichment releases us from partiality; it allows us to have a higher and wider understanding of beliefs; it fortifies the intellect and very often it leads us to a deeper experience of the truth and to a very advanced level of our growth in the presence of the divine revelation.
>
> (Ecumenical Patriarch Bartholomew I 2007)

This message referred not only to the Greek–Turkish conflict, which is to some degree informed by religious differences, but also to the wider divide perceived to exist between the 'West' and the 'Islamic world'. Bartholomew has also been vocal on this issue. For example, the Ecumenical Patriarchate has frequently organised events promoting interreligious dialogue with emphasis on issues such as the environment. These have included various symposia on environmental protection, including one on board a vessel on the Amazon river in July 2006 and another held in Greenland the following year. Interlocutors have included major figures of Islam in Turkey, including Fethullah Gülen and leaders of American Jewry such as Chief Rabbi David Rosen, President of the International Jewish Committee on Interreligious Consultations. Overall, such activities have earned Bartholomew great respect while increasing his international influence, in contrast to his continuing weak domestic position in Turkey.

Explaining the difference

Such a sharp difference between the approach of the Ecumenical Patriarchate and the Church of Greece on Greek–Turkish relations can be explained by allusion to various factors. First, we can point to an instrumentalist explanation for the position of the Ecumenical Patriarchate. That is, the Patriarchate and Turkey's Greek minority have both paid a very high price because of the long-term tension in Greek–Turkish relations. It is no coincidence that the decline of the Greek minority population in Turkey was positively correlated with the emergence and escalation of the Cyprus question after the Second World War. Discriminatory measures and attacks against Turkey's Greeks were seen in both Turkey and Greece as a form of 'retaliation' against anti-Turkish Cypriot incidents in Cyprus between the 1950s and 1970s. This brought Turkey's Greek minority to the brink of extinction and the Ecumenical Patriarchate under unprecedented pressure, as it became unable to manage its property or educate its clergy while facing serious difficulties in performing even its most basic functions. It was hoped that improvement of Greek–Turkish relations would help defuse the pressure traditionally exerted on Turkey's Greek minority and the Patriarchate and also pave the way for Turkey's European integration, as Greece, historically the biggest opponent of the improvement of EEC–Turkey relations, became an ardent supporter of Turkey's EU membership. Shortcomings in minority rights protection, however, never distanced the Patriarchate from the strategic target of Turkey's European integration. A European Turkey, with a thriving economy and a fully democratic political system, would, it was believed, be a much more suitable host country for an institution of the international stature of the Patriarchate.

Nonetheless, instrumentalist reasoning is insufficient to explain overall the position of the Ecumenical Patriarchate on Greek–Turkish relations. One also needs to consider the role of leadership and agency. At the theological level, Bartholomew consistently advocated the Christian principles of toleration, peace and reconciliation against Greek or Turkish nationalism. He also realised that the European Union was a political project, which stood for the reconciliation of the

European peoples and the overcoming of nationalist conflicts in the European continent. He understood that Turkey's EU membership could greatly contribute not only to the reconciliation of Turkey with Greece, but also to the much greater task of building bridges between Muslims and Christians. This position gained Bartholomew greater international respect and recognition, manifested for example in May 2008, when he was included in the *Time* magazine annual list of the world's 100 most influential people. The Archbishop of Canterbury and Head of the Anglican Church, Rowan Williams, justified the *Time* decision as follows:

> Patriarch Bartholomew, however, has turned the relative political weakness of the office into a strength, grasping the fact that it allows him to stake out a clear moral and spiritual vision that is not tangled up in negotiation and balances of power. And this vision is dominated by his concern for the environment.
>
> (Williams 2008)

In addition, while Turkish authorities insisted on viewing him as the religious leader of a tiny religious minority of Turkey, Bartholomew was officially received and visited by heads of states, prime ministers and religious leaders throughout the world. In this regard, it is appropriate to mention, for example, his visit to the United States in March 2002, when he was received by the US president with head-of-state honours.

As regards the Church of Greece, one needs to consider its growing political voice in order to understand its position on Greek–Turkish relations. The increased political voice of the Church of Greece has followed its closer affiliation with the state. Church officials felt empowered to make their positions known on a range of political issues, which – in most cases – resembled positions taken by parties on the far right of the Greek political spectrum, such as the Popular Orthodox Rally (Laikos Orthodoxos Synagermos, LAOS). This trend became stronger under Archbishop Christodoulos. The adoption of a populist, nationalist and xenophobic agenda was condemned by a large part of the Greek intelligentsia, while having considerable appeal among many conservative voters who saw Christodoulos as a political leader who did not hesitate to defend narrowly defined Greek national interests at all costs. In that context, Greek–Turkish rapprochement efforts were often seen as a foreign ploy to promote a fake reconciliation between Greece and Turkey at the expense of Greek national interests. Given the key role Orthodoxy has played in the formation of Greek national identity, Christodoulos was eager to play a leading role in Greek nationalist mobilisation. The conciliatory stance of the Ecumenical Patriarchate was conveniently ignored or undermined, regarded as a product of foreign pressure or even as 'treason'. Christodoulos' political agenda allied him with the right of the Greek political spectrum, and this inevitably meant his identification with this strand of Greek public opinion on the issue of Greek–Turkish rapprochement. The conflation of religion with nationalism, populism and direct political involvement may have led to short-term political gains and appeal among a part of Greek population, but in the long term it helped to undermine his religious soft power. In other words, his ability was reduced to influence and persuade more widely, by setting a moral paradigm based on religious principles.

The failure of this policy was implicitly accepted by the prelates of the Church of Greece. After the death of Archbishop Christodoulos in January 2008 the Holy Synod elected Bishop Ieronymos as his successor. The new Archbishop was the best-known opponent of Christodoulos' strategy to claim a key political role for the church, including issues of foreign policy generally and Greek–Turkish relations specifically. In his enthronement speech, Ieronymos underlined that he was an ecclesiastical leader and not a politician. In the first months of his tenure, he followed a line distinctly different from that of his predecessor. He refrained from interventions in foreign policy affairs – including Greek–Turkish relations and Turkey's EU candidacy – and restricted his activity to strictly religious issues. One of the first tasks was notably the restoration of good relations between the Church of Greece and the Ecumenical Patriarchate. His appointment also raised hopes that a reconsideration of the relationship between the Greek state and the Church of Greece was possible.

Conclusions

Given the strong imprint of Orthodoxy on the definition of Greek national identity, the divergent positions of the Ecumenical Patriarchate and the Church of Greece on Greek–Turkish relations illustrate how both institutions have over time suggested alternative versions of what it means to be Greek. The Church of Greece under Christodoulos saw the continuation of Greek–Turkish rivalry as a substantial part of Greek national and Orthodox religious identity and opposed any rapprochement efforts and Turkey's EU integration. The Ecumenical Patriarchate, however, did not consider Greek–Turkish conflict as a defining element of Greek identity. A more inclusive, tolerant version of Greekness was championed, which was not built on animosity towards Turkey. Instead, this stance highlighted the potential merits of Turkey's EU accession for both Greeks and Turks, including the key prize of resolution of existing disputes between the countries. In addition, it became clear how the interaction between the Greek state and the Orthodox Church could very easily facilitate the instrumentalisation of religion for nationalist purposes in foreign policy-making. This highlights how state-affiliated religious actors may side with state positions, which in some cases are characterised by both nationalist bias and a realist, bleakly Hobbesian, view of international relations.[10] Under these circumstances, religious actors may behave more like state officials or politicians promoting state interests or the views of their own political clientele, rather than encouraging conflict resolution, peace and toleration. On the other hand, lack of links with a state may be a necessary but not sufficient condition for the development of positions loyal to religious principles such as peace and conciliation. Lack of alignment with state interests allows for the adoption of different positions on issues of foreign policy, which may be closer to a cooperative Kantian view of international relations.

The autonomy of religious institutions from the state apparatus may be considered as an additional reason for their support for conflict resolution and reconciliation. Under these conditions, religious leaders may underplay the importance of secular nationalist concerns and address foreign policy questions on the basis of religious principles. Moreover, we also need to address the importance of agency. For example, the personality of a religious leader can have a major impact on the formation of the position of the religious institution on various issues, including foreign policy. Finally, it appears that in the long run success in the use of religious soft power depends on consistent adherence to clear religious principles. Consistency between political goals and religious principles may lead to enduring or even increasing soft power of religious actors. Religious actors who prefer to serve a radical political agenda and make policy choices inconsistent with religious values such as peace, toleration and conciliation may have to face a decrease of their ability to persuade wide segments of the society that their position is one they should support. Judging by the evidence presented in this chapter, viewing religion as an agent of pacification and conflict resolution is not only consistent with religious principles, but also may earn considerable religious, social and political appeal.

Notes

1 The *millet* system was the main political framework according to which the Ottoman Empire ruled its subjects, based on their religious affiliation. On this see Braude (1982).
2 For more on this, see Hirschon (2003).
3 Among several grievances, one could highlight the official rejection of the Patriarchate's ecumenical character and legal personality. This included the legal personality of numerous Orthodox pious religious foundations. This paved the way for systematic confiscations and usurpations of immovable assets.
4 Interestingly there was no differentiation between Orthodox and Catholic Christians, despite the identification of the *Rum millet* with Orthodoxy. Apparently this stance aimed to co-opt the Greek-speaking Catholic population of the Aegean, as well to avoid antagonising the Western powers. However, the identification of Greek national identity with Orthodoxy became clear following independence in 1830.
5 For more information on the *millet* system, see Braude (1982).
6 The case of Cyprus and the religious–political rule of Archbishop Makarios from the 1950s to the 1970s is a highly indicative late survival of the Ottoman convolution of religious and political authority.
7 The doyen of Greek Enlightenment, Adamantios Korais, was a primary advocate of such ideas.
8 For more information on the relations between Greek nationalism and the Ecumenical Patriarchate in the nineteenth century, see Matalas (2002).
9 The term *Rum* included all the Orthodox subjects of the Ottoman Empire, regardless of their ethnic origin and language. The term 'Greek' referred to the Orthodox subjects which embraced the Greek nationalist project.
10 For a comparison between Hobbesian and Kantian approaches to Greek–Turkish disputes, see Kirişçi (2002).

Bibliography

Bailis, P. (2003) 'Christodoulos' Frenzy: He Attacked From the Pulpit "Barbarian" Turks [Παραλήρημα Χριστόδουλου: Επιτέθηκε από Άμβωνος Κατά Των "Βαρβάρων" Τούρκων]', *Τα Νέα* [*Ta Nea*], 5 December.

Bailis, P. (2005) 'Anti-Turkish Explosion … Christodoulos Characterised the Turkish People as "Villain"' [Αντιτουρκική Έκρηξη … Ο Χριστόδουλος Χαρακτήρισε "Κακούργο" τον Τουρκικό Λαό]', *Τα Νέα* [*Ta Nea*], 10 October.

Birand, M. A. (2007) 'Ekümeniklik Neden Bizi Rahatsız Ediyor?' *Posta*, 3 July.

Braude, B. (1982) 'Foundation Myths of the *Millet* System' in B. Braude and B. Lewis (eds), *Christians and Jews in the Ottoman Empire: The Functioning of a Plural Society*, New York: Holmes & Meier, pp. 69–88.

Çarkoğlu, A. and Kirişçi, K. (2004) 'The View from Turkey: Perceptions of Greeks and Greek–Turkish Rapprochement by the Turkish Public', *Turkish Studies*, 5, 1, pp. 117–53.

Christodoulos, A. (2005) 'Interview', *Πολιτικά Θέματα* [*Politika Themata*], 17 October.

Ecumenical Patriarch Bartholomew I (1999) 'Είναι Αίρεση ο Εθνικισμός-Βλάπτει την Ορθοδοξία' [Nationalism is a Heresy – It Harms Orthodoxy], interview with Stratis Balaskas, *Ελευθεροτυπία* [*Eleftherotypia*], 29 March.

Ecumenical Patriarch Bartholomew I (2007) *Speech to the Plenary of the Parliamentary Assembly of the Council of Europe*, Strasbourg: Council of Europe.

Ekşi, O. (2004) 'Psikopat Değilse Nedir?' *Hürriyet*, 27 August.

Evin, A. O. (2004) 'Changing Greek Perspectives on Turkey: An Assessment of the Post-Earthquake Rapprochement', *Turkish Studies*, 5, 1, pp. 4–20.

Evin, A. O. (2005) 'The Future of Greek–Turkish Relations', *Journal of Southeast European and Black Sea Studies*, 5, 3, pp. 395–404.

Giannaras, C. (1999) 'Μυκτηρίζουν τη Μόνη Λύση' [They Mock the Only Solution], *Καθημερινή* [*Kathimerini*], 26 October.

Grigoriadis, I. N. (2006) 'Turkey's Accession to the European Union: Debating the Most Difficult Enlargement Ever', *SAIS Review of International Affairs*, 26, 1, pp. 147–60.

Grigoriadis, I. N. (2007) 'Türk or Türkiyeli? The Reform of Turkey's Minority Legislation and the Rediscovery of Ottomanism', *Middle Eastern Studies*, 43, 3, pp. 423–38.

Grigoriadis, I. N. (2008) 'On the Europeanization of Minority Rights Protection: Comparing the Cases of Greece and Turkey', *Mediterranean Politics*, 13, 1, pp. 23–41.

Hellenic Parliament (2001) *The Constitution of Greece*, Athens; available at www.parliament.gr/english/politeuma/syntagma.pdf

Hirschon, R. (2003) 'The Consequences of the Lausanne Convention: An Overview', in R. Hirschon (ed.), *Crossing the Aegean: An Appraisal of the 1923 Population Exchange between Greece and Turkey* New York: Berghahn Books, pp. 13–20.

Kerinçsiz, K. (2006) 'Σε Δύο Χρόνια Θα Κλείσουμε το Πατριαρχείο' [We Will Close the Patriarchate within Two Years], interview with Anna Andreou, *Τα Νέα* [*Ta Nea*], 8 July.

Kirişçi, K. (2002) 'The "Enduring Rivalry" between Turkey and Greece: Can "Democratic Peace" Break It?' *Alternatives: Turkish Journal of International Relations*, 1, 1, pp. 38–50.

Matalas, P. (2002) *Έθνος και Ορθοδοξία: Οι Περιπέτειες μιας Σχέσης. Από το 'Ελλαδικό' στο Βουλγαρικό Σχίσμα* [Nation and Orthodoxy: The Adventures of Relation. From The 'Greek' to the Bulgarian Schism], Rethymnon: Crete University Press.

Mavrogordatos, G. T. (2003) 'Orthodoxy and Nationalism in the Greek Case', *West European Politics*, 26, 1, pp. 117–36.

Molokotos-Liederman, L. (2003) 'Identity Crisis: Greece, Orthodoxy and the European Union', *Journal of Contemporary Religion*, 18, 3, pp. 291–315.
Nye, J. S. (2004) *Soft Power: The Means to Success in World Politics*, New York: Public Affairs.
Williams, A. R. (2008) 'Bartholomew I', *Time 100*, p. 5.
Yıldırım, T. and Tuna, T. (2006) 'Bergama Bazilikası'nda Ayine "Kızılelma" Protestosu', *Milliyet*, 8 May.

Part II
Secularisation

4 Religion and secularism in Israel

Between politics and sub-politics

Guy Ben-Porat

Introduction

Contemporary Israel is characterised by a secular–religious clash, sometimes described as a 'culture war', a highly volatile example of a world trend. This religious–secular struggle involves, on the one hand, a territorial debate over the future borders of Israel and, on the other hand, a struggle over the shape of the public sphere. The border debate concerns the future of the territories captured by Israel in the 1967 Six-Day War. Israeli politics is divided between 'doves' who support a territorial compromise and the formation of a Palestinian state and 'hawks' who oppose territorial compromise. Opposition to Israel's withdrawal from the territories is often based not only on security concerns but also on a significant religious ideology, which negates any compromise over the 'promised land'. The struggle over the public sphere concerns both the status of Israel as a *Jewish* state and the role of religion in public life. While secular Israelis feel constrained by religious rules and regulations, religious Israelis are concerned with the weakening of religion's influence in public life and the consequential secularisation of Israeli society. Overall, in Israel religion and politics are perceived as intertwined in both ways and, consequently, supposedly underline the tense relations between religious and secular in Israel, as well as the perceived growing potential for a 'culture war'.

The territorial debate and the struggle over the public sphere, however, as will be argued below, do not necessarily constitute a 'culture war'. In the debate over territory, not only do dovish and hawkish positions gradually overlap with secularism and religiosity but, in addition, these positions are played out centrally in the political arena. But, conversely, struggles over the role of religion in public life are often absent from the formal political arena and are determined elsewhere in what is referred to here, following Ulrich Beck (1994, 1997), as 'sub-politics'. Interestingly, until the late 1960s, politics and religion in Israel centred on the public sphere, where religious political parties sought to maintain their power, relatively indifferent to territorial questions. It was only after the 1967 war where a dynamic religious camp emerged, perceiving itself as leader and standard bearer of 'true Zionism', which brought the territorial debate to centre-stage. Over time, however, struggles over the public sphere have not disappeared or lost significance but, for reasons explained below, have, at least partially, shifted towards 'sub-politics'.

Interactions between religion and politics in Israel, as this chapter demonstrates, are complex, dynamic and do not adhere to the strict contours of a 'culture war' where political and social hostility are rooted in different systems of moral understanding translated into competing sets of principles and ideals (Hunter 1991: 42). I will begin by establishing the theoretical connections between religion and politics through discussion of the 'culture war' scenario. The second part will describe two developments that supposedly highlight the culture war in Israel: (1) collapse of the secular–religious *modus vivendi* in the public sphere – known as the 'status quo' – and (2) strong links that have developed between religion and politics on the issue of the future of the occupied territories. While the latter emerges as a political event that resonates with a culture war, the former translates into different struggles – such as Sabbath, non-kosher meat and marriage – that gradually shifted from 'politics' to 'sub-politics'.

Religion, secularism and the 'culture war'

Tensions between religion and secular tendencies have been described as one of the characteristics of the post-Cold War era (Jurgensmeyer 1995). Religious fundamentalist movements across the globe seek to reclaim authority for religion and demand reinstatement of religion into the public policy decision-making process (Shupe and Hadden 1989). Religions in this context are 'de-privatised' (or 'politicised'), according to Casanova (1994: 6), as they seek to re-enter the public sphere, not only to defend their 'traditional turf' but also to

> participate in the very struggles to define and set the modern boundaries between the private and the public spheres, between system and life-world, between legality and morality, between individual and society, between family, civil society, and state, between nations, states, civilizations, and the world system.
>
> (Casanova 1994: 6)

The rise of religious fundamentalism, on the one hand, and the politicisation of religion, on the other, amount, according to some observers, to a 'culture war'. American sociologist James Hunter (1991: 42–4) describes a situation of culture war where political and social hostility are rooted in different systems of moral understanding. Competing sets of principles and ideals – polarisingly defined as 'Orthodox' and 'progressive' – provide a 'source of identity, purpose and togetherness for people who live by them' (ibid.). While Orthodoxy, related to religion, is distinguished by its belief in the existence of an 'external, definable and transcendent authority', progressivism defines moral authority 'by the spirit of the modern age, a spirit of rationalism and subjectivism' (ibid.). This divergence of world views translated into political struggles has also been described as a crisis of moral authority, a new religious war and a conflict between an approach to citizenship based on rights and one based on duties (Johnson 1995). The struggle between religious and secular is essentially a cultural conflict translated into various disagreements over procedural norms and legal codes that define limits of personal behaviour and collective action, the nature and extent of political responsibility and the regulation of interactions between different parties in the political arena (Hunter 1991: 52).

The use of the term 'culture war' implies a clash between opposing principles and uncompromising political positions. In reality, however, the relations between secular and religious often present a more complex, multilevel picture. First, secularism and secularisation processes tend to be multidimensional rather than unified and coherent. Consequently, second, secularism and religion engage in different struggles with the investment of differing levels of commitment and political energy. And, third, some of these struggles take place outside or beyond the formal political sphere. The multidimensionality of secularisation refers to the different levels where religion's authority declines, from various institutions that gain autonomy from religious control to a popular decline in religious involvement, religious belief and religious practices (Chaves 1994). In more simple terms we can differentiate analytically between two processes: 'institutional secularisation' that refers to formal, legal changes of the status of religion and 'private secularisation' that refers to personal beliefs and practices.

Secularisation translates into a 'bricolage', a construction of beliefs, practices and values, observed in many Western societies, where people often make differing choices, sometimes incoherent and at times contradictory (Beckford 2003; Luckman 1967). Because secularisation is not linear or coherent, it often follows that the secular–sacred boundary is blurred as the religious becomes less obviously religious and the secular less obviously secular (Heelas 1998). Indeed, the distance between secular and religious is often less than its proponents are willing to acknowledge. Secularism presents itself as crucial to private freedom, democracy, individual rights, public reason and an ideological battle against the supposed dogmatism of religion that ended in church–state separation. But secularism is as much a consequence of changes in social structure, economy and technology as a result of secularist ideology (Wilson 2001). Thus, secularisation can be in part the result of an emerging consumerist society, whose practices often contrast with religious way of life, yet that has little to do with ideology. In his study of commercial activity on Sundays in Britain, Philip Richter (1994) finds that people who shop on that day may also attend church and perceive no contradiction in such behaviour. Similarly, Ben-Porat and Feniger (2009) find that in Israel secular practices such as shopping on the Sabbath are often detached from wider political goals and commitments.

For Bruce (2003: 9), 'politics' includes not only the nature and actions of states and governments, but also what political parties and various groups do, trying to influence government policies, including the basic liberties that they are supposed to protect and defend. Many people would agree that this is indeed the substance of politics, so when religious (or secular) issues are politicised they become part of the public debate and part of the political struggle to shape the public or the common good. On the other hand, exclusive focus on the decline of traditional forms of participation ignores the new participation styles that are rapidly rivalling the old ones (Gundelach 1984). According to Ulrich Beck, the security concern of many citizens that governments either do not understand or cannot control, leads not necessarily to political apathy but sometimes to new political channels: 'on the one hand, a political vacuity of the institutions is evolving, on the other hand, a non-institutional renaissance of the political' (Beck 1994: 17). Instead of focusing exclusively on formal politics, Beck suggests, scholars should pay attention also to 'sub-politics', the 'new' politics that is sometimes hidden from the eye (ibid.). Sub-politics practices seek to fill the political gap described above, where citizens lose faith in political institutions and political institutions lose their capacity to govern. What Holzer and Sorensen (2001) define as 'active subpolitics' implies responsibility taking by citizens in their everyday, individual-orientated life arena that cuts across the public and private sphere (Micheletti 2003: 25).

Secular and religious activists may find formal politics unsatisfying and search for other channels of influence. These forms of political participation that bypass the formal political arena translate into different initiatives and struggles, and sometimes into unofficial compromises and solutions. In the Israeli case, discussed below, a political paralysis in religious–secular affairs is manifested in an inability both to mediate the conflict or to govern. This paralysis is related, at least partly, to the involvement of religion in the territorial debate and the consolidation of this schism as the axis of contemporary Israeli politics. However, as other religion/church–state relations that pertain to everyday life remain unresolved, secular and religious activists move away from traditional political channels that they find unsatisfying to new initiatives that can be described as sub-politics. Thus, while religion is politicised in the territorial debate it also shifts to the less formal channels of sub-politics in other areas.

From status quo to paralysis

Since the early period of Zionism at the turn of the nineteenth century, the controversy over the status of religion has been conducted under the threat of an internal breakup between the religious and secular camps (Horowitz and Lissak 1989). The potential conflict between the largely secular Zionist movement and the religious parties within the movement was largely avoided by a series of concessions, trade-offs, deferral of issues that threatened to tear apart the delicate consensus and a 'division of labour' between the leading religious and secular parties. The dominant force in Israeli politics in pre-statehood and the first thirty years of statehood – Mapai (the Labour Party) – established a working relationship with the National Religious Party (NRP). This working relationship was based on a division of labour: NRP left Mapai to make decisions on issues of foreign affairs and security, while the NRP had an influential voice in various issues involving religion and religious affairs.

Pragmatic, consociational type, compromises established in the early years of statehood, an arrangement that came to be known as the 'status quo', established various rules related to the public sphere. The rules, both formal and informal, included the observance of *kashrut* (Jewish dietary rules) in public institutions; declaration of the Sabbath as an official day of rest; establishment of a separate religious school system; granting religious Orthodoxy a monopoly over various issues, including marriage arrangements, conversion to Judaism and burial; and the exemption of ultra-Orthodox men and religious women from mandatory army service. While the status quo did not resolve all issues of conflict it did create some flexible guidelines that acted as a starting point for negotiations. 'They present a kind of a default position with presumptive validity. Deviation is clearly possible, but it requires cogent justifications' (Cohen and Susser 2001:19). Thus, the issues at stake between religious and secular in the earlier years of statehood were not foreign policy and territorial questions but internal questions regarding the role of religion in public life and the observation of the status quo. Essentially, the religious politicians were concerned with maintaining their monopoly over significant aspects of public life such as marriage, kosher licensing and burial.

In the early 1970s significant changes gradually undermined the division of labour and the cooperation between the parties. First, the future of the territories occupied in 1967 became a dividing issue between the moderate Labour Party and the NRP, which became a leading hawk on the issue. And, second, economic and demographic changes gradually eroded many of the status quo arrangements. According to some scholars, the early consociational agreements gave way to a crisis-dominated relationship between secular and religious Jews. 'Rather than an accommodation of each other's needs in the interest of preserving national unity, a majoritarian, winner-take-all style has grown more and more dominant' (Cohen and Susser 2001: xxi). In short, the breakup was the result, on the one hand, of the territorial debate and, on the other hand, of struggles in the political sphere. Combined, over time the issues underscored a growing perception: development of a 'culture war' (*kulturekampf*) in Israel between religious and secular Jews.

Those who reject the *kulturekampf* thesis often point to a large if relatively silent category of 'traditionalists' who provide support for the spirit of consociational agreements and, consequently, help prevent the potential for culture war. Studies conducted in both 1991 and 1999 (the Guttman report) support the existence of a middle category between secular and religious, the 'traditional'. About a third of the national sample of 2,446 respondents (36 per cent) described themselves as observant/highly observant, 40 per cent as somewhat observant and only 20 per cent described themselves as non-observant. In addition, 78 per cent defined themselves as 'traditional' or 'non-religious' compared to a minority who defined themselves as 'secular' or 'religious' (Levi *et al.* 2000). This demonstrates that the putative religious–secular divide is actually a continuum wherein many people select which rituals to participate in and the commandments to obey. Another related argument against the *kulturekampf* thesis refers to the existence of a common set of symbols or imagery that most Israeli Jews share. This, it can be argued, serves to transcend many of the differences, providing a basis for common discourse (Liebman 1997). Specifically, the values of Jewish peoplehood and the 'religion of security' are two central belief systems that provide a basis for broad consensus that exists among many Israeli Jews and may be said to override the divisions.

But the existence of a middle category of traditionalists does not by itself provide a bridge between opposing positions, nor does it rule out polarisation between groups with very different, sometimes frictional, ways of life. It is argued that such separate ways of life in Israel serve to underscore growing alienation between religious and secular and, consequently, polarisation of Israeli society (Schweid 1997). The polarisation thesis is supported by opinion polls in which religious and secular display a negative attitude towards each other. For example, in the Guttman report, cited above, in spite of a large centre of traditionalism, the majority of respondents (82 per cent) described the relationship between religious and secular as negative.

The centrality of the religious–secular cleavage is, however, undeniable, at least in the perceptions of many Israelis (Levi *et al.* 2000). But, as I argue below, the cleavage is only partly politicised and, consequently, far from a culture war. Not only do different struggles with varying levels of commitment and involvement involve the religious and the secular, but in addition the central struggles have largely shifted towards sub-politics. Interestingly, as the territorial question became an important indication of the engagement of religion and politics, significant issues of public life, previously the core of religious–secular politics, have shifted to a considerable degree away from the formal political sphere. These two developments, I argue, are related. This is because the political sphere had become overburdened and stagnant, unable to deal with new challenges and demands, and 'alternative politics' – that is, sub-politics – emerged. In the rest of this chapter I show, first, how the territorial issue became the main dividing line of Israeli society and religion's role in this. Second, I demonstrate how to a considerable extent sub-politics replaced formal political forms of participation. Specifically, non-Orthodox marriage, commerce activity on the Sabbath and the sale of non-kosher meat emerged less through a political struggle and more through alternatives that bypassed the political system and its regulation and, to a large extent, bypassed political conflict.

The occupied territories: religion meets politics

In the last week of March 2007 about 3,000 people, mostly young Jewish religious settlers, marched to Homesh, a settlement in the northern West Bank evacuated in the summer of 2005 as part of the government's disengagement plan from the territory. Prior to their march, they were given directions by their spiritual leaders. 'The Holy One Blessed Be He is the main partner, and it is to Him that we appeal for help, because without Him there is no chance,' read the leaflet distributed to the thousands of zealots. Rabbi David Dudkevitch, the rabbi of the Yitzhar settlement in the West Bank, urged them to go to Homesh,

> because that is the most natural and essential thing to do. In doing this, we are making a statement about the strength of the covenant between us and God, as it is written in the Torah. We are Jews who have come to inherit the land that God gave to our ancestors, and to realize our right of return.
>
> (Ben-Simon 2007)

This was not an uncommon sight or statement. Since the late 1990s, the Israeli public has become used to the involvement of religious leaders in the struggle over the future borders of the state and the use of religious commandments in the struggle. Some of these religious leaders explicitly argue that the commitment to the land and to 'greater Israel' overrides government decisions and stands outside the parameters of democratic political debate.

The war of 1967 ended with a decisive military victory for Israel. It led to the holding of new territories, adding a Palestinian population greater than that within Israel, about 750,000 in the West Bank and 400,000 in Gaza. The issue of the occupied territories became not only a major factor of the Israeli–Arab conflict but also became from the late 1970s the most contentious issue of Israeli politics. Despite the declaration of the Israeli government after the war that Israel had no intention of expanding its territorial boundaries, the 'temporary' occupation was gradually entrenched through the settlement of Israeli citizens in the territories. Not only were the newly occupied territories valued strategically but also their religious and sentimental value was popularised. For some Israelis the occupation of the old city of Jerusalem, the West Bank and the rest of the territories was seen as the fulfilment of a divine promise and the establishment of Israel in its 'natural' borders.

It was the younger generation of the NRP that soon became at the forefront of a movement to settle the territories and de facto annex them to Israel. 'The movement for the greater land of Israel', established shortly after the war to encourage the government to annex the territories, was made up of Labour Party hawks, but soon young Orthodox religious Jews came to dominate the movement. Early attempts of settlement of the territories by religious-nationalist Jews were, however, sporadic and included the involvement of a small group of Orthodox Jews who in 1968 squatted in the Arab town of Hebron. The movement only gained real momentum with the formation of Gush Emunim (Bloc of the Faithful) in 1974. This movement, comprising primarily young members of the NRP, adopted a messianic concept of religion and politics based on the redemption of the land and the nation. Between 1974 and 1977 Gush Emunim launched a settlement drive and pressurised the government to authorise settlements, even those established without permission. In demographic terms this drive did not amount to much – by the beginning of 1977 fewer then 4,000 Jews lived in the West Bank in four settlements – but an important precedent was set.

In 1977, for the first time in Israel's history, the Labour Party lost the elections to the Likud, a party favouring territorial maximalisation. Menachem Begin, Israel's new prime minister, was quick to declare his commitment to the territories and stated that 'Samaria and Judea [the Jewish name for the West Bank] are an inalienable part of Israel'. The Likud embarked on a wide-ranging initiative to institutionalise beliefs in the legitimacy of the new boundaries. Its pattern of Jewish settlement in the territories carved up the territories by settlements in such a disparate fashion that any future partition agreement would necessarily require removal of established settlements. Nevertheless, despite efforts to blur the border between the occupied territories and Israel by Jewish settlements and the attempts of Gush Emunim to present itself as the bearer of true Zionism, the territories remained a deeply divisive issue.

The growing political, economic and moral costs of occupation – especially since the Palestinian uprising in 1987 – led to a realisation among many Israelis, including policy-makers, that territorial compromise must be sought. The victory of the Labour Party in the 1992 elections and the peace process between Israel and the Palestinians that began a year later placed Gush Emunim in a defensive position. The desire of policy-makers to 'normalise' Israel through peace and global integration was, however, an anathema to the religious right, hawkish religious Israeli Jews. The religious right, which believed Israel to be a 'nation that dwells alone', rejected the idea of peace based on territorial compromise. Gush Emunim, which fought against the withdrawal from Sinai in 1982 and lost, led mass demonstrations against the Labour government determined to prevent any territorial compromise in the West Bank and Gaza. To them, territorial compromise was a betrayal of the essence of both Zionism and Jewish values. Accordingly, the language used in the anti-Oslo campaign described the government harshly, as 'traitors'. Some demonstrations turned violent, and tensions peaked with the assassination of Prime Minister Yitzhak Rabin in November 1995 by a student, a religious zealot.

During the 1990s overlap between the religious–secular and the hawk–dove cleavages was discernable in both political life and academic research. While many Jewish settlers in the West Bank and Gaza came primarily for subsidised housing, the overall tone was set by the religious ideologues of Gush Emunim, who tended to settle in more remote areas. In addition, many young religious students followed their religious leaders on demonstrations and helped establish illegal settlements. During Israel's disengagement from Gaza in the summer of 2005, when for the first time settlements were evacuated, many religious settlers resisted the efforts of soldiers and police to remove them with the help of religious youth who came from different places to support the settlers. Also, for the first time, extremist rabbis ordered their pupils who served in the army to defy orders they called 'illegal'.

Overall, this indicates that in recent years religion in Israel became part of a wider territorial ethno-national conflict, influencing policy-makers and constituents, not only a source of legitimacy for decisions concerning territorial compromise or annexation but also the major dividing line of Israeli politics.

Politicisation of religion and religionisation of politics are salient in the territorial debate. Not only have the religious–secular and the older, secular left–right debates overlapped, as religious people tend to identify themselves with the vision of 'greater Israel', but also religious symbols, language and commandments became part and parcel of the debate. Formation of a political religious camp, however, was matched by creation of a self-contained secular camp. It was also checked by international developments that prevented the *de jure* annexation of Palestinian territories and even threatened to reverse the settlement drive. This deadlock not only kept the territorial question undecided but also meant that the questions that pertain to everyday life and the public sphere remained unsettled. Over time, the territorial debate became the core of Israeli political life, the central issue on which government coalitions are formed (and fall apart). Other religion–state issues remain controversial, but Israeli governments, as demonstrated below, have neither sufficient energy nor capacity to resolve them. In this deadlocked formal political arena, the rules of the game established by the status quo arrangements can be neither enforced nor changed.

The public sphere – the rise of sub-politics

The role of religion in public life was at the heart of the struggles, decisions and compromises between religious and secular people in Israel until the 1990s. The status quo arrangements included the observation of *kashrut* (Jewish dietary rules) in public institutions, observance of the Sabbath as the official day of rest, and an Orthodox domination over matters of marriage and divorce. These arrangements, however, began to lose their relevance in the 1990s in the context of two significant developments: the mass immigration of Russians from the former Soviet Union and the advance of global consumer culture, a partial consequence of globalisation. In the past, struggles against the status quo were largely ideologically driven by a minority that held what might be called 'liberal' values, such as freedom of marriage or, in general, freedom of and from religion. The new economic and demographic developments, however, rendered many of the religious–state arrangements irrelevant with little ideological fervour, simply by creating 'new facts on the ground'. Against the background of a weakening state, increasingly unable to enforce rules or to regulate, changes to the status quo regime were all but inevitable, although not necessarily through the formal political sphere. In many cases, conventional politics proved ineffective, paving the way for the increased significance of alternative politics or, as I term it here, sub-politics.

During the 1990s, Israel's economy experienced a wave of growth resembling that of the East Asian 'Tigers' and living standards of many Israelis advanced, edging near to those of the rich Western democracies. In addition to these economic developments there was an increased 'Americanisation' of Israeli society, which involved deepening of consumerist behaviour and values and leisure activities and entertainment patterns and lifestyles that collectively transformed the hitherto relatively closed Israeli society. From a poverty-stricken society in the 1950s, Israel was now a relatively affluent society with more 'hedonistic' values, open to foreign cultural influences, and deeply engaged in consumption and consumerism. By the 1990s, when the state of Israel responded to globalisation's economic processes by reducing taxes on private businesses and on foreign goods, the cultural changes of Israeli society were striking. American fast food and retail chains were established across the country, a new language imbued with English words and slang was commonly used, while rock music and other (mostly) American musical influences and multi-channelled commercial television were ubiquitous. Overall, these developments linked all sorts of Israelis of to the wider Western and American world of plenty (Markowitz and Uriely 2002).

Mass immigration from the former USSR in the early 1990s was another striking change affecting Israel's society. More than a million immigrants arrived in a decade, many of them not Jewish according to Orthodox definition (determined by the mother's religion), and the vast majority of them secular. These immigrants had a strong influence on consumer patterns as they increased demand for non-kosher products (see below), often oblivious to religious constraints. The non-Jewish immigrants also challenged existing arrangements regarding rituals of marriage. Since they were not recognised as Jews by the Orthodox rabbinate and were unwilling in most cases to go through conversion, the state had to provide solutions that would allow them to perform essential services.

Commercialisation and immigration also created new challenges to existing religion–state and religion–society arrangements, as well as overall relations between religious and secular. And, as mentioned above, struggles over the public sphere that were central to the relationship between religion and politics in recent years were added to the pre-existing territorial debate. This combination overburdened the political system, more and more occupied by the territorial debate and, consequently, hardly able to regulate everyday life issues of religious–secular relations. The overburdened state failed to change the system of marriage or to provide an acceptable solution for the Sabbath. This led to alternative political struggles that served to render many of the old arrangements increasingly irrelevant. Debates over the role of religion in public life, however, did not disappear or diminish. Rather, they shifted from the realm of formal politics to that of sub-politics.

Sabbath – time for shopping?

The Jewish religion prohibits both work and commerce on Saturday – the Jewish Sabbath. The sacredness of the Sabbath is mentioned several times in the Bible, in Exodus (20: 8–10) for example:

> Remember the sabbath day, to keep it holy. Six days shalt thou labour, and do all thy work; but the seventh day is a sabbath of the Lord thy God: in it thou shalt not do any work, thou, nor thy son, nor thy daughter, thy manservant, nor thy maidservant.

These commandments were translated into a variety of prohibitions on travel and work on the Sabbath that in modern times seemed to define levels of religiosity, while separating observant from non-observant Jews and, in the context of Jewish statehood, underscored and informed many secular–religious debates. In particular, commercial activity on the Sabbath is a striking example of the crumbling status quo. While in the early years of statehood commercial activity was severely restricted, by the early 1990s out-of-town shopping centres were common, catering to the growing public desires.

Struggles over the Sabbath between religious and secular Israelis in the 1980s served to worsen relations between them. One significant struggle was that against the decision in February 1984 to open a cinema in the town of Petach Tikva on Friday nights. Attempts to persuade the mayor to prevent the opening of the cinema failed and appeals to the court fared no better. Religious leaders called on their supporters to demonstrate against the decision. About 10,000 demonstrators responded to the call and gathered on the first Friday night of the cinema's operation to protest. But neither this demonstration nor others that followed changed the decision. The demonstrations against the cinema lasted for three years and at times turned violent, but eventually, the Orthodox community lost this struggle, and the cinema (and others that followed) continued to operate on Saturday (Gutkind-Golan 1990). According to the Guttman survey of 1999, around two-thirds of Israelis (between 64 and 72 per cent) support the secularisation of Saturday, including in the cities the opening of film theatres and shopping centres. Most people regard Saturday as a free day in the Western sense of the word, and as individuals many like to spend the day as a holiday. This attitude of the individualistic Saturday is in contrast with the public Saturday ('status quo') that limits individual freedom and accords with the desire of the religious public to maintain the status quo.

The change of values and the new secular desires were not matched in the political sphere where the decision neither to change the laws nor to enforce them was made. Accordingly, secular desires to change the rules of the Sabbath were translated, not into formal political actions, but into various initiatives that can be described as sub-politics. Shopping centres built outside the cities became a popular site of family leisure. Like elsewhere, off-centre retailing is popular in Israel because of economic costs and easy access. However, in Israel these shopping centres also enjoy the advantage of being able to operate on Saturdays, whereas within the cities the municipalities have the ability to restrict their operation. A 2001 survey, conducted by a research marketing group, estimated that an average of 600,000 people participate in commercial activities on the Sabbath and the revenue of shops open on the Sabbath is reported to be three times greater than on weekdays (Brandman 2001). Therefore, there is a great commercial advantage if out-of-town shopping centres open on the Sabbath. Religious parties' demands that the government enforce the law and shut down businesses that operate on the Sabbath led to some political controversies but because, on the one hand, a limited budget was allocated to enforcement agencies and, on the other hand, many stores manage to circumvent the laws by hiring non-Jewish workers for the Sabbath, the commercialisation of the Sabbath continues. As one store manager explained: 'These are the facts of life. In Israel, Sabbath is the only day for family time. Some go to the synagogue, others go to the swimming pool, and many prefer to spend the day shopping' (quoted in Ben-Porat and Feniger 2009).

Religious attempts to shut down commercial activity on Saturdays through formal political channels have so far failed. Even when the Ministry of Labour was run by the religious parties (1996–2000, 2001–3) and businesses were fined for employing Jewish workers on Saturday by Druze workers employed by the Ministry, the shopping centres continued to operate. Failed attempts by religious leaders to persuade the government to enforce the laws that seek to protect the sanctity of the Sabbath only encouraged new activists, ideas and strategies that sought to challenge the business profits from operation on the Sabbath. Attempts to use consumer politics to protect the Sabbath are based on the belief that a committed religious public can employ boycotts to persuade businesses not to operate on the Sabbath and achieve what government regulation has thus far failed to achieve (Shamir and Ben-Porat 2008). In January 2005, thousands of Orthodox Jews gathered to protest against commercial activity on the Sabbath. Rabbi Raphael Halperin, the owner of a large optical retail chain, who organised the event, described the current status of the Sabbath as a 'cancer in the nation's body' and called for strict enforcement of the laws. He urged his listeners to take the initiative and not count on law enforcement: 'We are a strong economic force of half a million people,' he informed his audience of about 324,000 Jews who signed a petition declaring they would not set foot in stores that operate on the Sabbath (IsraelNationalNews.com, www.inn.co.il/news.php?id=100041).

In conclusion, secular consumers' demands for more shopping on the Sabbath were met by a growing number of stores opening on that day. The Orthodox religious public sought to change this by using its purchasing power of boycott. A close-knit community, the Orthodox religious have the social capital, the leadership and the commitment to challenge the policy. But the greater size of the secular public and its changing patterns of leisure and consumption has created major incentives for many businesses to operate on the Sabbath. In the course of the struggle, the issue has shifted from formal politics – that is, involving attempts to legislate for and against commerce on the Sabbath – to the economic realm and the choices of consumers – that is, the realm of sub-politics. Next we turn to a similar development: the issue of non-kosher meat.

Non-kosher meat

Non-kosher meat, especially pork, is a sensitive issue for the religious and also for some of the non-religious public in Israel. In Jewish tradition pork is not only strictly forbidden but is also a sign of oppression of the Jewish people, forced at various historical points to eat pork. Consequently, many Jewish Israelis who describe themselves as traditional or even secular avoid eating pork and support the restrictions. In the early years of statehood the consumption of pork was limited, with pork raised mostly in the more radical kibbutzim as a cheap supply of meat. In 1958 a law was passed that forbade raising pigs on Jewish land. Most of the kibbutzim closed down their operations, except two which found ways to circumvent the law by moving the pigs elsewhere and opening pork meat factories. Their operations, however, were mostly small-scale and low-key. Pork meat was found not in supermarkets but in small delicatessens where those interested could meet their needs and in some non-kosher restaurants that often used to call it 'white steak'.

In the late 1980s the religious parties which played a pivotal role in the government, attempted to restrict the rules and prevent the commerce of pork except in designated areas. Factories and shop owners whose businesses were in danger and liberal-minded activists joined forces in a struggle to prevent the new legislation, using both economic logic (the money invested in the industry and the employment it provided for hundreds of people) and liberal arguments of freedom of choice. But what decisively changed the situation was not the demonstrations and political struggles for or against the pork industry, but mass immigration from the former Soviet Union. The immigrants created new demands for pork and other non-kosher products and the market responded quickly. Large numbers of small shops and several large chain supermarkets began to cater to these demands. However, on the formal political level not much changed. For example, an attempt by secular entrepreneurs in 1992 to challenge the law that prevents the import of non-kosher meat to Israel in the Supreme Court, failed. Nevertheless, the commerce in non-kosher meat has proliferated and practically rendered old legal arrangements irrelevant.

The arrival of a million immigrants from the former USSR significantly raised the demand for pork meat. In addition, however, many other Israelis have also changed their perceptions and tastes. This was in part the effect of the increasingly globalised Israeli society noted above, and the associated thriving consumer culture. Israelis began in the 1990s increasingly to consume various food products, regardless of kosher restrictions, looking for both quality and good taste, and often caring little for religious restrictions on their diet. For example, Tiv Ta'am ('Good Taste') is a supermarket chain formed in the early 1990s, initially for Russian immigrants but later for all Israelis. Since 2000 it has gradually turned into a gourmet supermarket that caters, according to one of the owners, to

> the global Israeli … who spends time abroad and wants to get the same products and enjoy the same shopping experience as in Europe or the US … We decided to offer the new Israelis a global supermarket and a culinary feast.
>
> (Mr Kobi Teibish, interview with author, 2007)

The supermarkets are located out of town or in secular neighbourhoods in order to avoid conflict with religious Jews. This, as a senior partner explained, is economic logic:

> I have no interest in conflicts. Aren't there enough locations I can open without conflict? I bring employment to many people, I pay city taxes ... if there is a risk of conflict in a certain location, we will not open a store. I consult with the mayor before I decide to open, why risk a fight? There is no conflict. Who needs a conflict?
>
> (Interview with author 2007)

Like commerce on the Sabbath, the struggles over the sale of pork are also localised as religious people attempt to keep non-kosher establishments out of their neighbourhoods. The words of a religious member of parliament indicate the change:

> I am not against the sale of pork. I mean, I would not want pork in this country but if we are talking about reciprocity, why not? Eat pork. But, as a Jew I am deeply offended when I see pork sold in my neighborhood. So, I am asking, you can sell it, but do it in the outskirts of town.
>
> (quoted in Barak-Erez 2003)

Here, again, demographic and economic changes rendered previous arrangements all but irrelevant, but found the government unable to enforce or change laws. Overall, the result, as in the case of the Sabbath discussed above, was not a political struggle per se but instead a new mode of operation that is reshaping the public sphere, usefully described in Beck's term as sub-politics.

Marriage

Marriage provides another example of the waning power of religion in the public sphere in Israel. Official arrangements remain formally intact but demographic, social and economic changes undermine their relevance. Under the status quo arrangements, registration of Jewish marriage was placed under the authority of the Orthodox Rabbinate, formed in 1921 under the British Mandate, while Muslim and Christian marriages are registered by their respective religious authorities. This arrangement, which underlines the Orthodox monopoly, not only prevents inter-faith marriage (requiring conversion of the couple to one faith) but also does not allow registration of civic marriage and of non-Orthodox Jewish marriage. These arrangements were first challenged by a series of struggles that can be described as liberal-principled against the status quo in favour of civic rights and, later, by a significant demographic change caused by the mass immigration of mostly secular Jews from the former USSR. This subsequently led to the embedding of the issue of marriage in sub-politics, creating new alternatives for marriage without a formal political struggle.

These liberal struggles were engaged in both by individuals and groups who either found the Orthodox rituals unsatisfactory and discriminatory towards women and/or desired non-Orthodox rituals, and by individuals who were prevented from marrying on religious grounds. Groups like the Association for

Civil Rights engage in political and legal attempts to allow civil marriage in Israel and abolish the Orthodox monopoly over marriage and divorce. Unequal treatment of women especially in divorce cases is often the trigger for such demands and struggles. Similarly, the Reform and Conservative Jewish movements, who perceive Judaism different than the Orthodox and are organised separately, demand that their rabbis be allowed to perform marriage rituals. But, the limited power of liberal groups and the political power of religious groups has so far prevented institutional change and the Orthodox monopoly currently (2009) remains intact. But for many of those uninterested or unable to marry by the religious Orthodoxy, an exit option now exists: registering marriage abroad or cohabiting without marriage.

In the early years of statehood the exit option was taken by relatively few, probably because of the costs of travel and the existence then of a rather traditional and conformist society. Since the 1990s, however, more and more couples have decided not to marry through the rabbinate. This change is partly the result of growing dissatisfaction with the Orthodox monopoly felt by many Israelis, people who are willing and able to pay the necessary costs to travel out of the country (mainly to Cyprus) to register their marriage. Legal changes also make it possible to cohabit and have children and avoid the need to register marriage. This is especially popular among the more affluent and educated sectors who often hold more liberal world views and enjoy related lifestyles. Since the 1970s the relative numbers of Israelis married by the rabbinate has been in decline, especially since the arrival of immigrants from the former Soviet Union.

The immigration, as mentioned above, was characterised not only by the secular characteristics of many who entered Israel from the former Soviet Union (FSU), but also by the large numbers of immigrants who were entitled to immigrate and naturalise because of their Jewish family yet who were not recognised as Jewish by the Orthodox rabbinate. Thus, not only did many of the immigrants find it difficult to relate to the Orthodox rituals, but also many were excluded from the possibility of marrying at all. In spite of the political organisation and power of the FSU immigrants, the Orthodox monopoly was not changed as legislative reforms consistently failed. The result was a more extensive use of the exit option as immigrants constitute over one half of the 1,600 Israeli marriages in Cyprus every year (Dovrin 2006). Organisations that struggle to change existing laws, like the Forum for Free Marriage, often use the examples of individuals unable to marry to explain the need for change (interview with author, 2007). But in practice the availability of several exit options, enhanced by market means, seems to limit the motivations for a struggle. A large number of entrepreneurs offer vacation packages in Cyprus that include marriage and others provide legal arrangements as an alternative to registered marriage. Where the Orthodox monopoly continues to matter is in divorce cases that still have to go through the rabbinate (even for marriages performed out of Israel!) but, as of 2009, this has had limited political effect.

In conclusion, changing patterns of marriage may have greater implications than the Sabbath and non-kosher meat for the unity of the Jewish people since, as is often remarked, religious Jews threaten that they will not be able to marry the offspring of non-Orthodox marriages Thus, despite the fact that existing institutions are no longer able to supply the needs and demands of many people, changing existing laws proves to be difficult. On the other hand, changes are gradually suggested and introduced among the Orthodoxy itself. For example, some Orthodox rabbis have openly raised the possibility of civic marriage, limited to those who cannot otherwise be married. Other Orthodox rabbis have formed a new organisation (Tzohar) that attempts to make the Orthodox ritual more to the liking of the secular public and improve the image of the rabbinate.

Conclusions

Israeli society, because of the combined impact of globalisation, consumerist culture and mass immigration, is rapidly secularising, turning against formal religion–state arrangements that still, however, remain formally intact. This can be explained, first, by the power that religious parties still hold in the increasingly unstable formal political arena, which is divided by the territorial question, where they often play a significant role in governing coalition negotiation and formation. And, second, it can be explained by the fact that most Israelis remain committed to the idea of a 'Jewish state', privileging the Jewish (or non-Arab) majority (Ben-Porat 2000). The challenges the changes present find an unresponsive political system largely unable to provide new solutions, enforce existing laws or provide comprehensive policy-making capacity. But this incapacity, as the examples above demonstrate, leads not to a culture war or even a sustained political conflict but instead to alternative channels of operation that can be described collectively, following Beck, as sub-politics. Thus, while religion and politics merge on the territorial question, they fragment on other questions, shifting to other realms and to alternative forms of politics.

The religious–secular divide in Israel is often described as a potential 'culture war' that threatens Israel's social fabric. Tension is strengthened by the connection between religion and politics over questions of territorial compromise. Thus, the right-wing maximalist territorial position also has a significant religious factor. But, when the religious–secular debate extends into other questions regarding the shape of the public sphere and the role of religion in public life a variety of goals, tactics and strategies is displayed. Consequently, we are witnessing not a culture war between two coherent poles but rather a multidimensional setting where the religious–secular debate can turn either to a political struggle or to initiatives outside the formal political realm.

The study of religion and politics, as this chapter has attempted to demonstrate, requires a look beyond the arena of conventional politics into new modes of organisation and action that help shape the public sphere. In Israel, in common with many other countries, conventional (or formal) politics is to some degree losing its salience while the religious–secular debate remains significant. As a result, the religious–secular struggle may eventually break down into various localised struggles, waged in different realms, by different constituencies with varying levels of intensity. Alternatively, the struggle may even disappear as options created by market forces and social entrepreneurs can dissipate, albeit temporarily, political energies and political conflicts. This is not necessarily good news for secular ideologues who find in Israel waning support for separation of religion and state.

Bibliography

Barak-Erez, D. (2003) 'The Transformation of the Pig Laws: From a National Symbol to a Religious Interest?', *Mishpatim*, 33, pp. 403–75 (Hebrew).

Beck, U. (1994) 'The Reinvention of Politics', in U. Beck, S. Lash and A. Giddens (eds), *Reflexive Modernization: Politics, Tradition and Aesthetics in the Modern Social Order*. Stanford, CA: Stanford University Press, pp. 1–26.

Beck, U. (1997) 'Subpolitics', *Organization & Environment*, 10, 1, pp. 52–65.

Beckford, J. (2003) *Social Theory and Religion*, Cambridge: Cambridge University Press.

Bell, D. (1980) 'The Return of the Sacred? The Arguments on the Future of Religion', in D. Bell, *The Winding Passage: Essays and Sociological Journeys 1960–1980*. Cambridge, MA: Alt Books, pp. 324–54.

Ben-Porat, G. (2000) 'A State of Holiness: Rethinking Israeli Secularism', *Alternatives*, 25, pp. 223–45.

Ben-Porat, G. and Feniger, Y. (2009) 'Live and Let Buy, Consumerism, Secularism and Liberalism', *Comparative Politics*, April, pp. 293–313.

Ben-Simon, D. (2007) 'Exercise in Futility', *Haaretz*, 31 March, p. B3.

Brandman (2001) 'Shopping on the Sabbath', Brandman Marketing Research and Consultancy, December.

Bruce, S. (2003) *Politics and Religion*, Oxford: Polity.

Casanova, J. (1994) *Public Religions in the Modern World*, Chicago: Chicago University Press.

Chaves, M. (1994) 'Secularization as Declining Religious Authority', *Social Forces*, 72, 3 (March), pp. 749–74.

Cohen, A. and Susser, B. (2000) *Israel and the Politics of Jewish Identity: The Secular–Religious Impasse*, Baltimore, MD: Johns Hopkins University Press.

Connolly, W. (1999) *Why I Am Not a Secularist*, Minnesota: Minnesota University Press.

Dobbalaere, K. (1981) 'Secularization: A Multidimensional Concept', *Current Sociology*, 29, 2, pp. 3–153.

Dovrin, N. (2006) 'Marriages of Israelis abroad', *Megamot*, 44, 3, pp. 477–506 (Hebrew).

Gundelach, P. (1984) 'Social Transformation and New Forms of Voluntary Associations', *Social Science Information*, 23, 6, pp. 1049–81.

Gutkind-Golan, N. (1990) 'Hichal Cinema Case as a Symptom to Religious–Secular Relationship in Israel in the Eighties', in C. Liebman (ed.), *Religious and Secular: Conflict and Accommodation between Jews in Israel*, Jerusalem: Keter, pp. 70–88.

Hadden, J. (1987) 'Towards Desacralizing Secularization Theory', *Social Forces*, 65, pp. 587–611.

Haynes, J. (ed.) (2006) *The Politics of Religion*, London: Routledge.

Heelas, P. (1998) 'Introduction', in P. Heelas, (ed.), *Religion, Modernity and Postmodernity*, Oxford: Blackwell, pp. 1–15.

Holzer, B. and Sorensen, M. (2001) 'Subpolitics and subpoliticians', Arbeitspapier 4 des SFB 536 Reflexive Modernisierung München, July 2001, available at www.lrz-muenchen.de/~bfh/papers/SFB_ap4-holzer_soerensen.pdf

Horowitz, Dan and Lissak, Moshe (1989) *Trouble in Utopia*, New York: SUNY Press.

Hunter, J. (1991) *Culture Wars: The Struggle to Define America*, New York: Basic Books.

Johnson, P. (1995) 'God and the Americans', *Commentary*, 99, 1, pp. 24–5.

Jurgensmeyer, M. (1995) 'The New Religious State', *Comparative Politics*, July, pp. 379–91.

Keddie, N. (2003) 'Secularism and its Discontents', *Daedalus*, 132, 3, pp. 14–30.

Lehman-Wilzig, S. (1991) 'Loyalty, Voice and Quasi-Exit: Israel as a Case Study of Proliferating Alternative Politics', *Comparative Politics*, 24, 1, pp. 97–108.

Levi, S., Levinsohn, H. and Katz, E. (2000) *A Portrait of Israeli Jewry: Belief, Observances and Values among Israeli Jews*, Jerusalem: Israel Institute of Democracy.

Liebman, C. (1997) 'Cultural Conflict in Israeli Society', in C. Liebman and E. Katz (eds), *The Jewishness of Israelis*, New York: SUNY Press, pp. 103–18.

Luckman, T. (1967) *The Invisible Religion: The Problem of Religion in Modern Society*, New York: Macmillan.

Markowitz, F. and Uriely, N. (2002) 'Shopping in the Negev: Global Flows and Local Contingencies', *City and Society*, 14, 2, pp. 211–36.

Micheletti, M. (2003) *Political Virtue and Shopping*, New York, Palgrave Macmillan.

Ravitzky, A. (2000) *Religious and Secular Jews in Israel: A Kulturkampf?* Jerusalem: Israel Democracy Institute.

Richter, P. (1994) 'Seven Days' Trading Make One Week? The Sunday Trading Issue as an Index of Secularization', *British Journal of Sociology*, 45, 3, pp. 333–48.

Schweid, E. (1997) 'Is There Really No Alienation and Polarization?' in C. Liebman and E. Katz (eds), *The Jewishness of Israelis*, New York: SUNY Press, pp. 119–85.

Shamir, Omri and Ben-Porat, Guy (2007) 'Protecting the Sabbath – Religious Consumerism and Public Policy', *Contemporary Politics*, 13, 1, pp.75–92.

Shupe, A. and Hadden, J. (1989) 'Is There Such a Thing as Global Fundamentalism?' in J. Hadden and A. Shupe (eds), *Secularization and Fundamentalism Reconsidered, Vol. III*, New York: Paragon, pp. 109–22.

Wilson, B. (2001) 'Reflections on Secularization and Toleration', in A. Walker and D. Martin (eds), *Restoring the Image*, Sheffield: Sheffield Academic Press, pp. 38–48.

5 Between mediation and commitment

The Catholic Church and the Basque conflict

Xabier Itçaina[1]

Introduction: the paradoxical effect of secularisation

The evolving relationship between religion and politics in Western societies offers three fields of research for political scientists. The first one hinges on *the political regulation of religion*. Drawing inspiration from a legal and sociological tradition, which is regularly updated (Madeley and Enyedi 2003), it uses an institutional approach, addressing the issue in a classical but axiomatic way. This analysis of the legal status of religion, far from being purely descriptive, sheds light on the various forms of political legacy and culture. The second approach focuses on *the religious regulation of politics*, mainly through the study of the impact of religion on various behaviours: individual (religion and voting), median (religion and activism) and collective (cultural effects of religion). While such an approach is very interesting, it offers only indecisive conclusions. The third field of research centres on the analysis of *the role of politics within religious institutions*, and tests the validity of the politico-institutional metaphor to analyse them (Lagroye 2006). Overall, the three analytical approaches tend to merge somewhat into a singular and empirical object, for example, in relation to the ethno-nationalist conflict in the Basque Country in France and, more significantly, in Spain.[2]

It is appropriate first to examine each approach in order to assess the role of religion in one of the last zones of violent ethno-nationalist conflicts in Western Europe: the Basque Country. *The political regulation of religion* has indeed offered a renewed form of activism for religious institutions – limited to the Roman Catholic Church in this context. In Spain, the revision, between 1976 and 1979, of the Concordat of 1953 that dated back to General Franco's regime (1939–75) limited the institutional clout of the church while offering it new freedom. It was obliged to adjust its praxis to the new political and democratic regime and to the rapid secularisation of Spanish society.[3] But this new arrangement did not mean that the church disappeared from the public sphere – quite the opposite. We can see *the religious regulation of politics* at work in the church's attempt at moralising in the public sphere in the new democratic Spain, especially on ethical questions, including ethno-territorial questions.

Along with other Spanish regions, the Basques share Catholicism's long-term religious and social domination. However, a long and specific history of interactions between religion, politics and territorial identity clearly gave its specificity to Basque Catholicism, at least from the time of the Carlist wars in the nineteenth century. This reminds us that it is important to remember that there are not one but many Catholicisms in Spain, and this internal pluralism can only be understood by overlaying a 'conservative–progressive' axis on a 'centre–periphery' axis. It is also notable that Basque nationalism has only recently freed itself from the hold of religion, part of a general process of secularisation (Itçaina 2007a). The ideological tenets of the Basque nationalist party (Partido Nacionalista Vasco, PNV), founded in 1894 in Bilbao, were indeed based on a strong Christian identity, thus relaying the anti-revolutionary mobilisation movement in defence of provincial privileges that marked nineteenth-century Spain (the Carlist wars) (MacClancy 2000). Excepting the Acción Nacionalista Vasca, a marginal secular nationalist movement in the 1930s, it was only in 1959, when the armed separatist organisation ETA (Euskadi ta Askatasuna, 'Basque homeland and freedom') was founded in the Spanish Basque Country followed a year later by the creation of Enbata in the French Basque region, that the first secular forms of Basque nationalism emerged. However, at this time the secularisation process was not complete, exemplified by the continued activism of some Christian groups (for example, a group of Christians in the Enbata movement in the early 1970s; Davant 1972) within the Basque political associations. However, Basque nationalism did eventually became a secular movement, with only implicit reference to religious affiliation in the Christian Democratic tenets of the Basque Nationalist Party (PNV), officially secular since 1977. On the other hand, interaction with religion did not totally disappear, since the church committed itself deeply to a new form of political regulation: mediation, through the search for a peaceful solution to the Basque conflict. In addition, this political activism revealed the internal divide within the Catholic Church, through a debate on Basque identity.

The central argument of this chapter is that the recent involvement of the Catholic Church in the quest for peace has allowed the church to regain some legitimacy as a social actor, thus symbolically distancing itself from its *problematic* historical past. However, this change was especially remarkable given that it took place in the context of *a more pronounced secularisation process* in the Spanish Basque Country, compared to the rest of Spain. This was exemplified, for example, by fewer and fewer seminarians in the Basque–Navarre region,[4] along with a regular but significant drop in church attendance – although in the 1960s and the early 1970s it had been the highest in Spain (Iztueta 1981). Surveys on religious attendance confirm this inversion: overall, the Basque exception stems from its society's high level of secularisation, compared to a more moderate process in the rest of Spain (Pérez-Agote and Santiago García 2005). According to Alfonso Pérez-Agote, rejection of the church by the Basque radical nationalists was a factor in helping explain the uninterest and/or hostility of younger people towards religion.

In terms of social trust, the church ranked only eleventh out of seventeen institutions in the Euskobarometro 2007 November survey.[5] The hypothesis developed by A. Pérez-Agote (Pérez-Agote 1986) at the end of Franco's regime, which argued that the central role of religion had been replaced by politics, was thus confirmed. Nationalism and language became gradually more important than religion in a secularised Basque society. In a quite paradoxical way, there seems to be a discrepancy between the social decline of religion, and a clear politicisation of the interventions of religious actors in the public sphere. In a general context of crisis of legitimacy experienced by various institutions (for example, party membership decline, voting decline, lack of trust in institutions, etc.), we can argue that the church, despite its social decline, is still perceived by most political actors among Basque nationalists *and* non-nationalists as an important provider of *meaning* in a public sphere in search of stabilised interpretation of society and politics.

Confronted with this phenomenon – which is somewhat less pronounced among Basques in France compared to those in Spain – the church was forced to reconsider its political and social positioning. It is a well-known fact that the massive support of much of the Spanish Catholic Church for the political transition from Francoism was one of the main factors in the emergence and consolidation of the new democratic regime, as it made possible the rallying of social groups which had hitherto been opposed to such a change. For example, some of the most conservative Catholics, including sectors of the army, were reassured by the inauguration of a parliamentary monarchy and by the democratic conversion of the church. It also illustrated the radical estrangement of the church from political power in the last years of the authoritarian regime (Pérez-Díaz 1993; Brassloff 2003). In a more tense context than in the rest of the country, the political transition in the Basque Country urged the church progressively to replace its leadership and adjust its rhetoric to the new political environment. It was indeed in its capacity as mediator that the Basque Church was given the opportunity of regaining its legitimacy as a social and functional actor. As an institution intrinsically predisposed to mediation (Palard 2006), the Catholic Church's interventionism was naturally adapted to a territory in which fundamental political cleavages had historically been shaped by religion. In such a context, the church played, and is still playing, an important role in its attempt at settling the conflict in the Basque Country. This activism in the Spanish Basque Country may be analysed from three complementary angles. First, it was precisely the persistence of uncompromising attitudes in the conflict that conferred on the church its legitimate and social role as a mediator, even if the results remained inconclusive. Second, acknowledgement of this social role also influenced the religious institution itself, affecting its internal cleavages. Finally, this ambivalent role of Catholic mediation should be placed in the wider debate over competing conceptions of democracy expressed by both religious and political actors. In that sense, promoting peace in the Basque Country was, for these religious actors, a way to reassert the impact of their own ethical code in a definitely secularised political and social environment.

Political intransigence and the church's mediating efforts

The persistence of uncompromising attitudes offered an unexpected opportunity for the Catholic Church. Through their absolute and intransigent claims in the identity crisis – including the persistence of claims of independence and of political violence and its repression – the result was political deadlock. As the political *arena* (the locus where decisions are made) was totally paralysed, some institutions originating in the *forum* (the debating locus) (Jobert 1995: 21) were called on by default, even after the political transition (1975–82), to involve themselves in political negotiations. The Catholic Church thus found itself involved in pursuit of a peaceful third way, through peace movements and mediating action between the two most radical actors of the conflict (on the one hand, Basque militants supporting armed struggle and, on the other, advocates of purely repressive responses). The actions of the church became political in as much as it substituted for the political actors either unable to break this deadlock or willing to maintain the status quo. These religious actors started working in the field of mediation, defined here as 'a consensual process of conflict management, in which a third party who is impartial, independent and without any decision-making capacity, tries to solve or to moderate conflicts through the organisation of exchanges between persons and institutions' (Faget 2008: 312). De Briant and Palau (1999: 36) consider that religious mediation is one of the 'traditional' or 'unnamed' forms of mediation. As in all other types of mediation, it implies that a connection is established between two persons through a third one, but in a specific and often informal way which is not always openly called mediation. Theologically founded on the figure of Christ in the Christian tradition, 'religious mediation' is, in the view of these authors,

> the perfect illustration of *the act of faith* – which mediation fundamentally is – a belief that individuals can overcome their differences of opinion, can see *the other as their neighbour*, especially the mediator, can listen to the other, but also can *hold to their word* and *grin and bear it*.
>
> (De Briant and Palau 1999: 40, emphasis in original)

As a political mediator, the church acted both as a generalist (*médiateur généraliste*) and as a broker (*médiateur courtier*) (Nay and Smith 2002). As a generalist, the mediator tries to bring together institutional milieus which do not share the same knowledge or the same representations (the cognitive dimension of mediation). As a broker, the mediator is looking for acceptable solutions between very different groups which have to find an interest in cooperating, while pursuing different aims and defending different interests (the strategic dimension of mediation). The Catholic Church played, and is still playing, this double role in the Basque Country, achieving better results in terms of cognitive mediation than in strategic mediation. The involvement of the church in the pro-peace mobilisations since the mid-1980s is the best illustration of this 'cognitive mediation'.

A generalist mediator: the church and social construction of peace

All the public mobilisation movements for peace, encouraged by the church, belong to the first type of mediation. The emergence of the peace issue as a major political stake in the mid-1980s furthered the church's involvement in the profound identity crisis experienced by the whole of Basque society with the persistence of violent conflict. The urgent need to settle the conflict and restore peace created a new political locus, saturated with specialised institutions (Reizabal Arruabarrena 1996) both in the Spanish and, to a lesser extent, in the French Basque Country. The institutionalisation of social movements within non-partisan structures (such as Elkarri [Together], Gesto por la paz [A move towards peace] and Gernika gogoratuz [Remembering Gernika], among many others) led to the emergence of a third locus where the church in its capacity as peace-making expert was called on to play an active role. This offered the church the opportunity of reintroducing itself into the public sphere because of its socially recognised competences, without trying to dominate things. The church and its agents (see below) were appealed to because of their expertise in conflict resolution and deliberation. We may here see the illustration of a commonly held view: religious actors can intrinsically create the necessary conditions for consensus-building and conflict-solving. According to Ramón Zallo (1998), Basque society is a deeply divided society that may be regarded from two different perspectives. For a first group of political parties and social movements ('constitutionalist' parties and the nationalist movement), Basque society is mainly composed of two loci (nationalist/non-nationalist), in constant opposition. For the second group (Basque Nationalist Party (PNV), pacifist movements, the ELA and LAB trade unions[6]), there are three loci in Basque society, with a mix of confrontation, negotiation and cooperation. The *abertzale* (Basque nationalist)/non-*abertzale* divide was thus attenuated by the emergence of a third way, a social movement for peace which could not be reduced to any of the two groups. There was a close link between the church's new form of interventionism, including not only the religious institution but also individual initiatives, and the emergence of a specific collective action. The third way, which was traditional for the Christians, thus enhanced the action of the church, both inside and outside the institution.

Internal generalist mediation

Some religious groups reorganised themselves with a view to achieving this objective. This evidenced the real, though hardly perceptible, influence of the public debate on the peace issue on the very organisation of the church. Perhaps the best illustration of this can be found in Guipuzcoa, a province where nationalist radicalism was firmly rooted. Within the diocesan structure, the social secretariat created when Monsignor Setién became Bishop of San Sebastián in 1979,[7] top priority was given not only to the nagging problem of unemployment but also to the restoration of peace. From 1992 onwards, the Gentza diocesan committee led both reflective and symbolic action on this issue, through its organisation of highly publicised operations such as the March for Peace to the Arantzazu sanctuary, which involved nearly 10,000 people. In addition, the Rally for Peace held in Armentia (Alava) on 13 January 2001, under the aegis of the four Basque and Navarre bishops, asked both that ETA should lay down its arms and that politicians should open negotiations. The leadership of the San Sebastián bishops, Monsignor Setién (1979–2000) and Monsignor Uriarte (since 2000), played an essential role in mobilising local people and neighbouring dioceses.

In the 'utopian margins' within the Catholic Church, the same commitment to the cause of peace was most obvious in the religious orders. The Jesuits could use their long experience in peace studies and peace-building, from Loyola to the entire Catholic world. The Franciscan community in Arantzazu (in the province of Guipuzcoa), which contributed so much to the promotion of Basque culture from the 1950s, was particularly active. In an attempt at restructuring its pastoral project around the question of peace, the pastoral council – which brought together both priests and laypersons – started in 1992 to take training and advisory initiatives on this theme, with the help and support of the diocesan authorities. The sanctuary regularly became an arena where representatives of the peace movements and political parties convened. Thus, together with symbolic moves such as prayers for each violent death and marches for peace, the Franciscan community contributed significantly to the emergence of new loci where each party could express their views, in spite of the methodological differences that occasionally cropped up between the church and the peace movements. Its action rested on the belief that intermediary bodies were presumably more efficient. As expressed by a friar from the Arantzazu community, 'We must not leave it only to politicians to find the solution, we must show them the way, hence the importance of pardon.'[8] This vocation was confirmed by the creation of Baketik (meaning 'from/through peace') in April 2006, a research and formation centre for peace and conflict-solving under the aegis of the Arantzazu Franciscans. Centred on the 'ethical elaboration of conflicts', Baketik has sought to contribute to the process of reconciliation within Basque society, albeit without intervening directly in the previous phases of 'preconciliation' and 'conciliation'. These more political steps were to be acted upon by more interventionist pacifist mobilisations, including Elkarri and Gesto por la paz. The Baketik experience, informed by both religious and lay factors, illustrates well the dynamics of a civil society 'which is at least ten years ahead of the political actors'[9] with respect to resolution of the conflict.

External generalist mediation

Outside the institutional structure of the church, Catholic actors also actively contributed to structuring the pacifist 'third sector' in the Basque Country. Far from monopolising the pro-peace movement, the Catholic initiatives were, among many others, part of a strongly mobilised civil society. While the Catholic Church could serve as one of the main models for political protest against Francoism (Iztueta 1981), it is no longer the case today. In his recent PhD on environmental protest in the Spanish Basque Country, Mario Zubiaga Garate (2008) underlines that many of today's pacifist movements borrow their repertoire of action (in terms of protest *and* mediation) from the environmental mobilisations of the early 1990s rather than from the church. For example, Elkarri, founded in January 1995, followed the initiative of the Lurraldea ('territory') collective group, created in 1986, to oppose the planned Irurtzun–Andoain motorway.[10] The actors of the pacifist third sector belonged to many different groups, composed of trade unions, forums and committees, which did not amount to an homogenous entity, while some were more or less under the influence of the political groups. In addition to the traditional opposition between the nationalist movement and the committees which criticised not only the use of violence but also the very foundations of Basque nationalism (Basta Ya ['it's enough'], Associations of the Victims of Terrorism), there was also an internal cleavage between various committees, including those composed of leftist nationalist dissidents (Elkarri), groups of prisoners' families and other, more 'moderate', groups. The regional autonomous government also took an active part in the process, thus weakening the local balance of power.[11] Some Christian groups also became involved, in a variety of ways. Some committed themselves openly in the name of their religious affiliation. Others were less outspoken and joined non-denominational groups. Gesto por la Paz was discreetly supported by the Bilbao diocese in its logistics and through the participation of diocesan groups of young Christians. There were also 'mutual consultations' between organisations such as Elkarri and the church.[12]

There was also another instance of informal cooperation between Christians, priests and pacifist organisations. Most nationalist-oriented peace movements and the associations of the victims of terrorism, especially after ETA broke the ceasefire in 1999, constantly appealed to the church. It was particularly the case of the Senideak ('the families', associations of prisoners' families) and the Gestoras pro-Amnistia, close to the nationalist left, which regularly invited the church to air its views on the problem of political prisoners, either by staging hunger strikes, with the support of some priests, or by directly questioning the diocesan authorities. That was the main motive behind the action undertaken by Senideak and the Gestoras in Arantzazu in September 1997[13] and in churches and cathedrals in June 1998,[14] as well as the symbolic fast undertaken by Herri Batasuna, the nationalist group, in Arantzazu in May 1998.[15] Senideak also took part in a meeting with the Christian Popular Communities and the coordination of Basque priests (Euskal Herriko Apaizen Koordinakundea, EHAK) in Arantzazu in March 1997, to talk about the situation of the prisoners.[16] In the view of the committees, the appeal to the church was justified for strategic reasons. 'We think that the church has a lot of power in our society,' declared one of the spokespersons at the June 1998 rallies.[17] The site of Arantzazu was regularly used as a meeting point.

By resorting to hunger strikes in churches, the nationalist organisations perpetuated a traditional means of action frequently used in the last years of

Franco's regime. Appealing for a more active political involvement of the church meant for them that the situation was far from normalised: that is, limited to a competition between well-defined and accepted organisations and political actors. The functionalist approach of the Franco years was reinvigorated, as the church substituted for a political regime whose democratic legitimacy was questioned. The church was called upon not in the name of its recognised Christian affiliation, but by default, thus revealing the deficiencies of political competition. The question of the prisoners fuelled this tension and furthered the specific interaction between the peace movements, the nationalist organisations and the religious groups. The church was not only appealed to by the *abertzale* (Basque nationalist) left or the committees of prisoners' families, but also by the associations of the victims of terrorism, who regularly asked the diocesan authorities to express clearly their opposition to nationalist violence. ETA took due note of this new trend. When it openly criticised the Basque Catholic Church in April 2001, it was precisely the new concerns of the church towards the victims of terrorism that were the butt of ETA's attacks, as there was a risk, in the armed nationalists' view, that 'if the Church follows this path, it will lose in the future the role of intermediary that it has traditionally had'.[18] All these examples show that the church has had to tread a difficult path between the various activist groups, who could hardly hide their differences behind a superficially common rhetoric of peace.

A broker: the church and impossible negotiations

The real social impact of the church's commitment for peace calls for a mitigated appraisal of its talents as a broker. Several times since the establishment of the Autonomous Region, members of the Catholic Church have been called or have proposed to act as intermediaries between the most antagonistic parties. Their mediation efforts have mainly, but not exclusively, concerned the Spanish government and ETA, thus bypassing the elected authorities of the Basque Country. Carlos Garaikoetxea, the former president of the Basque Autonomous Community (1980–5) and now a member of the moderate nationalist party EA (Eusko Alkartasuna [Basque solidarity]) mentions in his memoirs an initiative undertaken by the Society of Jesus in 1984 with a view to initiating new negotiations (Garaikoetxea 2002: 179–80). The Basque episcopal authorities have also regularly proposed their help, as for instance the Bishop of San Sebastián, Monsignor Setién, in 1986–7,[19] then in November 1997,[20] or the Bishop of Bilbao in October 1996. After a failed attempt at resuming negotiations, ETA made public the names of four intermediaries who had taken part in the organisation of meetings with the Spanish government. Under the Socialist government, it was a former Nobel Peace Prize laureate of 1980, the Argentine writer Adolfo Pérez Esquivel – whom ETA accused of having relinquished his role as 'intermediary' for a role of 'counsellor' – who was in charge. When the conservative Popular Party came to office in 1996, Harry Barnes, a member of the Carter Foundation played the role of intermediary.[21] According to ETA, the representatives of the

Spanish government were reluctant about this kind of mediation, which turned the conflict into an international one. The extradition of two ETA representatives from Santo Domingo to Spain put an end to negotiations in August 1997. The Roman Catholic community of Sant'Egidio also offered its mediation services. Specialised in conflict management, for example in Mozambique, Sant'Egidio allegedly held secret meetings with ETA and the Spanish Minister of the Interior. The rumour of a potential police operation ended these talks. During the ETA ceasefire in 1998–9, Monsignor Uriarte, then Bishop of Zamora before becoming Bishop of San Sebastián, was also said to have taken part – unsuccessfully – in negotiations between the armed organisation and the Popular Party government.[22]

Some representatives of the church did not limit their mediation efforts to bilateral contacts between ETA and the Spanish government, but also acted in order to further dialogue between the moderate nationalists and the Spanish executive, as well as between moderate and radical nationalists. This initiative was undertaken by senior members of the Catholic hierarchy. In late September 2000, on the occasion of the canonisation of María Josefa del Corazón de Jesús Sancho de Guerra Maria, talks were held between the head of Vatican diplomacy, Monsignor Tauran, and the president of the Basque government, Juan José Ibarretxe, on the one hand, and the Spanish Minister of the Interior, Jaime Mayor Oreja (Popular Party) on the other, in order to analyse 'the present and future prospects of a peaceful solution ... together with the potential contribution that the Catholic Church can offer'.[23] For the Spanish Foreign Affairs Minister, Josep Piqué, this proposed 'collaboration' did not mean that the church was to act as a mediator, as 'nobody can serve as a mediator between a democratic State and murderers'.[24] Beyond the inevitable political controversy, the Vatican acted in its capacity as an expert in peace-seeking, which it had already done in other circumstances.

The new political context, after the banning of the Basque radical nationalist party Batasuna (Unity) in June 2002 in Spain, favoured the emergence of a new form of mediation. Talks took place within the nationalist camp between the moderate PNV and EA parties, the ELA and LAB trade unions, the 'environment' of Batasuna (the political, cultural and economical entities and social movements supporting the ideas of the Basque leftist and radical nationalism), Udalbiltza (the association of municipalities) and some *abertzale* lawyers. These talks were symbolically initiated by, among others, Alec Reid who, as an Irish priest, a member of the Redemptorist Roman Catholic missionary order, had played a significant part in the 1998 Good Friday Agreement in Northern Ireland.[25] He proposed a 'tactical ceasefire' to ETA in order to put forward a common proposal for the resumption of negotiations with the Spanish state. He was helped in his task by members of the Bilbao diocese and supported by the Bishop of San Sebastián. Alec Reid had previously taken part in the peace conference organised by Elkarri in October 2001 and 2002, as a guest expert, together with a member of the Sant'Egidio community.[26]

The church came back to activism after the announcement by ETA of a ceasefire on 22 March 2006. On 3 April 2006, Monsignor Uriarte, Bishop of San

Sebastián, presented to the Vatican the efforts of the Church of the Basque Country in favour of peace. Two days later, Pope Benedict XVI exhorted the congregation gathered in St Peter's Square 'to pray in order that everybody will intensify their efforts for the consolidation of the horizons of peace that seem to appear in the Basque Country and in all Spain, and to overcome the obstacles that could appear'.[27] Despite a very cautions attitude (promoting peace is *not* mediating in the conflict), the intervention of the Pope had a considerable symbolic impact, as it helped put the Basque issue on the universalistic Catholic agenda. However, a lot of these hopes disappeared when ETA started killing again from December 2006 onwards.

Three partial conclusions drawn from these brokering mediation efforts

First, perceived – at least by political and institutional actors – as an institution which could be trusted, the church was still a sufficiently committed social actor to be recognised as a legitimate mediator in the pursuit of peace. At the same time, the recent but effective secularisation of Basque society helped the church ward off any accusation of proselytism or hegemony. Churchmen indeed benefited from their relative neutrality, able to exploit their in-depth knowledge of the situation – for example, some of them had family ties with political leaders or had taken an active part in many political actors' former socialising process in religious schools and/or in seminars (Itçaina 2007a: Ch. VII).

Second, mediation failed, with hardly any concrete results in the resolution of the conflict. The religious mediators acted more as 'facilitators' than 'formulators' or 'manipulators'.[28] They served essentially as media of communication between the most polarised actors in the conflict. However, this lack of real power or influence may have given some legitimacy to the religious actors, as exemplified in other contexts by the 'power of weakness' assumed, for instance, by Quaker mediators (Faget 2008: 320). Since the end of the ceasefire with ETA in November 1999, the nationalist conflict had once again become more radical, and the response from the Spanish state showed the limits of mediation efforts. The failure of the new ceasefire declared by ETA between March and December 2006, in a radically different context from the years 1998–9, was also a good illustration of the uncompromising positions of the political actors. The intermediaries are exemplified by Monsignor Uriarte in 1998–9, who acknowledged the limited impact of his action, reduced as he was to the role of a mere go-between trying to reconcile two parties which could hinder any progress if they refused to make compromises.

Catholic mediation must finally be comprehended within the more general framework of the bilateral relations at play behind the institutional and democratic political scene in the Basque Country. The church's legitimacy was different from the democratic legitimacy guaranteed by elections, and the religious actors assumed the role of 'recognized moral authorities' (Pace 1998: 157), sufficiently remote from the conflict to remain neutral, and committed enough in

Basque society to be trusted. If we consider the total failure of the institutional response to the conflict, an unexpected opportunity was thus offered to the church.

The backlash: internal polarisation within the Catholic sphere

Mediation efforts carried out by the church also had a significant impact in terms of internal polarisation and, more globally, in its relation with the public sphere. The church could hardly hide its internal cleavages behind its unitarian rhetoric. The question of its commitment to peace revealed a high pluralism in the Catholic sphere. As a religious institution, the Catholic Church entertains a double relation with political power. It is both a 'cause' group – that is, committed to the defence of various causes – and a sectional pressure group. In addition to its universalist mission, the church defends the interests of the section of the population which adheres to its beliefs and practices. Its legitimacy rests on its capacity for turning the particular interests of these factions – denominational schools, social services, status of the clergy, etc. – into political and generalist claims concerning the society as a whole. At the same time, the church is able to mobilise beyond the limited circle of Christians on greater social causes. In short, the church's mediation actions in relation to the Basque question do not originate in a neutral structure which has only recently relinquished its dominant position in Basque and Spanish society.

The Spanish debate

In a more significant way, the church suffered from the repercussions of political competition in the context of its own internal debates. The Church of the Basque Country – a better expression than the questionable 'Basque Church' – had to face up to a double source of internal tension. On the one hand, the Basque bishops opposed the majority of the Spanish Episcopal College, and on the other hand, the Basque clergy were divided on the problem of Basque identity. Such a double cleavage weakened the superficial unity of the Spanish Episcopal College. The core–periphery divide added to the more traditional opposition between conservative and progressive bishops on sensitive issues such as family or education, especially under socialist majorities (Brassloff 2003; Itçaina 2007b). In spite of the apparent unity within the College, the analysis of the positions taken by the Episcopal Conference of Spain revealed profound differences. There was no real consensus, and no position became dominant. Much hyped in the press, these internal divisions showed how segmented the institution was.

As an example, in February 2002, the Spanish Episcopal Conference publicly expressed its opinion relative to the lack of support by the Spanish bishops on the anti-terrorist plan jointly defended by the Popular Party (PP) and the Socialist Party (PSOE), in order to spare the Basque bishops.[29] In May 2002, the three bishops of the Autonomous Community of Euskadi published a pastoral letter in which they criticised the Spanish law on political parties, passed in order to ban the nationalist party Batasuna. Over 300 Basque priests issued a critical manifesto against this law. This statement, justified by the bishops on account of the risk of mounting divisions that this law would trigger, caused an outcry in the whole country. In June 2002, the Episcopal Conference refused to condemn the Basque bishops. In November 2002, however, the Conference published a memorandum condemning infra-territorial separatism, thus aligning itself with the position of the government, which immediately led to an official declaration by the Bishop of San Sebastián, who refused to condemn any form of nationalism a priori.

The Basco-Navarrese debate

The church's unity was furthered weakened by the internal divide within the Basque–Navarre clergy. Since the democratic transition, the clergy had indeed been divided over the question of identity and its territorial consequences. In Guipuzcoa, the church was very active in its mediation efforts whereas, conversely, the Navarrese diocesan authorities had adopted a more moderate position on the very concept of joint territoriality shared between the Basque and Navarre provinces. These diverging opinions only mirrored the distinctive nature of the political debate within each province. For their part, the clergy and the Christian organisations split into different groups. The *abertzale* tendency was most perceptible in three organisations, which were both close to each other yet quite distinct: the Coordination of the Priests of the Basque Country (Euskal Herriko Apaizen Koordinaketa, EHAK), the popular Christian Communities (CCPs) and the magazine *Herria 2000 Eliza* ('People/country 2000 church'). Created in 1976, EHAK took up the clerical rhetoric of anti-Franco rebellion. But its vision of the territory was different, as it transformed an essentially Biscayan and Guipuzcoan movement during Franco's dictatorial regime into a wider organisation that gathered priests from the seven provinces, thus recreating in its very structure the territorial unity of the Basque Country.[30] The higher number of Navarre and French Basque members in early 2000 illustrated the prevalence of provinces in which Basque nationalism was in the minority and dominated by the most nationalistic factions. The coordination of the delegations was made by an inter-diocesan commission composed of representatives elected by the priests and accountable to the assembly.[31] From the beginning, the Coordination wanted to adopt a prophetic and anticapitalist pastoral of liberation in favour of a Basque population freed from any form of oppression. However, and despite such radical positions, the Coordination was not intent on creating a parallel church. Thirty years later, the theoretical references are little changed: EHAK still abides by a liberation theology adapted to the European and Basque context; it does not see itself at odds with the church hierarchy, but rather wants to promote grassroots activists. Its aspiration for an *incarnated* church – that is, a church firmly rooted in local cultures, following the Vatican II Council in 1965 – is the same: 'We are a *herri*,[32] and this reality must shape our evangelising action.'[33] Such diverging opinions and interpretations between this movement and the Episcopate regularly crystallise on recurrent issues such as the creation of a unified Basque ecclesiastical province or during elections.

The Coordination was joined by the Popular Christian Communities (CCPs), which started coordinating their actions in 1976–7. Drawing their inspiration from the Chilean model of the Cristianos para el socialismo (Christians for Socialism), they progressively organised themselves, with a strong influence exerted by the Navarrese, as in the case of the Coordination. The magazine *Herria 2000 Eliza* was first the mouthpiece of the CCPs, but soon created its own collective. In his theology doctoral thesis, Felix Placer contends that the political commitment and religious belief of these groups can be seen as an alternative way to live and express their Christian identity within the Church of the Basque Country (Placer Ugarte 1998: 25). The CCPs and EHAK, from different backgrounds[34] but with a common desire to promote grassroots activism, developed an ecclesiastical alternative which was based on the idea of a popular Basque Church. There were obvious links with the socio-political situation 'which made it possible for the hopeful emergence of a popular process in the Basque Country, at the social, political and cultural level, in which CCPs and EHAK wanted to participate on account of their specific liberation and Christian choices' (Placer Ugarte 1998: 178). Much like the clergy in the 1960s, EHAK defended avant-gardist intra-ecclesiastical claims. It took a particularly active part in the social forum for peace. In 2003, *Herria 2000 Eliza* managed to organise a meeting with J. I. Ibarretxe, the president of the Autonomous Basque Community, some academics, trade union members and political actors from various origins, in order to debate the presidential project of sovereignty association.[35] The title given to the book which was then published, *Tiempo de soluciones* ([Time for solutions] *Herria 2000 Eliza* 2003), similar to *Time for Peace* in Ireland, clearly showed their will to promote mediation *and* their desire to have a Basque *herri* recognised.

The Roman debate

The actions of the Vatican, as the central institution of Roman Catholicism, took a special meaning in this context. Different voices emanating from very distinct sectors of the Basque society appealed to the Vatican over this matter: Catholics asking for the official recognition of a Basque ecclesiastical province, or, on the other side, victims of terrorism asking for a clearer condemn of violence *and* of Basque nationalism, pacifists, etc. Periods of ETA ceasefires seem to have constituted favourable moments for the expression of generalist messages from the Vatican in favour of peace in the Basque Country. The exhortation of Benedict XVI in April 2006 testifies to this trend. The evocation – even if very cautious – of the Basque conflict by the head of the Catholic hierarchy could contribute to an internationalisation of the Basque question, despite all those trying to limit it to a French and Spanish domestic public order issue. The strong presence of churchmen of Basque origins in the Roman curia and in the missionary orders may have influenced the Holy See's policy on the Basque question. However, we lack solid data to go further in that direction, and to analyse better the role played by key Roman figures of Basque origins with a strong experience of mediation on other conflicts.

The church, politicisation and criticism of procedural conceptions of democracy

What is really at play in the mediation efforts of the church is its place in the public sphere and its wider relation to politics, politicisation and democracy in the Basque Country and in Spain.

Competing conceptions of politicisation

Acknowledging the political dimension of a problem means turning it into a conflict issue that might be solved through 'conversations' within the public sphere. The Catholic Church's commitment in the peace process is buttressed by its adherence to the principle of subsidiarity. It legitimises the role of intermediary bodies in conflict resolution, especially as the so-called political actors and institutions have proved unable to arrive at any effective solution. Many Christians are also deeply motivated by their refusal to participate in violence and politics. The enduring conflict and persistent uncompromising attitudes may have shaken Christians out of their apolitical positions which traditionally did not induce them to get involved in politics (Braud 1998: 39–40). The church's reluctance to commit itself in the political arena has influenced the various mediation efforts carried out by the clergy and the peace movements. According to Brother E., Arantzazu, a Franciscan from the Arantzazu community, there is a specific Christian approach to peace:

> In our reflection group on peace, there are two tendencies: for some, we must work with Herri Batasuna, with Elkarri. Elkarri is active in 200 villages and organizes extensive debates. It is not always successful. Their method consists of bringing out the differences between people. *On the contrary, the method of the church is to smooth away the differences.* Elkarri has developed a specific methodology: first everybody speaks, then there are explanations, and finally the discussion really starts. For the other group, we should rather turn towards Monsignor Setién's speech and the methodology of the vicar-general on the peace process, in addition to the teachings of St Francis of Assisi.[36]

Mees highlights the fact that the diverging opinions on the political sphere *as* a conflict issue may account for the differences among the peace movements. Contrary to Gesto por la paz, Elkarri considers that the debate is political, not ethical (Mees 2003: 97). In that respect, the source of violence must be found in the conflicting opposition between a significant part of the population and the

Spanish state on issues such as power-sharing and self-determination. Mees also points out that there is a double risk in the openly political dimension of Elkarri's action, since its efficiency depends on the support of the political parties. Elkarri may also be criticised by all those who feel reluctant about the intervention of non-elected organisations.

In addition to these diverging interpretations that go beyond the restricted circle of people who are close to the church, the Catholic actors have finally been submitted to a double and paradoxical process of politicisation – both internal through the emergence of factions, and external with the arrival of a third sector for peace, which is also politically divided. The impossibility for the Christians to adopt a neutral stance is also due to the pressure exerted by the most polarised actors in the conflict. ETA criticised the rally for peace organised in April 2001 by the Basque–Navarre bishops in Armentia, accusing the church of trying to 'depoliticise the conflict' to go back to the period 'before the Lizarra pact', while recalling the mediating role of the church during the 1998–9 ceasefire. The discrepancy between the interests of the various parties and the mediation objectives has led to contradictions and to a deadlock.

Competing conceptions of democracy

This activism may also implicitly reveal a critical approach to certain forms of democracy. When working in favour of peace, the church rejects a purely *procedural* conception of democracy, which would consider that the legitimacy of political decisions only stems from the way they are adopted, particularly from majoritarian rule. Following this critical perspective, the majoritarian procedure may be seen as useful for the adoption of temporary compromises, not for the durable resolution of deeply rooted conflicts such as the ethnonationalist one. Many pacifist movements also criticise the *constitutional* conception of democracy, which attributes to the institutional arrangements made of rules and procedures a socio-political virtue in terms of political and social stabilisation. In the Basque Country, the institutional order linked to the Spanish Constitution of 1978 has proved to have serious difficulties in dealing with the claims for more political recognition of Basque identity. Meanwhile, the promotion of a generalised social dialogue around peace turns the Catholic Church into the vector of a *deliberative* conception of democracy that would give more importance to the process of dialogue preceding the decision itself. In the majoritarian procedure, on the other hand, the aim is to measure the balance of power, without aiming at modifying the positions of each one. Only the deliberative model would allow, following Gutmann and Thompson (2004) to resolve moral conflicts, since this kind of conflict mobilises irreconcilable positions.[37] In a deliberative process, all the dimensions of the problem become salient and are discussed. Identity conflicts are both political conflicts *and* moral issues, which is what makes them so difficult for any democratic regime to resolve.

If we reduce this theory *ad absurdum*, we might be tempted to find some parallel – which we shall immediately refute – between the approaches to democracy by the religious actors and the most radical actors of the conflict. Both buttress their action by a relativist conception of democratic rule. The radical leftist Basque nationalists refuse the institutional and territorial arrangement established by Spanish democracy after Franco. The Basque autonomous status is regarded as an illusion. The church's approach to democracy is much more complex, but is also concerned by an implicit criticism of the current institutional order. Politically committed Christians are confronted with the task of surmounting the contradiction between the logic of democratic public deliberation – laws are made from the collective will of the citizens – and the absolute primacy of the binding religious law for everybody, whether they adhere to it or not (Hervieu-Léger 1996: 367). There are 'superior' Christian values that cannot be reduced to the majoritarian rule. For the church, the *nature* of the law has often been more important than its *form*, in accordance with its conformity to the Catholic conception of common good. During the Spanish democratic transition, some values of democratic governance such as tolerance and acceptance of the Other were encouraged by the church, while other aspects were ethically challenged in spite of their institutional ratification (Anderson 2003). What applies to family policies, ethical questions (Barreiro 2001) or immigration (Itçaina 2006, 2007b) is also valid on the question of identity. In a sense, compromises and negotiations which are inherent in a democratic regime may have had destabilising effects on the church. Of course, this parallelism is negated as soon as it is formulated. The means and objectives of an armed organisation are by essence totally opposed to the Christian doctrine. The fact remains that some form of common scepticism towards a purely institutional response may bring diametrically opposed actors round to adopting similar views in their attempt at creating a new political space for deliberation.

Basque bishops repeatedly expressed themselves in favour of such a demanding conception of democracy, especially in Guipuzcoa, where radical nationalism is firmly rooted. In a recent book, Monsignor Setién (2007), former bishop of San Sebastián, expresses the complexity of the pressure exerted on the church in his diocese. By rejecting both the violence of ETA and the purely repressive positions of the state, the bishop examines the controversies involving the Basque Church: visits of the bishops to *all* the prisoners, rights of the victims, polemic about funerals and memorial masses, different interpretations between Basque and Spanish bishops during the ceasefire of ETA in 2006, debate over the equivalence of violence. Peace, according to Monsignor Setién, cannot be reduced to a matter of public order. Such a vision tries to bring together a deeply religious conception of peace, based on reconciliation and forgiveness, and an assumption of the political nature of the Basque conflict, which cannot be reduced to its violent counterpart. According to Monsignor Setién (2007: 197), the two processes (end of violence and political normalisation) have to be, at the same time, distinguished *and* considered together in order to reach a real pacification. Such a position was opposed both to an armed organisation claiming for the recognition of the so-called inalienable rights of the Basque people, and to those assimilating terrorism and any claim for identity. In the same vein, Monsignor Setién (ibid.: 202) questions both the 2002 law on political parties, which provoked the banning of Batasuna, and the persistent refusal of Batasuna to condemn the violence of ETA. This ethical approach of the conflict was perceived by the Basque radical nationalists *and* by their more radical opponents either as abusively liberal, since it assumed the legitimacy of *all* the ideologies, or as too committed, because he (Setién) recognised the political nature of the conflict.

Conclusion

Sociologists and those specialising in the political roles of religion use two sets of variables to analyse relations between religion and politics (Bréchon 2000). In their view, the strategies adopted by the church have alternated between *withdrawal* (that is, a monasticism, whereby one renounces worldly pursuits in order to fully devote one's life to spiritual concerns), *consent* (conformism towards power) and *protest* (worker priests, for example). But, in all cases, the action of the religious institutions within the public sphere has been either discreet or visible. The rallies for peace organised by the Basque bishops are good illustrations of such a 'visible' strategy. Conversely, the bilateral talks organised by some religious figures – acting as brokers – with the Spanish Minister of the Interior and ETA representatives have been carried out in the strictest secrecy. In strategic terms, the mediating efforts made by the Catholic Church in the Basque Country have evidenced its refusal to withdraw within itself and adopt a purely religious and non-political approach to the peace process. It should be noted that the regular clergy – the religious institution which is sometimes said to be the most cut off from the rest of the world – has also taken an active part in mediation. The Arantzazu Franciscans, for instance, have justified their political commitment on the grounds of their own theological references. It is much more difficult to determine whether the church's action is a sign of consent or protest.

It is therefore necessary to assess the real impact of Catholic mediation. Unquestionably the church has significantly contributed to structuring public deliberation (the *forum*) on the peace process. Nevertheless, such activism does not necessarily mean that the church has been present in the political *arena* – the locus of negotiation and decision-making. Can we thus say that all mediation efforts made by the church have been in vain? It is much too early to know if these efforts will eventually be instrumental in the emergence of a real debate between the actors concerned. The radicalism of the separatist movement or the excessively repressive positions adopted by the Spanish authorities in a general context of political violence bode ill for a peaceful resolution of the conflict. The church may well seize such an opportunity to recover some social legitimacy, even if it is not part of a deliberate strategy on its part. It is much more doubtful whether it will effectively contribute to finding a durable solution, i.e. the stabilisation of competing interpretations of the identity question in a non-violent and democratic political game.

Appendix 1

The Basque question

A recent chronology (1988–2008)

- 1988–98: Ajuria–Enea Agreement between political parties (with the exception of Basque radical nationalists) on the development of the statute of autonomy and the end of violence.
- 1994–5: a Council for Development and a Council of Elected Officials are set up in the French Basque Country.
- 1997 (17 July): kidnapping and assassination of Miguel Angel Blanco, a young local councillor of Ermua (Vizcaya), by ETA. Huge mobilisation against ETA.
- 1998 (March): the president of the Basque Autonomous Community Ardanza issues his official peace proposal.
- 1998 (September): Lizarra–Garazi agreement, continuing the Foro de Irlanda. The Lizarra–Garazi is an agreement between Basque nationalist parties, trade unions and social movements. The agreement backs dialogue and negotiation to put an end to the conflict. The Lizarra–Garazi is perceived as a sovereignist agreement and rejected by non-Basque-nationalist formations.
- 1998 (18 September): announce of ceasefire by ETA.
- 1999 (winter): calling off of the ceasefire.
- 2000 (January): killings by ETA.
- 2000–5: *Acuerdo por las Libertades y contra el Terrorismo*, anti-terrorist agreement between Partido Popular and PSOE at the Spanish level, which will lead to a series of measures against Basque radical nationalism and its political, cultural and social environment.
- 2001: The Council for the Basque Language (Conseil de la langue basque) is set up in the French Basque Country.
- 2001 (May): autonomous elections in the Basque Autonomous Community. A new autonomous government is set up between the moderate nationalist parties Partido Nacionalista Vasco and Eusko Alkartasuna and the leftist Izquierda Unida-Ezker Batua.
- 2002 (June): new law on political parties in Spain.
- 2003: Batasuna becomes illegal, in application of the new law.
- 2004 (11 March): Islamist bombings in Madrid; 191 people are killed and 1,500 are wounded.
- 2004 (13 March): the PSOE wins general election in Spain.
- 2004 (November): the Anoeta Proposal, *Orain herria, orain bakea* ('The country/people now, peace now'), by Batasuna.
- 2004 (December): the Ibarretxe (president of the Basque Autonomous Community) Proposal for the Reform of the Political Status of the Autonomous Community of Euskadi is approved by the Basque parliament.

- 2005 (1 February): the Ibarretxe Plan is rejected by the Spanish parliament.
- 2005 (April): elections in the Basque Autonomous Community. Victory of the moderate Basque nationalist coalition (PNV/EA).
- 2005: in the French Basque Country, the Council for the Basque Language becomes the public office for the Basque language.
- 2006 (March): ETA ceasefire.
- 2006 (May): J. L. Rodriguez Zapatero's proposal for talks between the Spanish government, ETA and the Basque political parties.
- 2006 (30 December): Madrid bomb attacks by ETA. Two Ecuadorian citizens are killed. The ceasefire is called off.
- 2007 (1 December): in Capbreton (France), two Spanish policemen (*guardia civiles*) are killed by ETA.
- 2007–8: frequent bomb attacks in the Spanish Basque Country, La Rioja and Cantabria against tourist areas, headquarters of the PSOE, judicial institutions and barrack buildings.
- 2008 (7 March): in Mondragón, a former socialist local councillor is killed by ETA.
- 2008 (9 March): Spanish general election, victory of the PSOE.
- 2008 (14 May): car bomb attack in Legutiano (Alava). A *guardia civil* is killed by ETA.
- 2008 (20 May): four top members of ETA are arrested in Bordeaux (France).
- 2008 (May): ETA dismisses the Ibarretxe referendum 'as a fraud'.
- 2008 (27 June): the Ibarretxe proposal of a referendum on the end of violence and self-determination is approved by the Basque parliament.
- 2008 (July): the Spanish government appeals to the Constitutional Court against the Ibarretxe referendum project.

Notes

1 I would like to thank Jean-François Allafort and Jeffrey Haynes who helped me with the translation of this chapter, and Anja Hennig, Jeffrey Haynes and the anonymous reviewers of the original book proposal for their comments.

2 The seven Basque historical provinces are currently divided among three territories: the Basque Autonomous Community and the Foral Community of Navarra in Spain, and the western part of the department of the Pyrénées-Atlantiques in France. Discussion in this paper will be centred on the Spanish side. For an analysis of religion and politics on the French Basque region, see Elgoyhen (2001) and Itçaina (2007a).

3 Whereas in France the church had already adapted, from the mid-1920s, to the secular regime of *laïcité* which had eventually proved to be a guarantee for its autonomy.

4 In 1968, 12.2 per cent of all Spanish seminarians came from the Basque–Navarre region. They were only 5.9 per cent in 1975 and 4.4 per cent in 1990 (Andrés-Gallego and Pazos 1998: 230). The number of seminarians in Spain declined by 30 per cent between 1987 and 2007 (from 1997 to 1387). The Basco-Navarrese dioceses were particularly concerned by this decline. The diocese of Vitoria provided only one seminarian in 2007 (119 for the diocese of Madrid) (Bellido 2007).

5 The church ranks after, in order, the Basque parliament, the autonomous government, the EU, the trade unions, the autonomous police, the king, the business organisations,

the Spanish government, the Congress of Deputies and the Senate. The church is ahead of the Constitutional Court, the political parties, the *guardia civil* and the national police, the justice administration, the armed forces and NATO. The church scores 3.7 on a 0–10 approval scale. The Basque parliament and government are the only ones to score higher than 5 (Euskobarometro 2007).

6 The ELA-STV (Solidaridad de trabajadores vascos [Solidarity of Basque workers]) was historically close to the PNV. LAB (Langile abertzaleen sindikatua [Nationalist workers' trade union]) had closer ties with the radical nationalists. The rapprochement of the two unions was one of the factors in the bringing together of the two nationalist movements, which was to lead eventually to the Estella–Garazi agreement and the ceasefire decreed by ETA in September 1998. This agreement, named after the Navarrese town of Lizarra (Estella) and the French Basque town of Donibane Garazi (St Jean-Pied-de-Port) took the form of a sovereignist manifesto. It was made on 12 September 1998 by twenty-eight Basque trade unions, social movements and political parties (nationalist parties but also the non-nationalist Carlist Party, Izquierda Unida [United Left] and the French Basque Greens. The declaration consisted of two parts. In the first, the example of the Northern Irish peace process (and especially the 1998 Good Friday agreement) was analysed. In the second part, the signers discussed the potential implementation of the Irish experience in the Basque case (Mansvelt-Beck 2005: 211).

7 Prior to his nomination, Mgr Setién had been auxiliary bishop in San Sebastián since 1972.

8 Interview with Brother E., Arantzazu, 1998.

9 Interview with a representative of Baketik, Arantzazu, June 2008. See also Fernandez (2007).

10 There is, however, an implicit reference to religion, since the former leader of Lurraldea and Elkarri eventually became the main animator of the Baketik centre.

11 In April 1998, the rejection by the Partido Popular (Popular Party) and PSOE (Socialist Party) elected representatives of the peace plan proposed by José Antonio Ardanza, the president of the Basque Autonomous Community, invalidated the pact of government in Vitoria and plunged the Basque Country into a profound political crisis.

12 For a classification of the Basque pacifist movements, see Mansvelt-Beck (2005: 214).

13 On the occasion of a religious feast celebrated in Arantzazu, the Gestoras pro-Amnistia urged Monsignor Setién to clarify the position of the church on the problem of political prisoners ('Setienen aurrean kexu' [Angry against Setién], *Egunkaria*, 10 September 1997).

14 *Egunkaria*, 12 June 1998.

15 *El Mundo*, 15 May 1998.

16 *Egunkaria*, 18 March 1997.

17 'Senideak pide la implicación de la Iglesia vasca. Los familiares de los presos realizaron concentraciones ante las catedrales' (*Egin*, 15 June 1998).

18 *Diaro Vasco*, 15 April 2001; *El País*, 16 April 2001.

19 'Entrevista realizada por Francisco Mora a Mons. Setién', *Interviú*, 569, 9 April 1987, pp. 19–23.

20 'La Iglesia vasca está dispuesta a mediar en el conflicto', *Egin*, 2 November 1997.

21 The Carter Center conflict resolution programme was interested in the Basque conflict from the early 1990s. In 1994, Elkarri and the Basque Studies Program of the University of Nevada in Reno approached the Carter Center to ascertain its possible interest in serving as a mediator should there be negotiations among the parties to the Basque conflict. On 14 November 1995, in San Sebastián, Elkarri and the Basque Studies Program signed an agreement creating the International Committee for the Basque Peace Process. In 1995, Harry Barnes, a former diplomat and member of the Carter Center, had contacts with Basque political parties, representatives of the Socialist party (PSOE) and ETA. In 1996, after the victory of the conservative Partido Popular

(PP) at the Spanish general elections, the foundation tried to inaugurate a new round of contacts, but in December President Aznar and Minister of the Interior Jaime Mayor Oreja prevented a meeting between PP members and the Carter Center. In May of 2003, members of the Carter Foundation had their first contacts with the associations of victims of terrorism (Fundación de víctimas del terrorismo, Fundación Miguel Angel Blanco, FAES, Fundación por la Libertad, Basta Ya) and with the Basque government service in charge of the victims of terrorism (Fernando Lazaro, 'La fundación Carter contactó con las víctimas del terrorismo a finales de Mayo', *El Mundo*, 6 July 2003, no. 4960). Harry Barnes also joined the permanent group of international advisors to the peace process set up by J. I. Ibarretxe, president of the Basque Autonomous Community, in January 2007, together with Joseba Azkarraga (Basque Minister for Justice, Employment and Social Security), Javier Madrazo (Izquierda Unida), Albert Reynolds (former Irish Taoiseach), Joanna Weschler (Human Rights Watch) and Rolf Meyer (South Africa's former Defence Minister) (*Le Journal du Pays Basque*, 30 and 31 January 2007).
22 *Gara*, 1 May 2000.
23 3 October 2000; see http://archimadrid.es/princi/menu/notdirec/notdirec/oct2000/03102000.htm.
24 Ibid.
25 Resumen diario de prensa, Arzobispado de Pamplona, 28 May 2003; see http://iglesianavarra.org/hemeroteca/20030528.htm
26 In the last stage of the Conference for Peace, in June–October 2002, Elkarri staged another seminar gathering international experts in conflict resolution, with A. Bartoli, head of the International Centre of Conflict Resolution, Columbia University, and a member of the Sant'Egidio community; W. D. Weisberg, member of the Programme for the Resolution of International Conflicts, Harvard; H. Barnes, former head of the conflict resolution programme in the Carter Center; and Alec Reid.
27 Luis R. Aizpeolea, 'El Papa apoyó el proceso de paz tras la mediación del obispo Uriarte ante el Vaticano', *El País*, 22 October 2006.
28 The *mediator–facilitator* is an intermediary between the opponents and has only a little control on the process itself; at its best, this diplomacy of 'good offices' can organise the logistic of the process. The contribution of the *mediator–formulator* is more substantial, since he or she exerts formal control when choosing the place, the number and the kind of encounters, when setting the agenda, when controlling the distribution of information and proposing solutions to the opponents. The *mediator–manipulator* can make propositions, but is also able to use his position and his resources in order to influence, to persuade and to give ultimatums (Faget 2008: 318).
29 *El País*, 20 February 2001.
30 Interview with a Guipuzcoan member of EHAK, San Sebastián.
31 'Zerbitzu honen oinarriak, Bases de este servicio' (Aguirre *et al.* 1978: 479).
32 The Basque word *herri* means 'people', 'country' or 'village', as does the Spanish *pueblo*.
33 Interview with a Guipuzcoan member of EHAK, San Sebastián.
34 Contrary to EHAK, which belongs to the protest movement of the clergy, the CCPs were rather inspired by the national and international context for the promotion and restoration of the Christian communities, after Vatican II.
35 This project, known as the Ibarretxe Plan, was an institutional proposal to alter the statute of autonomy of the Spanish Basque Country by giving it greater autonomy. It was inspired by the sovereignty-association approach of the Parti Québecois in Quebec. The project was presented by the Basque government in 2003 and approved by the Basque parliament on 30 December 2004. In January 2005, the Plan was sent to the Spanish parliament for them to debate and vote, being refused on 1 February by 313 votes to 29, with two abstentions.
36 Interview with Brother E., Arantzazu.

37 Gutmann and Thompson (2004: 7) define deliberative democracy

> as a form of government in which free and equal citizens (and their representatives) justify decisions in a process in which they give one another reasons that are mutually acceptable and generally accessible, with the aim of reaching conclusions that are binding in the present on all citizens but open to challenge in the future.

Bibliography

Aguirre, R., Aguirrebaltzategi, P. and Basurko X. (1978) *Herria-Eliza, Euskadi, pueblo-iglesia*, Zarautz: Itxaropena.

Anderson, J. (2003) 'Catholicism and Democratic Consolidation in Spain and Poland', *West European Politics*, 26, 1, pp. 137–56.

Andrés-Gallego, J. and Pazos, A. (1998) *Histoire religieuse de l'Espagne*, Paris: Éditions du Cerf.

Barreiro, B. (2001) *Democracia y conflicto moral: la política del aborto en España e Italia*, Madrid: Istmo.

Bellido, J. (2007) 'Creciente caída del número de vocaciones en España', Camineo.info, Noticias católicas en Internet, 19 February 2007, available at www.camineo.info/news/119/ARTICLE/1919/2007-02-19.html (accessed 2 July 2008).

Brassloff, A. (2003) *Religion and Politics in Spain: The Spanish Church in Transition, 1962–1996*, Basingstoke, UK: Palgrave Macmillan; New York: St Martin's Press.

Braud, P. (1998) *Êtes-vous catholique?* Paris: Presses de Sciences Po.

Bréchon, P. (2000) 'Conclusion', in P. Bréchon, B. Duriez and J. Ion (eds), *Religion et action dans l'espace public*, Paris: l'Harmattan, pp. 287–300.

Davant, J.-L. (1972) 'Foi et politique', *Enbata*, 275, 2 (November), pp. 4–5.

De Briant, V. and Palau, Y. (1999) *La Médiation: définition, pratiques et perspectives*, Paris: Nathan.

Elgoyhen, M. (2001) *Le Clergé du diocèse de Bayonne face à la question basque: 1964–1998*, Toulouse: GRHI.

Euskobarometro (2007) *Estudio periódico de la opinión pública vasca*, Leioa: Euskal Herriko unibertsitatea.

Faget, J. (2008) 'Les Métamorphoses du travail de paix. Etat des travaux sur la médiation dans les conflits politiques violents', *Revue française de science politique*, 58, 2, pp. 309–33.

Fernandez, J. (2007) *Being Human in Conflicts. An Ethical Reflection after Direct Experience of the Basque Conflict*, Arantzazu: Baketik.

Garaikoetxea, C. (2002) *Euskadi, la transición inacabada: memorias políticas*, Barcelona: Planeta.

Gutmann, A. and Thompson, D. (2004) *Why Deliberative Democracy?* Princeton: Princeton University Press.

Herria 2000 Eliza (ed.) (2003) *Tiempo de soluciones: proyectos políticos, análisis y sugerencias*, Getxo: Herria 2000 Eliza.

Hervieu-Léger, D. (1996) 'Croire en modernité: au-delà de la problématique des champs religieux et politique', in P. Michel (ed.), *Religion et démocratie*, Paris: A. Michel, pp. 361–81.

Itçaina, X. (2006) 'The Roman Catholic Church and the Immigration Issue. The Relative Secularization of Political Life in Spain', *American Behavioral Scientist Journal*, 49, 11 (July), 1471–88.

Itçaina, X. (2007a) *Les Virtuoses de l'identité. Religion et politique en Pays Basque*, Rennes: Presses universitaires de Rennes.

Itçaina, X. (2007b) 'Vers une nouvelle régulation religieuse du politique? Catholicisme, espace public et démocratie en Espagne et en Italie', in F. Foret (ed.), *L'Espace public européen à l'épreuve du religieux*, Bruxelles: Éditions de l'Université de Bruxelles, pp. 91–108.

Iztueta, P. (1981) *Sociología del fenómeno contestario del clero vasco: 1940–1975, (análisis de las causas de la radicalización del clero vasco en el período 1940–1974)*, Bayonne, San Sebastián: Elkar.

Jobert, B. (1995) 'Rhétorique politique, controverses scientifiques et construction des normes institutionnelles: esquisse d'un parcours de recherche', in A. Faure, G. Pollet and P. Warin (eds), *La Construction du sens dans les politiques publiques: débats autour de la notion de référentiel*, Paris: l'Harmattan.

Lagroye, J. (2006) *La Vérité dans l'Église catholique. Contestations et restauration d'un régime d'autorité*, Paris: Belin.

MacClancy, J. (2000) *The Decline of Carlism*, Reno: University of Nevada Press.

Madeley, J. T. S. and Enyedi, Z. (eds) (2003) Special Issue on 'Church and State in Contemporary Europe. The Chimera of Neutrality', *West European Politics*, 26, 1.

Mansvelt-Beck, J. (2005) *Territory and Terror. Conflicting Nationalisms in the Basque Country*, London: Routledge.

Mees, L. (2003) *Nationalism, Violence and Democracy: The Basque Clash of Identities*, London: Palgrave Macmillan.

Nay, O. and Smith A. (2002) 'Les Intermédiaires en politique. Médiation et jeux d'institutions', in O. Nay and A. Smith (eds), *Le Gouvernement du compromis: courtiers et généralistes dans l'action politique*, Paris: Economica, pp. 1–21.

Pace, E. (1998) *La Nation italienne en crise: perspectives européennes*, Paris: Bayard.

Palard, J. (2006) 'Médiation et institution catholique', *Archives de sciences sociales des religions*, 133, pp. 9–26.

Pérez-Agote, A. (1986) 'The Role of Religion in the Definition of a Symbolic Conflict: Religion and the Basque Problem', *Social Compass*, 33, 4, pp. 419–35.

Pérez-Agote, A. and Santiago García, A. (2005) *La situación de la religión en España a principios del siglo XXI*, Madrid: CIS.

Pérez-Díaz, V. (1993) *The Return of Civil Society: The Emergence of Democratic Spain*, Cambridge, MA: Harvard University Press.

Placer Ugarte, F. (1998) *Creer en Euskal Herria: la experiencia creyente de las comunidades cristianas populares y de la coordinadora de sacerdotes de Euskal Herria, 1976–1996*, Bilbao: Herria 2000 Eliza.

Reizabal Arruabarrena, L. (1996) *Bakearen dimentsio kulturala Euskal Herriko uste sistema eta pertzepzioetan*, Leioa: Universidad del País Vasco, Servicio Editorial.

Setién, J. M. (1998) *Obras completas, t.1, Dios, política-paz*, San Sebastián: Idatz.

Setién, J. M. (2007) *Un obispo vasco ante ETA*, Barcelona: Crítica.

Wehr, P. and Lederach, J.-P. (1991) 'Mediating Conflict in Central America', *Journal of Peace Research*, 28, 1, pp. 85–98.

Zallo, R. (1998) 'Teoría y práctica del tercer espacio', *Egin*, 24 January.

Zubiaga Garate, M. (2008) 'Boteretik eraginera: mekanismoak eta prozesuak Leitzarango eta Urbina/Maltzagako liskarretan', unpublished PhD thesis, Department of Political Science and Administration, Leioa: Euskal Herriko unibertsitatea.

6 *E unum pluribus*

The role of religion in the project of European integration

John T. S. Madeley

Introduction

The ongoing resurgence of the religious factor in politics across the world is most frequently traced back to changes which occurred in the turbulent 1970s. Thus, for example, Gilles Kepel in his 1994 volume *The Revenge of God: The Resurgence of Islam, Christianity and Judaism in the Modern World* pointed to changes occurring in 1977, 1978 and 1979 as indicating a decisive reversal of modernising and secularising trends which had dominated the post-Second-World War era: the electoral breakthrough of Israel's Likud Party in May 1977, the election of Pope John Paul II in September 1978, and the return of Ayatollah Khomeini to Tehran leading to the proclamation of Iran's Islamic Republic in February 1979 (Kepel 1994: 6–7). Also writing in 1994, as the introduction to this volume points out, José Casanova adopted a similar chronology with his claim that '[w]hat was new and became "news" in the 1980s was the widespread and simultaneous character of the refusal to be restricted to the private sphere of religious traditions … in all three worlds of development' (Casanova 1994: 6). It might, however, be claimed that the single most significant contribution of religious actors to the world of politics – in Europe at least – occurred approximately three decades earlier with the launching of the project of European integration under Christian Democratic auspices. The reason why this might have been overlooked in claims about a supposed 'religious resurgence' in recent decades is that the latter is now associated with such spectacular events as those of 9/11 in 2001 or, in the case of Europe, 11 March 2004 in Madrid and 7 July 2005 in London. Compared to the demonstration effects of events such as these, the origins of the European Union (EU) in the European Coal and Steel Community (ECSC) some fifty years earlier appear ostentatiously humdrum. If the degree of dramatic effect has affected the resurgence claims it might be that the timing of Kepel's *Revenge* and Casanova's 'news' is wrongly calibrated or even wrongly identified at least so far as Europe is concerned. It might even be the case that what is being witnessed in Europe at the start of the third millennium of the common era is not so much a rise in the influence exerted by religious forces in politics as a rise in the salience of religious or religion-related issues regardless of outcome. This is consistent, to be sure, with a purported progressive refusal of religion to be restricted to the private sphere, but it suggests a different dynamic from that proposed by Kepel and Casanova – not so much a resurgence of the religious factor as heightened incidence of controversies in which religious groups and individuals have become involved – a level of incidence which has only been amplified by a growing resistance to religious influence on the part of secular liberals. In short, increased salience of religion-related issues might as much reflect the incidence of struggles to neutralise as to maximise religious influences in politics.

The relevance of such developments to issues of citizenship, secularisation and democracy is patent and wide-ranging in its possible ramifications. This chapter will touch on only a few of these as they have arisen in connection with the political project of European integration. It looks at the involvement of religious–political actors (both individual and collective) in the launching of the political project of European integration after the Second World War and over the fifteen years from 1992, when the EU's ambit was extended northwards and eastwards from a membership of fifteen countries to one of twenty-seven. The comparison suggests that the impact of religious–political actors, in particular political parties of religious inspiration, which ranged themselves in support or opposition to the project, varied markedly between those two time periods in both degree and direction. In attempting to understand these variations, three explanatory hypotheses are briefly reviewed which suggest that one of the reasons for the hypothesised rise in secular(ist) resistance to religious influences of recent years is associated with the revival of intra- as well as inter-confessional differences among the religious themselves. In short, it would appear that instead of religious voices having greater impact in Europe recently than they had in the 1945 to 1965 period, the issue is now more and more whether religious voices – themselves progressively seen as discordant and conflicting – should have a significant role in public affairs at all.

Without doubt, fifty years on from the signing of the Treaty of Rome on 25 March 1957, the place of religion and the role of religious actors in the halting process of European integration remains controversial. Thus there has been the debate about a possible *invocatio deo* (literally, an invocation of God, in particular a reference to the contribution to European culture and values of the Christian religion) in the draft preamble to the stalled Constitution for Europe, the objections raised on religious or religion-related grounds to the eventual admission of Turkey to the EU, and the failure at the jubilee anniversary of the Treaty of Rome itself explicitly to acknowledge the importance of religious influences in the beginnings of the Union. These have each caused hackles to be raised and harsh things to be said which seem to belie the notion that such skirmishes are merely symbolic or even essentially trivial. With the rest of the world, including the USA, in Peter Berger's words seeming – against common expectation – to have become 'more furiously religious than ever', it cannot be easily assumed that in Europe these should be regarded as mere 'noises off' which can be readily ignored (Berger 1999: 2). While Norris and Inglehart's analysis of secularising and de-secularising trends across the world supports the view that Western

Europe continues to defy an otherwise widespread shift towards a resurgence of religion as such *and* as a factor in politics, others argue that claims about European exceptionalism are overdone (Casanova 1994; Davie 2002; Greeley 2003; Norris and Inglehart 2004). In addition, it is the principal thesis of the 2006 Bynes and Katzenstein edited volume, *Religion in an Expanding Europe*, that the process of 'European enlargement will feed rather than undermine the importance of religion in the EU' as 'transnational religious communities in the European periphery are reintroducing religion into the center of Europe' (Byrnes and Katzenstein 2006: 2). Even if this thesis proves to be well founded, it can be argued that such a political resurgence of the religious factor is only likely at best to recapitulate, albeit under very different circumstances, the shift which occurred in the immediate post-war period when Christian Democracy first emerged as a – or perhaps *the* – central party actor on the stage of West European politics.

European integration: a Christian Democratic project?

For many participants and contemporary commentators, religion was often acknowledged to be a significant contributory influence in framing the project of European integration, as it took form and gained ground in the late 1940s and 1950s when Europe was struggling to surmount the challenges of post-war reconstruction. In particular, the formative role of a core group of Catholic 'founding fathers' was clearly evident since most were leading members of the Christian Democratic parties that had emerged or re-emerged in the six continental states of Germany, Italy, France and the Benelux countries after the war and taken on central roles in government (Buchanan and Conway 1996). In the big three countries (Germany, Italy, France), reform-minded Catholics had long been excluded from the centres of power. So it was something of a novelty that in the immediate post-war period, Konrad Adenauer (German chancellor 1949–63), Alcide de Gasperi (prime minister of Italy 1945–53) and Robert Schuman of France (a holder of high office as, alternatively, finance minister, foreign minister and prime minister, 1947–52) should combine key positions in the three states with their own strong Catholic backgrounds. Commenting on the so-called Schuman Plan, which had actually been developed by Jean Monnet, Schuman went so far as to suggest to his fellow European Christian Democrats that

> [t]his project will be our pride, for us French and German Christian Democrats to have transposed in the first European institution the very principles that comprise our Christian ideals of charity, peace and social justice ... To decide to apply the Schuman plan is, in one word, to ensure the triumph of Christian Democracy.
>
> (Schuman to Nouvelles Equipes Internationale (NEI) representatives in 1950, quoted in Gonzalez 2005 from the minutes held in the NEI archives)

Triumphal accents of this sort were, however, mainly for private consumption among members of the NEI, the Christian Democrat international network, and

the plan itself was sold to the wider world on the more pragmatic – if still vision-
ary – grounds that it provided a guarantee for preserving peace in Europe after
the devastations of the recently concluded war.

The rather technical and functional proposal to place coal and steel production under a common supranational authority did not seem at the time to be
freighted with religious–political significance at all. But, as Monnet protested to
the later British prime minister, Harold Macmillan, when the latter made a
counter-proposal designed to protect the prerogatives of the nation-state,

> The Schuman proposals are revolutionary or they are nothing. For centuries
> we Europeans have tried to solve our common problems either through
> diplomacy or through war, but, in the context of present-day Europe, agree-
> ments between national states for the preservation of strictly national inter-
> ests are wholly inadequate ... The Schuman proposals provide a basis for
> the building of a new Europe through the concrete achievement of a supra-
> national regime ... I have felt it necessary ... to emphasize that the indis-
> pensable first principle of those proposals is the abnegation of sovereignty.
> (From a copy of a letter to Macmillan sent by Monnet to Bidault, 8 August
> 1950; ibid.)

The willingness selectively to dispense with the principle of state sovereignty
which was generally understood to have been the cornerstone of the modern
state system since the 1648 Peace of Westphalia had been most systematically
set out in Jacques Maritain's influential 1951 book, *Man and the State*. The book
was quoted by Christian Democrats in many of the debates around key decisions
on European integration – for example, by Theo Lefevre during the final debate
in the Belgian Parliament on the European Defence Community in December
1953.[1] In retrospect, had the Gaullists, rather than the Christian Democratic
Mouvement Républicain Populaire (MRP), been in control of French foreign
policy in the late 1940s the key initiatives which led to the setting of this cornerstone of what is now the EU would surely not have seen the light of day.

Historians and other analysts of the history of European integration now generally acknowledge the critical role of Europe's Christian Democrats during the
project's gestation and birth (Lücker and Hahn 1987; Greschat and Loth 1994;
Gehler and Kaiser 2004; Philpott and Shah 2006; Kaiser 2007). While early neo-
functionalist and later liberal intergovernmentalist accounts tended to stress
national economic and security interests, more recent research has given greater
prominence to the role played by the leaders of European Christian Democracy
with their ostensible 'Christian inspiration'. With the focus on what is most
properly regarded as the foundational moment, the creation in 1950 of the ECSC
with its supranational High Authority, the role of these 'founding fathers' comes
out most clearly. According to Marks and Wilson, 'Christian Democratic parties
have been more closely associated with the founding of the European Union than
any other party family' (Marks and Wilson 1999: 451). Hanley pointed to their
'longstanding attachment to European integration as a means of overcoming

nationalism' (Hanley 1994b: 4). In Irving's words, the Christian Democrats had 'been untiring advocates of European integration', while Pridham noted that the German and Italian parties shared a 'strong ideological attachment to [the] values' associated with European integration.(Irving 1979: 249; Pridham 1976: 147). The supporting historical evidence was strong, no less for critics than for supporters of the project:

> It was the leaders of the three main Christian Democrat parties, Adenauer, de Gasperi and Robert Schuman, who, together with the technocrat Jean Monnet, brought the European Community into existence. And to this day it is the Christian Democrat parties of Europe who push hardest for the creation of something resembling a common European state.
>
> (Malcolm 1996: 60–1)

In 2006 José Casanova claimed that there was still a widespread tendency in Europe to ignore this 'forgotten history' and to refuse to recognise that

> the initial project of a European Union was fundamentally a Christian Democratic project, sanctioned by the Vatican, at a time of a general religious revival in post-World War Two Europe, in the geopolitical context of the Cold War when 'the free world' and 'Christian civilization' had become synonymous.
>
> (Casanova 2006: 66)

And for George Weigel, quoting J. H. H. Weiler, failure to acknowledge this historical debt was rooted less in some rival reading of history than in a 'Christophobic' mind-set committed to the progressive marginalisation of religious influences in Europe's public life (Weigel 2005).

The Christian Democratic parties at the time of the founding of the European Coal and Steel Community were in government in all six of the original member states, providing the prime minister in four (Haas 1958: 153). They alone of the main party families voted unanimously in all six legislatures for ratifying the Treaties of Paris and Rome in 1951 and 1957, reservations seeming to arise more from the sense that the treaties did not go far enough politically, rather than that they went too far. Throughout the 1960s the Christian Democrats of the Six continued to press for greater economic integration across the European Common Market, for strengthening its institutions, and for enlarging its membership, albeit largely without success because of the opposition of President de Gaulle. When the European People's Party (EPP) was created in 1976 to bring together the Christian Democratic parties of the member states Leo Tindemans, its first president, announced that the 'major task of our new party will be to breathe new life into the idea of European union; to fight to ensure that European unity is eventually achieved' (Irving 1979: 249).[2] The EPP has moreover remained loyal to this task and continued to be the most consistently federalist European grouping. Thus, for example, in October 2003 the EPP approved *A Constitution for a Strong Europe* at its conference in Estoril, Portugal – a strongly federalist document (although in deference to the non-Christian Democrat (CD) conservative parties it fudged the question of the European Executive): 'The peoples who joined the European integration process based on their free decision, declare to [*sic*] create a close and federal European Union' (Gonzalez 2003).

It is easy to overstate the case for the central role of the Christian Democratic parties and their leaders in launching and carrying forward the European integration project. It is, for example, the case that commitment to the project progressively ceased to be a distinguishing mark of the Christian Democrats as other party families moved to support the cause, even if Christian Democratic attachment to it has tended to outstrip that of other party families.[3] It should also be recognised that the first inspiration for the project itself long pre-dated the full emergence of the Christian Democratic parties after the Second World War; Pan-Europeans and Federalists with only incidental links, or none, to the forerunners of Christian Democracy had argued for it through much of the inter-war period. Progenitors and champions once it finally got under way in the 1950s included figures from other, contrasting, political traditions, including representatives of the centre and the left such as Paul-Henri Spaak, the Belgian Socialist, and Altiero Spinelli, the Italian former communist. It can even be argued that the Christian Democrats' own commitment to integration was less heartfelt than *faute de mieux* the product: that is, more of the need to have something distinctive to stand for when 'Christian values' and 'democracy' seemed insufficiently determinative to mark a separate political brand (Irving 1979: xix). In spite of all these qualifications, however, Wolfram Kaiser's archival research has recently traced the origins of the European Union to the network of Christian Democratic cross-border connections which developed rapidly after 1945 and confirmed the key role of these religious–political entrepreneurs (Kaiser 2007).

European integration: a Catholic rather than a Christian Democratic project?

A different gloss which can be put on the Christian Democratic roots of European integration is, however, that it represents not so much a Christian Democratic project as a carrying forward of an older tradition of continental political Catholicism with its distinctive long-standing concerns (Chenaux 1990; Nelsen and Guth 2003b). Schuman's previously noted commitment to the creation of a supranational body to administer the ECSC with its abrogation of state sovereignty in the sphere of coal and steel production was in fact in direct line with a long-standing Catholic critique of nation-state sovereignty (Pulzer 2004; Philpott and Shah 2006). One of the distinctive features of post-war Christian Democracy was that it attempted to transcend the old confessional division between Catholics and Protestants thrown up by the Reformation and Counter-reformation. While this feature was electorally unimportant in four of the original signatories to the Treaties of Paris and Rome because of their overwhelmingly Catholic colouration, it was very important in Germany and had some significance in the

Netherlands, two countries with historically dominant Protestant confessions. In the then West Germany, the Christlich Demokratische Union (CDU) was from the first a cross-confessional party even though its support was always markedly stronger among Catholics than among Protestants. In the Netherlands in December 1945 the former Roman Catholic State Party changed its name to the Catholic People's Party (KVP), redrafted its statutes so that it was no longer necessary to be a Catholic to join, and appealed for support from all Belgian citizens regardless of their confession. The continuing strength of the principal Protestant parties (the Anti-Revolutionary Party (ARP) and the Christian Historical Union (CHU)) blocked the KVP's ambition to gain significant Protestant support within the context of Dutch *verzuiling* ('pillarisation') but the reorientation reflected a continuing willingness to cooperate with Protestant parties in government.[4] For Casanova the formation of the ECSC and the EEC, launched in 1951 and 1957 respectively, was 'predicated upon two historic reconciliations: the reconciliation between France and Germany ... and the reconciliation of Protestants and Catholics within Christian Democracy' (Casanova 2006: 71). While it seems to be the case that the main Protestant parties of the Netherlands lent strong, if not quite full, support to European integration – and in the case of the ARP developed an intellectually sophisticated body of thought around such supportive concepts as 'sphere sovereignty' which chimed well with the Catholic concept of subsidiarity – other Protestants were typically less supportive. In both Germany and the Netherlands there were early (and in part continuing) distinct pockets of resistance; thus, Erhard, Schröder and von Hassel, all CDU Protestants who between them dominated German foreign policy-making in the mid-1960s, were frequently criticised as more Atlanticist than European. Meanwhile in the Netherlands, Protestants who did not support the ARP or the CHU maintained a separate presence in smaller parties which vocally expressed a strongly Eurosceptic perspective (Freston 2004; Vollard 2006).

The idea that Protestantism fosters Euroscepticism – or is at least significantly ambivalent about European integration – is reinforced when attention is shifted to the countries which have been historically overwhelmingly Protestant since the sixteenth century: the countries of Scandinavia and the United Kingdom (UK). Both Denmark and the UK, the first of these countries to join the European Union in 1974, have often played the role of reluctant – and even obstructive or 'awkward' – partners within the EU (Miljan 1977; George 1990; Gstoehl 2002). The only other one of these countries to negotiate terms of entry, Norway, actually voted not to join after a bitterly divisive referendum campaign in 1973 – an experience and an outcome which was repeated some twenty years later in 1994 (Madeley 2000; Vignaux 2003). Sweden joined in 1995 but, unlike Britain and Denmark, despite having negotiated no opt-out from monetary union, failed to join the Euro after the proposal was defeated in a further referendum. Alone among these countries, Finland, which joined at the same time as Sweden, has 'made a go' of EU membership, recording a good if not overwhelmingly large majority in favour of entry at its referendum in 1994, signing up to the Euro and generally involving itself to good effect for such a small country in EU internal politics (Jensen *et al.* 1998). It is significant, however, that even there the Finnish Christian Democratic party (as it is now called) expressed deep opposition to EU entry to the point of resigning from a coalition government in protest in 1994 and only later modifying its opposition (Madeley and Sitter 2003). The fact that the overwhelmingly Protestant Scandinavian countries on the one hand and the historically Protestant-dominant United Kingdom on the other have at one time or another harboured considerable reserves of Euroscepticism supports the hypothesis of a connection with their Protestant heritage.[5] Further supporting this implicitly 'confessional' hypothesis, it is after all the case that few overwhelmingly Catholic countries, even those that share with the Protestant countries a location relatively peripheral to the original six members of the EEC – countries such as Ireland, Poland and the Iberian states – exhibit similar levels of Euroscepticism. In a number of studies using Eurobarometer survey data, which confirm the linkage between confessional affiliation and attitudes to European integration at the level of individual correspondents, Brent Nelsen and his collaborators have documented that support for the European Union during the quarter-century between 1973 to 1998 was consistently stronger among Catholics than among Protestants, even when controlling for other relevant factors (Nelsen *et al.* 2001; Nelsen and Guth 2003a).

If attention is more narrowly focused on the religious parties that are to be found among the Protestant populations of Europe, such as the Finnish Christian Democratic Party, the linkage between Protestantism and Euroscepticism appears (on the surface at least) to be even more strongly marked. Protestant religious parties in Europe have historically failed to match the electoral success which their Catholic counterparts or the post-war Christian Democratic parties achieved. Given the fissiparous tendencies of Protestantism generally even in the Scandinavian countries where membership of state churches accounts, in nominal terms at least, for the vast majority of their native-born populations, this is perhaps not surprising (Bruce 1996: 43). While typically less strong and in places almost completely absent – or present only as micro-parties – Protestant political parties nevertheless do exist in surprisingly large numbers, as Paul Freston's global survey demonstrates, and there has been a tendency in recent decades for these numbers to increase and for some of the parties actually to prosper (Freston 2004: Madeley 2000). Most of them, furthermore, are judged to be Eurosceptic, as Table 6.1 reveals. This is in stark contrast to the Europhile profile of all the predominantly Catholic Christian Democratic parties of Europe. Taggart's 1998 survey of Euroscepticism in ten Western European party systems confirms this picture; comparison of his principal tables reveals that six of the seven parties with marked anti-EU positions that belong to religious party families are to be found in the Protestant countries – and if one adds the Northern Ireland Democratic Unionist Party (DUP), which it can be argued is as much, or more, religious than ethno-regionalist, then the proportion moves to seven out of eight, i.e. 87.5 per cent.[6] Unlike a number of the parties surveyed by Freston, furthermore, none of these are mere 'flash' parties or factions, or micro-parties which have never achieved national representation; all eight are deemed by

Table 6.1 Extant Protestant political parties of Europe identified by Freston and their stances on European integration *c*.2000.

Country	*Party name*	*Founded*	*Stance re EU*
Denmark	Kristen Demokratene (KD)	1970	Mod Eurosceptic
Estonia	Isamaaliit (Pro Patria Union)*	1988/1995?	Pro-EU
	Eesti Kristlik Rahvepartei (EKRP)	1998	Hard Eurosceptic
Finland	{Kristillisdemokraatit/	1958	Mod Pro-EU
	{Kristdemokraterna (KD)		
Germany	Christliche Mitte (CM)	Late 1980s	Eurosceptic?
	Partei Bibeltreue Christen (PBC)	1989	Eurosceptic
Latvia	Kristigo Tauta Partija (KTP)	1990?	
	Latvijas Pirma Partija (LPP)	2002	Mod Pro-EU
Netherlands	Staatkundig Gereformeerde Partij (SGP)	1918	Hard Eurosceptic
	ChristenUnie (CU)**	2000	
Norway	Kristelig Folkeparti (KrF)	1933	Mod Eurosceptic
Sweden	Kristdemokraterna (KD)	1964	Pro-EU
Switzerland	{Evangelische Volkspartei der Schweiz (EVP)	1919	Hard Eurosceptic
	{Parti Evangelique Suisse	1975	Hard Eurosceptic
	{Partito Evangelico Svizzero		
	{Eidgenössische-Demokratisch Union (EDU)		
	{Union Democratique Federale		
United Kingdom	Democratic Unionist Party	1971	Hard Eurosceptic
	Christian People's Alliance	1999	Mixed***

Notes
Coding of parties' 'Stance re EU' is taken from Taggart (1998) and/or from Freston (2004).
*The Isamaaliit (Pro Patria Union) was formed by a merger of Isamaa, itself a merger in 1992 of five parties, including the Eesti Kristlik Demokraatlik Erakond (EKDE) and the Eesti Kristlik Demokraatlik Liit (EKDL) both founded in 1988, the latter of which 'claimed to be the ideological heir of the Christian People's Party which had existed during Estonia's brief period of independence between the wars' (Freston 2004: 45).
**This party was formed by the merger of Gereformeerd Politieke Verbond (GPV), founded 1948, and the Reformatorische Politieke Federatie (RPF), founded 1975.
***Freston comments 'Different positions on European integration (not unique to the CPA) may be manageable' (ibid.: 55).

Taggart to be 'Established parties' as opposed to 'Single-issue' or 'Protest' or 'Factions of established' parties.[7]

The link between Euroscepticism and Protestantism seems so clear at both aggregate and individual respondent levels that a number of authors have assumed it and moved on to explain its nature. Thus, for example, Susan Sundback, writing about the Nordic countries, pointed to presumed differences between Protestant and Catholic value systems:

Protestant values such as freedom, individualism, rationalism and localism are often seen as opposed to Catholic [values] such as devotionalism, solidarity and universalism ... Ultimately Catholic values can be seen as more supportive of EU central power, because the political centre is an analogy of the position held by Rome within Catholicism. The problem with Protestantism is simply that it is a culture, which fails both to serve legitimation of the union and solidarity between nationalities within it.

(Sundback 1995: 8)

In similar vein Nelsen roots Protestant Euroscepticism in a particular view of the state:

To the Protestant mind, the state was not the cause of Europe's tragic propensity to engage in self-destruction. On the contrary, individual states were the bulwarks against coercive, homogenizing forces, whether they issued from the Vatican, Napoleonic Paris, Hollywood – or Brussels. States had saved for Protestants what was most important in the sixteenth century; states could still be trusted to save what was most important in the twentieth ... A distrust that was forged in the religious conflicts of the sixteenth century still echoes down the corridors of Brussels.

(Nelsen 2004: 18–19)

Some participants or close observers have also reported hearing these echoes. For example, in 2002 Stephen Wall, who was head of the European Secretariat in the UK Cabinet Office and Tony Blair's most senior advisor on Europe from 2000 to 2004, compared the British opponents of closer European Union integration to the anti-Catholics of the Reformation. He claimed that there was a common thread running from the anti-papist movement of the sixteenth century to the present-day critics of the EU: 'Our whole history as an island is an important factor. There are certain aspects of the Reformation and anti-popery that find an echo in modern euro-scepticism' (Times Online, 12 March 2002). The idea that contemporary British Euroscepticism represented a national tradition of anti-Catholicism which has somehow survived modern secularising trends has also been suggested by Linda Colley's analysis of the origins and development of Britishness in the eighteenth and nineteenth centuries. Her thesis is that from the early eighteenth century and for long after,

Protestantism was the dominant component of British religious life. Protestantism coloured the way that Britons approached and interpreted their material life. Protestantism determined how most Britons viewed their politics. And an uncompromising Protestantism was the foundation on which their state was explicitly and unapologetically based.

(Colley 1992: 19)

Even though features of the British Constitution, which *inter alia* makes the monarch the 'supreme governor' of the Church of England and accords membership of the upper house of the legislature to the twenty-six most senior Anglican bishops, suggest that the British state is anything but fully secularised. British society and culture by contrast can be shown to be much more secular (Norris and Inglehart 2004). Nor is Britain alone among Protestant majority countries in combining a lack of institutional state secularisation with a social and cultural surfeit of secularisation – the Nordic countries broadly exhibiting the same pattern (Madeley 2003; Fox 2008). However, there are other reasons for doubting the adequacy of the simple Protestant confessional hypothesis as an explanation of the relative Euroscepticism of Britain and Scandinavia.

European integration: a mainstream religious project opposed by fundamentalists?

As Grace Davie has pointed out, it cannot be Protestantism as such which explains the Euroscepticism of the British and the Nordics as, on a closer look, there is so much variation among Protestants in their attitudes towards European integration (Davie 1994: 106–8). After all, in Finland, Sweden and Norway, where the great majority of the population retain at least nominal membership of the national Lutheran churches, respectively 56.9 per cent, 52.3 per cent and 47.7 per cent voted in favour of EU membership in the 1994 referendums (Jensen *et al.* 1998). In this context therefore, where – as in Finland and Norway – the Christian parties with their strong Protestant profiles aligned themselves with other Eurosceptic forces from the political right, left and centre, they can only have contributed a minor or modest portion of the anti-EU votes that were cast. Furthermore as Table 6.1 shows, even across the limited array of Europe's Protestant political parties there is variation: some are markedly less Eurosceptic than others – within the Nordic group of countries, for example, the Swedish Christian Democratic party has been distinctly less Eurosceptic (indeed, for a significant period positively Europhile) than its counterparts in Norway and Finland (Madeley and Sitter 2003).

Eurobarometer survey evidence can also be used to illustrate the extent of the variation in attitudes to the EU which exists both within and between the different confessional traditions. Thus, Nelsen, Guth and Fraser were able to show from their analysis of cross-time series that during the period 1973 and 1992 across Europe devout Protestants actually tended to be less anti-EU than 'conventional' or 'nominal' Protestants; 'being Protestant does make one less supportive of the EU, but a few regular church attendees [*sic*] may sometimes get a strong dose of Christian internationalism that is missed by more nominal Protestants'. (Nelsen *et al.* 2001: 200). If the conventional assumption is made that, in some sense at least, devout Protestants are 'more religious' than nominal Protestants, it would seem then that, as is the case with Catholics, degrees of Protestant religiosity correlate positively, not negatively, with pro- (or less anti-) EU attitudes. The more fine-grained cross-sectional analysis of the larger data set available for 1994, the year of the Nordic referendums, revealed a rather fuller picture of differences among Protestants however. Paradoxically, this indicated *grosso modo* that greater Protestant devotion as measured by a larger battery of variables 'actually encourages Euroskepticism ... church-going Protestants are much more likely to mention "loss of national identity" as a major fear about the integration process supporting our theory that connects Protestantism and the nation state' (Nelsen *et al.* 2001: 206–7). One explanation for the conflicting findings based respectively on the time-series and the in-depth 1994 data is that the latter tapped differences among the so-called devout, differences observable between sectarian or fundamentalist and what might be called – following Scandinavian usage – 'churchly' Protestants. Nelsen *et al.* imply a similar analysis:

> Our theory ... suggests that sectarian Protestants should be the most opposed to European integration. In fact, where we can identify such groups in a few early Eurobarometers, that is exactly what we find: very devout Calvinists in the Netherlands and Northern Ireland and other Protestant minorities are much more hostile than are Catholics or those with no denomination.
>
> (Nelsen *et al.* 2001: 207–9)

Other analyses support the same conclusion. From these it appears that the leaders of most mainline Protestant churches, the broad membership of which dwarfs that of the sectarian Protestant groups (whether these are to be found inside or outside the formal membership of these churches), have tended to be pro-EU, something which is perhaps unsurprising in an era of continuing ecumenical efforts to transcend confessional divisions (Philpott and Shah 2006: 63). Thus, for example, Sundback concludes:

> The Nordic churches did not authoritatively, publicly or unanimously declare themselves as being for or against the EU in 1994, but many influential theologians recommended the people to vote 'yes' in various forums. Several Swedish bishops and the Finnish archbishop did so. In Sweden, Finland, Denmark and Norway spokesmen for Lutheran churches stated that Christianity, as a universal religion, had an important ethical mission in the EU and that it was necessary to depart from national forms of theology.
>
> (Sundback 2003: 196)

Similarly, as Rusama notes: 'The Finnish Lutheran Church had no official policy about EU membership. Yet it was clear that the church leadership was strongly in favour of membership' (Rusama 1994: 86). But as both Rusama and Sundback also report, despite the fact that the higher circles of the Nordic Lutheran churches could be identified as lending at least covert support for EU membership, other anti-EU religious sentiments were also to be heard, voiced by some from less elevated positions. As Sundback points out:

> Fundamentalist Christians, who often shared anti-Catholic fears, stood in sharp opposition to the church leaders. They based their statements on special interpretations of the Bible, but were almost totally without political influence in the Nordic countries. Their opinions did not reach out to the majority in the same way as, for example, the statements of a bishop may.
>
> (Sundack 2003: 196)[8]

Rusama mentions a Finnish case:

> Before the Finnish referendum on 16 October [1994] an earnest Finnish country pastor publicly preached of the dangers of Catholicism. He claimed that the Pope's role would become all too great and finally even the reading of the Bible would no longer be possible as it will be the only Church, that is the Roman Catholic Church, that has the whole truth, meaning the sole right to teach about Christianity and interpret the Bible.
>
> (Rusama 1994: 87)

In Norway and Sweden similar things were being said in the religious periphery, away from the establishment centres, among groups described variously in terms of Protestant fundamentalism or sectarianism or, more broadly, evangelicalism: 'Within Nordic Protestantism, EU negativism increased the further one went from the centre of the national churches. Free churches and evangelicals were negative towards the EU in all Nordic countries' (Sundback 2003: 198; see also Bjørklund 1982; Mathieu 1999; Hagevi 2002).

If attention shifts to the Eurosceptic Protestant political parties outside the overwhelmingly Lutheran Nordic area, the picture of contrasting stances on European integration among Protestant populations is clear. These contrasts are perhaps starkest in the case of the Netherlands, where the small Calvinist parties have long adopted stances radically at odds with those of the former mainstream Protestant parties, ARP and CHU (since 1977 incorporated along with the Catholic former KVP members in the cross-confessional Christian Democratic Appeal, CDA). According to Freston, some of Europe's micro-parties, such as the German PBC (see Table 6.1) which declares – along with its Christian Zionism – that a unitary European government is 'incompatible with biblical standards', or the Swiss EDU with its opposition to EU entry (and UN membership), also ground their Euroscepticism in religious arguments – in particular in those that relate to apocalyptic ideas about the current era being an end-time when the return of Christ can be expected at any time. It is in Northern Ireland, however, that religion-rooted Euroscepticism has had its most ample (and amplified) exposure through the medium of the Democratic Unionist Party (DUP) under its leader until 2007, Ian Paisley. The founder in the 1950s of a separatist Free Presbyterian Church, which in 1979 still had fewer than 10,000 adherents (at a time when he was able to attract over 170,000 votes), Paisley was able to dominate Northern Ireland's DUP for almost three decades and use his election to the Northern Ireland Assembly, the Westminster House of Commons, and the

European Parliament to broadcast the most vigorous and intransigent strain of religious Euroscepticism to be heard in all of Western Europe (Bruce 1986). Nor can his views be dismissed as mere idiosyncratic fulminations driven by a larger-than-life personality who seems to belong to another age; they represent instead a very distinct and long-standing tradition of radical sectarian belief which can be traced back at least to Scotland's Covenanters of the seventeenth century, the Anabaptists of the Reformation period or, if Norman Cohn is to be believed, right back through virtually two millennia of apocalyptic hopes and expectations. (Cohn 1957) However outlandish they may seem to most Europeans, they represent beliefs which are shared in one form or another by large numbers of adventist sects (such as Jehovah's Witnesses, adventists of many varieties, Mormons and others) and – perhaps more significantly – by increasing numbers of evangelicals, 'born-again' Christians, Pentecostalists and other conservative Protestant tendencies who currently represent between them the most success-fully resurgent forms of religion in the Western world, not least in the USA where sectarian Protestant traditions continue to thrive (Freston 2004).

Paisley's Euroscepticism is no mere local prejudice which might be expected to wane as UK membership of the EU becomes increasingly accepted. It might wane but it is not merely local: it connects instead with a long tradition of 'premillennial dispensationalism', a stance according to which the growth of the EU is seen as presaging the terrible end-time which will usher in the long-awaited return of Christ (Bruce 1986: 227–8). In 1979, the year he was elected to the European Parliament, Paisley delivered four sermons on the biblical sig-nificance of the then Common Market in the light of the prophecies of Daniel and the book of Revelation. For him it was clear that the woman referred to in Revelation on whose forehead was written 'Mystery, Babylon the Great, the Mother of Harlots and Abominations of the Earth' and who was seen by the prophet ' "riding upon the beast, who has spread herself and her influence and her control and the domination over the beast" was the Catholic Church … And the EEC was the beast which she rode and controlled' (Molony and Pollak 1986: 405).[9] These ideas and identifications are widely shared on the sectarian Protes-tant fringe, also in parts of the evangelical underbelly of the mainstream Protes-tant churches in the Anglophone countries – and they are occasionally to be encountered in Scandinavia, as Rusama, Mathieu and Sundback indicate, and the historically Protestant parts of continental Europe (Rusama 1994; Mathieu 1999; Sundback 2003).[10] Their potential political resonance is greatly reduced by the tendency of many of the sectarian groups with these ideas to forswear political involvement of any kind – just as they also refuse to do military service, to use the courts to gain redress for wrongs committed against them, and in other ways to involve themselves with state institutions. For many of them with continually rehearsed memories of religious persecution it is all forms of state power – and not just the EU – which is viewed as demonic. Freston's (2004) survey indicates in addition, however, that these ideas are also shared by marginal groups in several parts of Protestant Europe who are politically active if, at the present time, on the whole generally ineffective.

If the contrast between the Europhile attitudes found in the leadership of the mainstream denominations and the extreme sectarian versions of Euroscepticism undermines the hypothesis that Protestantism as such generates anti-EU sentiments, the observation that similarly hostile sentiments are to be found also among sections of Catholic, Orthodox and Islamic opinion weakens it further. To illustrate the point it is only necessary to consult the contents of the recent Byrnes and Katzenstein (2006) edited volume. There, Casanova identifies a category of 'Catholic europhobes' in Poland 'who are against European integration because today's Europe has lost its Christian identity and therefore its secularist, materialist, hedonist values represent a threat to Poland's Catholic identity and values' (Casanova 2006: 69). Ramet writes of 'Orthodoxy's war with the EU' which has been directed against the enshrining of liberalism within the EU's projected Constitution – with liberalism understood as

> an amalgam of select features associated with the liberal project (tolerance of homosexuality, neutrality of the state in matters of religion), pathological symptoms of social decay (pornography, drug abuse), and an assortment of groups of whom [Orthodoxy] disapproves (Jehovah's Witnesses, prostitutes, and advocates of globalization).
>
> (Ramet 2006: 166)

And in the same volume Tibi argues that the Islamists among Europe's burgeoning Muslim diaspora population support a version of Islamisation, which regards Europe's states gathered together within the EU as irredeemably corrupt, and aims at their eventual incorporation into *Dar-al-Islam* (the House of Islam) an ambition which, he argues, 'runs totally counter to Europeanization' (Tibi 2006: 208). On the basis of these observations alone it is clear that Eurosceptic sentiments of the most vigorous sort are to be found across all the principal confessional families represented in Europe: Protestant, Catholic, Orthodox and Islamic.

Conclusion

It is tempting to relate the associated patterns of division over attitudes to Europe, which are internal to the different confessions, to the distinction between fundamentalist and liberal forms or sub-traditions within each. But this might be more appropriate for some contexts than for others. The concept of fundamentalism has been promiscuously used in political discourse and journalism in ways which have contaminated its usefulness. The aetiology of the term, deriving as it does from a very particular coinage in the USA just prior to the First World War, is complex and controversial (Marty and Appleby 1993). While it is probably appropriate and correctly descriptive when applied to Ian Paisley, who wears the term as a badge of honour and not shame, it is arguably quite inapposite when applied to, say, the circles from which the Norwegian Christian People's Party emerged (MacIver 1987: 359; Madeley, 1994). Its use in the Islamic context is also controversial since it can be cogently argued that while there are many different shades and varieties of Islam (such as Salafist, Sufi, Wahhabi, Liberal, even Euro-), all are 'fundamentalist' in the sense of maintaining the inerrancy of the Qu'ran and the unique sacred standing of the Prophet Mohammad (Zubaida 1993).

A more useful set of terms for identifying the contrasting tendencies found across all the confessions can be found in the work of Woodhead and Heelas (Woodhead and Heelas 2000). Avoiding the term 'fundamentalism' because of the confusions associated with it, they distinguish instead between three principal varieties or styles of religion in modern times, each of which they claim can be found across all traditions: 'religions of difference', 'religions of humanity' and 'spiritualities of life'. The three are presented as located at different points 'on a spectrum of understandings of the relationship between the divine, the human, and the natural order' (Woodhead and Heelas 2000: 2). Two of these which seem best to fit the opposed tendencies identified above (associated in Europe with Eurosceptic and Europhile opinions) are respectively 'religions of difference', which distinguish sharply between God and the human and natural sphere, and 'religions of humanity' which attempt to hold the divine, the human and the natural in balance.[11] In adopting these terms, the suggestion would be that religious Euroscepticism should be seen as an outgrowth of the first variety (or style), a characteristic expression of it in the field of understanding 'the world' and the believer's place in it. For Woodhead and Heelas, religions of difference attribute authority first and foremost not to human beings or to nature, but to the transcendent; they locate the source of all goodness and truth in the transcendent, maintaining that humans are saved by a God outside rather than a God within; they manifest a duality which lays emphasis on the sinfulness, weakness, incompleteness, imperfection or corruption of the human race and the world; they believe in the reality of sin and typically hold that redemption can come only through divine intervention; and they believe that we are living in an era which has fallen away from some past golden age (Woodhead and Heelas 2000: 27). While few if any of the cases of religion-based Euroscepticism which have been referred to above could be said to meet all the criteria implied by this characterisation, each can be claimed to share at least some.

Religious–political actors have over the six decades since the end of the Second World War adopted significant roles in the political struggles around the European integration project. On the one hand they have, in the persons of the so-called founding fathers, been the launchers of the project and the major Christian Democratic parties of which they were leading figures have subsequently maintained their support, despite recent disappointments over Pope John Paul II's campaign to press forward a re-evangelisation of Europe, the abortive constitutional treaty and the patent failure of Jacques Delors' ambition somehow to instantiate a 'Soul for Europe'.[12] On the other hand, religious actors of a very different formation have by contrast played the roles of inveterate critics and foes of the project. They have also, either directly or in some cases through their activity in smaller, especially Protestant, religious parties, sustained this adversarial position, as have vigorously oppositional minorities within Roman

Catholicism, Eastern Orthodoxy and European Islam. In both cases the religious aspect of the contrary pro- and anti-EU tendencies has been close to the surface and the conflict between them has had more than a suggestion of the *odium theologicum* which has traditionally accompanied religious–political conflict, despite the efforts of ecumenists and others who campaign to transcend the differences. As suggested above, one reason for the durability of the tensions arising from these conflicting orientations towards the EU might be that the two exemplify different and largely incompatible varieties or styles of religion, whose mutual antagonism is probably exacerbated by the fact that they typically occur within the ambit of each of the main confessional families – Protestant, Catholic, Orthodox and Islamic. The survival of these antagonisms between as well as within the confessions, albeit mostly at the margins of Europe's political systems, has arguably stimulated secular liberals again to contest the legitimacy of importing religious views and arguments into political discourse with the effect that, far from recent decades seeing a resurgence of religious influences in politics, there has been a determined resistance which threatens to neutralise or in some other way marginalise such influences in the interest of civil peace.

Notes

1 It was rare, however, for quotations to be made of some of Maritain's more extreme claims made in that book, for example:

> In the eyes of a sound political philosophy there is no sovereignty, that is, no natural and inalienable right to transcend or separate supreme power in political society. Neither the Prince, nor the King, nor the Emperor was really sovereign, though they bore the sword and the attributes of sovereignty. Nor is the State sovereign; nor are even the people sovereign. God alone is sovereign.
>
> (Gonzalez 2005: 9)

Man and the State was published first in English in 1951 and only published in French translation in 1953.

2 Irving (1979: 249). The new party federation's statutes committed it to achieve this aim by championing the creation of a Federal Union of Europe.

3

> [A]llegedly distinct features of CD doctrine, such as belief in an integrated Europe, are much poorer guides to the specificity of CD politics, not least because they are nowadays so widely shared by other families, especially, liberals and social democrats.
>
> (Hanley 1994b: 4)

See Featherstone (1989).

4 Bone commented in 1962 that 'neither in terms of politics nor of electoral support has there been any noticeable difference between the pre- and post-war period, and the party has continued as the political spokesman of the Catholic "camp" in the Netherlands' (quoted in Irving 1979: 201). Cross-confessionalism was only finally achieved in 1977 when the three main religious parties combined to form the Christian Democratic Appeal. Irving notes of the French MRP that it 'was certainly an essentially Catholic party in spite of its attempts to embrace non-Catholics' (ibid.: 218). See Buchanan and Conway (1996) for similar points about most of the continental Christian Democratic parties.

5 Of the six countries that had above-average EU disapproval ratings in 1995, four (Sweden, the UK, Denmark and Finland) were predominantly Protestant (Taggart 1998: 375).

6 This simple calculation ignores the one religious/Christian Democratic group which figures as a faction rather than a full party: the anti-EU faction of the Portuguese Social Democrats. The Swedish Christian Democratic Party is not listed as Eurosceptic, unlike its three other Nordic counterparts. It is true that the party was formally committed to supporting EU membership, but it was internally divided and a majority of its supporters actually voted against membership in the referendum. Had this party been accounted Eurosceptic the proportion would have been even higher The consignment of the Nordic Christian parties to the Christian Democratic party family is controversial to some – see Kersbergen 1995: 254–5. For the 'religious' credentials of the DUP see below.

7 It should be noted also that all seven of the eight are also themselves overwhelmingly Protestant and do not represent non-Protestant minorities.

8 The quotation continued:

> A European Protestant synod had been organized by Evangelical Christians resisting a development towards what they saw as a growing Catholic dominance. It was a direct reaction to the vision about a re-christianized Europe which the Pope had published in 1989.

Given the relatively narrow margins between the 'yes' and 'no' camps in the Norwegian and Swedish referendums and the connections between sectarian Protestant traditions and the Christian parties in each country, Sundback's conclusion about 'their total lack of political influence' is, however, open to question.

9 More or less directly related expositions of ideas like these can be accessed via the internet for example via www.euro-sceptic.org/index.asp?RNG=2&PRT=1 Here is a representative sample: 'The Conspiracy behind the European Union: What Every Christian Should Know' at eips_info@yahoo.co.uk or 'Why the EU Needs to Be Destroyed, and Soon' by Baron Bodissey at http://gatesofvienna.blogspot.com/2006/06/why-eu-needs-to-be-destroyed-and-soon.html. Googling the phrase 'The Pope has been appointed the spiritual head of this New Holy Roman Empire by the head of the European Council' gives 116 links. A representative gobbet is:

> The Pope has been appointed the *spiritual head* of this New Holy Roman Empire by the head of the European Council, Jacques Delors. And since the Holy Roman Empire was '*Church over State*' this places him at the head of the coming world government.

10 According to Rifkin,

> 40 percent of the American people believe that the world will end with an Armageddon battle between Jesus and the Antichrist. Forty-seven percent of those who believe in Armageddon also believe that the Antichrist is on Earth now, and 45 percent believe that Jesus will return in their lifetime.
>
> (Rifkin 2004: 20)

His reason for reporting this is to draw the contrast between American religiosity and European secularity – but these beliefs continue to be held in Europe also, albeit very much more on the margin.

11 They relate these differences to the sociological distinction developed by Troeltsch between 'church' and 'sect' type communities – the former inclusive and willing to accommodate itself to worldly institutions, the latter 'exclusivistic, demanding voluntary commitment from its members and adopting a critical stance towards those

people and institutions who remain outside' (Woodhead and Heelas 2000: 29). The fact that this distinction derives entirely from Christian points of reference makes it unsuitable for general use, however.
12 'If in the next ten years we haven't managed to give a Soul to Europe, to give it spirituality and meaning the game will be up,' President Delors, 'Speech to the churches', Brussels, 4 February 1992.

Bibliography

Banchoff, T. and Smith, M. P. (eds) (1999) *Legitimacy and the European Union: The Contested Polity*, London: Routledge.

Berger, P. (ed.) (1999) *The Desecularization of the World: Resurgent Religion and World Politics*, Grand Rapids: Eerdmans/Ethics and Public Policy Center.

Bjørklund, T. (1982) *Mot Strømmen: Kampen mot EF 1961–1972*, Oslo: Universitetsforlaget.

Bruce, S. (1986) *God Save Ulster! The Religion and Politics of Paisleyism*, Oxford: Oxford University Press.

Bruce, S. (1996) *Religion in the Modern World: From Cathedrals to Cults*, Oxford: Oxford University Press.

Buchanan, T. and Conway, M. (eds) (1996) *Political Catholicism in Europe 1919–1965*, Oxford: Clarendon Press.

Byrnes, T. A. and Katzenstein, P. (eds) (2006) *Religion in an Expanding Europe*, Cambridge: Cambridge University Press.

Casanova, J. (1994) *Public Religions in the Modern World*, Chicago: University of Chicago Press.

Casanova, J. (2006) 'Religion, European Secular Identities, and European Integration', in T. A. Byrnes and P. Katzenstein (eds), *Religion in an Expanding Europe*, Cambridge: Cambridge University Press. pp. 65–92.

Chenaux, P. (1990) *Une Europe Vaticane? Entre le Plan Marshall et les Traites de Rome*, Brussels: Éditions Ciaco.

Cohn, N. (1957) *The Pursuit of the Millennium*, Oxford: Oxford University Press.

Colley, L. (1992) *Britons: Forging the Nation 1707–1837*, Yale: Yale University Press.

Davie, G. (1994) 'The Religious Factor in the Emergence of Europe as a Global Region', *Social Compass*, 41, pp. 95–112.

Davie, G. (2000) *Religion in Modern Europe: A Memory Mutates*, Oxford: Oxford University Press.

Davie, G. (2002) *Europe: The Exceptional Case. Parameters of Faith in the Modern World*, London: Dartman, Longman and Todd.

Featherstone, K. (1989) *Socialist Parties and European Integration: A Comparative History*, Manchester: Manchester University Press.

Fox, J. (2008) *Religion and the State: A World Survey*, Cambridge: Cambridge University Press.

Freston, P. (2004) *Protestant Political Parties: A Global Survey*, Aldershot: Ashgate.

Gehler, M and Kaiser, W. (eds) (2004) *Christian Democracy in Europe since 1945. Volume 2*, London: Routledge.

George, S. (1990) *An Awkward Partner: Britain in the European Community*, Oxford: Oxford University Press.

Gonzalez, N. (2003) 'Back to the Future? Locating Christian Democratic Normative Theories of Federal Constitution – Implications for the European Convention', paper for

ECPR Joint Sessions Workshop 'Legitimate Federation? Normative Political Theory and Institutional Design in the EU', Edinburgh.

Gonzalez, N. (2005) 'Ideas, Preference Formation, and Federalism in European Integration: The Case for Postwar Christian Democracy', paper for Visiting Scholars Forum, Center for European Studies, New York University, January.

Greeley, A. (2003) *Religion in Europe at the End of the Second Millennium*, New Brunswick, NJ: Transaction Publishers.

Greschat, M. and Loth, W. (eds) (1994) *Die Christen und die Enstehung der Europäischen Gemeinschaft*, Stuttgart: Kohlhammer.

Gstoehl, S. (2002) *Reluctant Europeans: Norway, Sweden, and Switzerland in the Process of Integration*, London: Lynne Rienner Publishers.

Haas, E. (1958) *The Uniting of Europe*, Stanford: Stanford University Press.

Hagevi, M. (2002) 'Religiosity and Swedish Opinion on the European Union' *Journal for the Scientific Study of Religion*, 41, 4, pp. 759–69.

Hanley, D. (ed.) (1994a) *Christian Democracy in Europe: A Comparative Perspective*, London, Pinter.

Hanley, D. (1994b) 'Introduction: Christian Democracy as a political phenomenon' in D. Hanley (ed.) *Christian Democracy in Europe: A Comparative Perspective*, London, Pinter, pp. 1–11.

Irving, R. E. M. (1979) *The Christian Democratic Parties of Western Europe*, London: Royal Institute for International Affairs.

Jensen, A. T., Pesonen, P. and Gilljam, M. (eds) (1998) *To Join or Not to Join: Three Nordic Referendums on Membership in the European Union*, Oslo: Scandinavian University Press.

Kaiser, W. (2007) *Christian Democracy and the Origins of the European Union*, Cambridge: Cambridge University Press.

Kepel, G. (1994) *The Revenge of God: The Resurgence of Islam, Christianity and Judaism in the Modern World*, Cambridge: Polity Press.

Kersbergen, K. van (1995) *Social Capitalism. A Study of Christian Democracy and the Welfare State*, London: Routledge.

Leustean, L. N. and Madeley, J. T. S. (eds) (forthcoming, 2009) *Religion, Politics and Law in the European Union*, London: Palgrave.

Lücker, A. and Hahn, K. (eds) (1987) *Christliche Demokraten Bauen Europa*, Bonn: Europa Union Verlag.

MacIver, M. (1987) 'Ian Paisley and the Reformed Tradition', *Political Studies*, 35, pp. 359–78.

Madeley, J. T. S. (1994) 'The Antinomies of Lutheran Politics: The Case of Norway's Christian People's Party' in D. Hanley (ed.), *Christian Democracy in Europe: A Comparative Perspective*, London: Pinter, pp. 142–54.

Madeley, J. T. S. (2000) 'Reading the Runes: The Religious Factor in Scandinavian Electoral Politics', in D. Broughton and H.-M. ten Napel (eds), *Religion and Mass Electoral Behaviour in Europe*, London: Routledge/European Consortium for Political Research, pp. 28–43.

Madeley, J. T. S. (2003) 'European Liberal Democracy and the Principle of State Religious Neutrality', in J. T. S. Madeley and Z. Enyedi (eds), *Church and State in Contemporary Europe: The Chimera of Neutrality*, London: Frank Cass, pp. 1–22.

Madeley, J. T. S. and Sitter, N. (2003) 'Differential Eurocepticism among Nordic Christian Parties: Protestantism or Protest?' paper presented at Scandinavian Politics Specialist Group, Political Studies Association Conference, Leicester, United Kingdom. April.

Malcolm, N. (1996) 'Conservative Realism and Christian Democracy', in K. Minogue (ed.), *Conservative Realism: New Essays on Conservatism*, London: Harper, pp. 44–67.

Maritain, J. (1951) *Man and the State.* Chicago: University of Chicago Press.

Marks, G and Wilson, C. (1999) 'The Past in the Present: A Cleavage Theory of Party Response to European Integration', *British Journal of Political Science*, 30, pp. 433–59.

Marty, M. E. and Appleby, R. S. (eds) (1993) *Fundamentalisms and the State. Remaking Polities, Economies and Militance*, Chicago: University of Chicago Press.

Mathieu, C. (1999) *The Moral Life of the Party: Moral Argumentation and the Creation of Meaning in the Europe Policy Debates of the Christian and Left-Socialist Parties in Denmark and Sweden 1990–1996*, Lund: Dissertations in Sociology.

Miljan, T. (1977) *The Reluctant Europeans: The Attitudes of the Nordic Countries Towards European Integration*, Montreal: McGill-Queen's University Press.

Molony, E. and Pollak, A. (1986) *Paisley*, Dublin: Poolbeg.

Nelsen, B. F. (2004) 'The Reluctant Europeans: Protestantism, Nationalism and European Integration', paper presented at the American Political Science Association Annual Meeting, Chicago, 2–5 September.

Nelsen, B. F. (2005) 'Europe as a Christian Club: Religion and the Founding of the European Community, 1950–1975, The Ideological Dimension', paper presented at the American Political Science Association Annual Meeting, Washington, DC, 1–4 September.

Nelsen, B. F. and Guth, J. (2003a) 'Religion and Youth Support for the European Union', *Journal of Common Market Studies*, 41,1, pp. 89–112.

Nelsen, B. F. and Guth, J. (2003b) 'Roman Catholicism and the Founding of Europe: How Catholics Shaped the European Communities', paper presented at the American Political Science Association Annual Meeting, Philadelphia, 28–31 August.

Nelsen, B. F., Guth, J. and Fraser, C. (2001) 'Does Religion Matter? Christianity and Public Support for the European Union', *European Union Politics*, 2, 2, pp. 191–217.

Nexon, D. (2006) 'Religion, European Identity, and Political Contention in Historical Perspective', in T. A. Byrnes and P. Katzenstein (eds), *Religion in an Expanding Europe*, Cambridge: Cambridge University Press, pp. 256–82.

Norris, P. and Inglehart, R. (2004) *Sacred and Religious. Religion and Politics Worldwide*, Cambridge: Cambridge University Press.

Papini, R. (1997) *The Christian Democratic International*, Lanham: Rowman and Littlefield.

Philpott, D. and Shah, S. (2006) 'Faith, Freedom and Federation: The Role of Religious Ideas and Institutions in European Political Convergence', in T. A. Byrnes and P. Katzenstein (eds), *Religion in an Expanding Europe*, Cambridge: Cambridge University Press, pp. 34–64.

Pridham, G. (1976) 'Christian Democracy in Italy and West Germany: A Comparative Analysis', in M. Kolinsky and W. E. Paterson (eds), *Social and Political Movements in Western Europe*, London, Croom Helm, pp. 142–74.

Pulzer, P. (2004) 'Nationalism and Internationalism in European Christian Democracy', in M. Gehler and W. Kaiser (eds), *Christian Democracy in Europe since 1945*, London: Routledge, pp. 10–24.

Ramet, S. (2006) 'The Way We Were – and Should Be Again? European Orthodox Churches and the "Idyllic Past" ' in T. A. Byrnes and P. Katzenstein (eds), *Religion in an Expanding Europe*, Cambridge: Cambridge University Press, pp. 117–47.

Rifkin, J. (2004) *The European Dream: How Europe's Vision of the Future is Quietly Eclipsing the American Dream*, New York: Penguin.

Rusama, J. (1994) 'Europe and the Churches', *Finnish Institute Yearbook*, London: Finnish Institute.

Sundback, S. (1995) 'Religious Integration and the Idea of a European Soul. The Pro-European Orientation of the Scandinavian Lutheran Churches', paper presented at the European Conference of Sociology (ESA), Budapest. 30 August–2 September.

Sundback, S. (2003) 'The Nordic Lutheran Churches and the EU Question in 1994', *Temenos: Studies in Comparative Religion*, 37–8, pp. 191–208.

Taggart, P. (1998) 'A Touchstone of Dissent: Euroscepticism in Contemporary West European Party Systems', *European Journal of Political Research*, 33, pp. 363–88.

Tibi, B. (2006) 'Europeanizing Islam or the Islamization of Europe: Political Democracy vs Cultural Difference', in T. A. Byrnes and P. Katzenstein (eds), *Religion in an Expanding Europe*, Cambridge: Cambridge University Press, pp. 204–24.

Vignaux, E. (2003) *Luthéranisme et Politique en Norvège: le parti chrétien du peuple*, Paris: l'Harmattan.

Vollard, H. (2006) 'Protestantism and Euroscepticism in the Netherlands', *Perspectives on European Politics and Society*, 7, 3, pp. 276–97.

Ward, K. (2000) *Religion and Community*, Oxford: Clarendon Press.

Weigel, G. (2005) *The Cube and the Cathedral: Europe, America and Politics Without God*, New York: Basic Books.

Woodhead, L. and Heelas, P. (2000) *Religion in Modern Times: An Interpretive Anthology*, Oxford: Blackwell.

Zubaida, S. (1993) *Islam, the People and the State*, London: I. B. Tauris.

Part III
Democracy

7 Political Islam and Islamic capital
The case of Turkey

Işık Özel

Introduction

In July 2008, the Constitutional Court of Turkey voted to come to a decision on banning the Justice and Development Party (AKP), Turkey's ruling party since 2002, as the 'party was seen a hub of anti-secular activities by the Constitutional Court'.[1] Six of the eleven judges of the Court voted to close the party, one fewer than would be required by the Turkish Constitution. Thus, rather than banning, the final verdict of the Constitutional Court was a warning to the AKP. It entailed a financial penalty: cutting state financial aid to the party. The Court's final verdict ended a long period of uncertainty which was based on the possibility that the ruling party – democratically elected by an overwhelming 46 per cent of the votes cast nationwide in 2007 – would be banned and its popular leaders prevented from standing for office.

This contentious case had begun with the so-called 'judicial coup' of spring 2008. The chief prosecutor of Turkey had prepared an indictment of the ruling AKP for violating the principle of secularism of the Turkish Constitution by allegedly undertaking a number of anti-secular activities. In its defence, the AKP, a party with Islamist roots, denied the charges of violating the Constitution's secular principles. For some, this signified the 'victory of democracy' over strict secularism championed by both the military and the judiciary of the Turkish state establishment; both consider the AKP government a serious threat to secularism in Turkey.[2] According to the secularist state establishment, in line with its close allies such as the Republican People's Party (CHP), the AKP's main opposition in parliament, the AKP is an agent of political Islam which cannot, in their view, coexist with secularism. These actors anticipate that although the ruling party does not openly associate itself with political Islam, it nevertheless allegedly aims to end or redefine secularism in the country, eventually Islamising Turkish society, politics and institutions. In sum, Turkish society is currently divided over various contentious political issues, including: the link between politics and secularism, the appeal of political Islam and its relationship with democracy. This situation is reminiscent of that which Ben-Porat describes in his chapter in this collection in relation to Israel: a situation of political polarisation in the society and state, which Kurtz (1995) refers to as a 'culture war'.

Global resurgence of religion is a widely discussed phenomenon (Thomas 2005; Haynes 2006). Keddie (2003) pinpoints a prevalent trend, whereby the rise of anti-secular ideologies and parties representing them is coupled with the process of secularisation, despite the common assumption that secularisation will *inevitably* diminish the demand for such politics. Emerging in different places as a reaction to secularisation, religious movements clash with secularising trends (Haynes 2006), giving rise to a process of 'de-privatization of religion' by relocating religion (back) into the political arena (Casanova 1994). Norris and Inglehart (2004) suggest that these common phenomena occur within the context of still proceeding secularisation.

The clash between the Islamist challenge to strict secularism and the secular state establishment in Turkey signifies a contested attempt to 'de-privatize' religion (Casanova 1994). Pointing out an extensive political resurgence of Islam, Haynes (1993: 64) suggests that Islam was the chief vehicle of political opposition in North Africa and the Middle East by the 1980s. In Turkey, such resurgence appeared in the 1990s, bringing an Islamist party to power in the early 2000s. The timing of this resurgence presents interesting puzzles for the Turkish case, not least because Turkey is a candidate for accession to the European Union (EU) (see Grigoriadis's chapter in this volume.) Furthermore, the accession negotiations are conducted by the AKP government, known to have Islamist roots, causing considerable concern within the Turkish state establishment which identifies itself with the West. How can we explain the rise of political Islam in Turkey in a context where Turkey has been in the process of trying to become part of the EU?

The rise of political Islam in Turkey is widely discussed, yet little has been written on the links between political and economic spheres: for example, how they bolster one another through religious networks, or how the ideas are spread through religious orders. I suggest that ideas spread by certain religious networks in Turkey play a central role in both the resurgence of what I call 'Islamic capital' and political Islam. In the political sphere, political claims promoted by such religious networks have helped bring Islamist parties to power, challenging the secular state establishment in an attempt to 'de-privatize' religion. In the economic sphere, such ideas have converged with discourses and practices of neoliberalism, facilitating the rise of what is known as 'Islamist business' within the context of intertwined processes of globalisation and liberalisation. In the realm of ideas, re-invention of *homo Islamicus* within the context of Islamic economics epitomises an ideational legitimacy in line with the dominant discourses of neoliberalism. In the context of Turkey, an ideational transformation, led and spread by certain religious orders, has played a key role in the expansion of Islamic capital. Focusing on Islamist business networks and the ideational changes such as the so-called 'quiet Islamic Reformation' or 'Islamic Calvinism' taking place in Turkey, this chapter sheds light on the relations between Islamic capital and a recent upsurge of political Islam. It explores the expansion of Islamic capital that began in the 1980s, and examines the links between such expansion and the unprecedented rise of political Islam.[3] In short, the chapter aims to understand intertwined processes: (1) the rise of Islamist business networks, which facilitate circulation of new ideas; and (2) connections between such networks and political Islam. It suggests, however, that these networks are far from monolithic and there is, indeed, a considerable competition between them, displayed through competing business organisations affiliated with certain religious networks.

I suggest that networks based on Islamic religious orders play a key role in the ideational transformation within the domain of religion in Turkey. Certain Islamic orders and communities facilitate the expansion of business networks along with the upsurge of political Islam through their promotion of distinct economic and political objectives. Such objectives include an attempt to challenge the status quo in the Turkish economy and politics, characterised by the hegemony of strictly secular big business in the former and the Kemalist state establishment with its strict secularism in the latter. Embracing neoliberal discourses, congruent with the teachings of certain Islamic orders, and benefiting from the space created by the neoliberal transition in Turkey, these business networks have recently expanded. In this chapter, I will particularly focus on two orders or communities: the Iskenderpaşa Community, affiliated with the Naqshibandi order, and the Gülen Movement.

Political Islam in Turkey

Political Islam in Turkey has evolved in reaction to strict secularism, a constitutional principle of the Turkish Republic, and has gone through considerable changes since the 1990s. For the first time in Turkish history, the country is now governed by a party with explicitly Islamist roots. The unprecedented victory of the AKP, the ruling party, in the 2002 and 2007 elections, granting it an overwhelming majority in parliament, opened an area of contestation regarding secularism in Turkey. Now, the country faces polarisation between the secularist state establishment and its allies in society, and the ruling party and its constituency. However, seeking to disengage from its Islamist pedigree, AKP now avoids any explicit association with political Islam and prefers the title of 'conservative democratic' (Öniş 2006). Nevertheless, secularists in Turkey commonly accuse the AKP of being engaged in anti-secular activities, with a secret agenda to take over state institutions in order to end the secular state and establish an Islamist one.[4]

Secularism was instituted as one of the foundational pillars of the Turkish Republic and became a constitutional principle. Although the strict secularism of the Turkish state establishment has always been subject to a certain degree of contestation, challenges increased after the initiation of a multi-party regime in 1950, generating various views and demands.[5] Brought about by such demands, origins of the current political parties with Islamist roots (the ruling Justice and Development Party, and the Felicity Party, SP) stretch back to 1970 when the first Islamist party was founded in Turkey. As Mardin (2006: 3) suggests, looking at post-2002 AKP governments, 'there had been precedents to the Islamisation of governments since the 1970s, but the overwhelming superiority of the

AKP Parliament was new'. Tepe (2006: 110) argues that 'Islam has performed a dual and contradictory role since the foundation of the Turkish Republic, as the state elite often relied on Islam as a common identity marker of the peoples who constitute the Turkish nation'. At the same time, Islam was perceived as an important threat by the same elite because of its anticipated capacity to challenge state power (Mardin 2006; Tepe 2006).

Starting from the transition to a multi-party regime in 1950, marked by accession to power of the Democrat Party (DP), centre-right parties have always attracted religiously conservative constituencies by deliberately employing religious symbols and attacking the strict secularism of the Kemalist state establishment. Such reaction to strict secularism signified a challenge to the state elite and its authoritarian modernist project by *peripheral* forces, which are predominantly religious. The identity of the DP was formed, based on such a stance gaining broad support.[6] Unsurprisingly, this stance triggered resistance from the state secularist bureaucracy, while the DP leaders claimed to represent the 'national will'. Thus, from the 1950s onwards, centre-right populist parties sought to address the tension between the so-called Kemalist elite – mainly the bureaucracy and military – and the 'people' by using both religious symbols and the secular vs anti-secular cleavage as a major point of reference, while numbering some supporters of political Islam within their ranks.[7]

Starting from 1970, Islamist parties competed with centre-right parties to attract the religiously conservative constituency's votes. The National Order Party (MNP, 1970–1) and the National Salvation Party (MSP, 1972–81) were the first two such parties.[8] Both parties were founded by Necmettin Erbakan, a prominent leader of political Islam in Turkey since the 1970s, and disciple of the Iskenderpaşa Community, the most prominent community within the Naqshi order in Turkey. The Iskenderpaşa Community has played a particularly important role in the emergence and evolution of political Islam in Turkey, as some of the most important political figures have been followers of this community, particularly its most influential leader, the late Mehmet Zahit Kotku. Prominent among such figures are not only Necmettin Erbakan and Tayyip Erdogan, current prime minister of Turkey, but also the late Turgut Ozal, former prime minister and president of Turkey, and his brother Korkut Ozal, one of the most important figures in the evolution of political Islam in Turkey. However, the roles of both Kotku and the Iskenderpaşa Community were not limited to encouraging the community's followers to make careers in the bureaucracy and politics, but also encouraged them to enter business. This community's penetration into the state institutions began in the 1960s with the Ozal brothers' working at the State Planning Organisation (SPO), a key centre of the economic bureaucracy until the 1980s.[9] For some, this was the beginning of a deliberate effort to 'capture the state' and then 'Islamise it'.[10] The careers of these individuals, most of whom later became politicians, were eagerly promoted by the leader of the Iskenderpaşa Community, Mehmet Zahit Kotku. Within the realm of its worldly activities, acquisition of the latest technological knowledge success in business (usually referred to as 'commerce'), and effective integration within global markets, were all fundamental tenets of the Iskenderpaşa Community. The late President Ozal was fully characteristic of this combination: a pious Muslim, an engineer, the architect of Turkish market reforms and neoliberalism, and a wholehearted supporter of Turkey's integration with globalisation.

As an interesting paradox, both the emphasis on modern science and technology, and the use of democratic political institutions put forward by the Constitution, were the basic tenets of the secular Turkish Republic (Mardin 2006). This shows the extent to which the modernisation project of the secular Republic has been internalised by a religious order/community which not only contested secularism but also challenged the secular state establishment. According to Mardin (2006: 16), 'Kotku had created a new version of the "operational code" of the Naksibendi, synchronised with the political code promoted by the Republic, that of constitutional legitimacy' and 'the positivistic support of the state came as a gift from the secular Turkish Republic', which emphasises the positive view of the state as an institution.

Military interventions and political Islam, a paradoxical link

The military intervention of 1980 and the subsequent military government (1980–3) brought about major consequences for both political Islam and Islamic capital. In the economic realm, it was the military government which de facto launched a thorough liberalisation programme, initiating a transition from a highly interventionist economy to a market-based one.[11] This transition was one of the facilitating factors behind the upsurge of Islamic capital, as it created a space for new entry into the market, which was fundamentally dominated by secularist big business until the 1980s. The striking congruence between the liberal economic principles and those promoted by the major Islamic orders in Turkey, such as the Iskenderpaşa Community of the Naqshi order, facilitated the expansion of Islamic business, as will be touched upon later.

During military rule in the early 1980s, Islam was used as a 'favourable' ideology against communism. Paradoxically, the secular military elite considered religion as a unifying identity thread which could help solve the pervasive fragmentation, polarisation and the resulting conflict in the Turkish society. Thus, the military elite played the religion card to try to diminish societal polarisation, especially in an attempt to curtail the left, a policy which paralleled United States foreign policy in Muslim countries more generally at the same time. The military opted for a synthesis – 'Turkish Islam' – which was an eclectic ideology which had been used by several centre-right political parties from the 1950s. In this context, the authority and funding of the state body, the Directorate of Religious Affairs, was enhanced, and religion classes became compulsory in primary schools. One result was that the contentious Imam Hatip schools, vocational schools which specialise in religious education and more specifically in training state-employed imams, saw major increases in numbers.[12]

An unintended consequence of this military intervention was, however, further fragmentation and polarisation. First, all political parties were banned, then successor parties were established after 1983, leading to greater ideological polarisation. The Motherland Party, which formed the first post-coup government (1983–91), represented an amalgam of several currents from centre-left and right, including Islamists who, later, left to form the Welfare Party (RP), the forerunner of the current AKP.[13] In sum, Islamist politics began to play a central role in the 1980s, bolstered by the military government and, after it, by Motherland Party rule.

By the 1990s, political Islam was transformed into a mass movement, mostly with an urban character, as its constituency was no longer limited to those of the MNP and MSP as it had been in the 1970s. The turning point in terms of indicating its mass character was the 1994 municipal elections when the Welfare Party won in all major cities, acquiring 19 per cent of the votes nationwide. Later, in 1995, the Welfare Party came to power in a coalition government with the True Path Party (DYP), when Erbakan became the prime minister. However, both the coalition government and some of its policies were deemed anti-secular by the secularist establishment. This led to a fierce reaction from the cadres of the secularist state elite, along with leading secularist groups in the society such as the Turkish Industrialists and Businessmen's Association (TUSIAD) and Association of Ataturkist Thought (ADD). The result was a wide-ranging secularist alliance against the government, endorsed by the most prominent business organisations. Following a warning to the government by the key state body, the National Security Council, the RP–DYP coalition collapsed in 1997. This so-called 'post-modern' coup gave rise to the 'February 28 Process', as a result of which the Welfare Party was banned and Prime Minister Erbakan ousted from power.

The February 28 Process also included a significant intervention in the economic arena, since a number of pro-Islamic businesses and financial institutions were subject to inspection. A stringent auditing process was launched, inquiring into the funds of these Islamist conglomerates, along with their ties with Islamist parties. The secularist state establishment declared a fierce war against these conglomerates (so-called 'green capital' – that is, capital owned by ideologically and politically Islamist actors) which had grown at an unprecedented level in the 1990s.[14] Through their ties with the Islamist parties, these businesses started competing with secular big business in various areas, including privatisation bids and state contracts. Such companies include: Kombassan, Yimpas, Kaldera, Kubra and Jetpa. For example, Kombassan Holdings, identified by the military as a 'serious threat' in 1997, won the bid for PETLAS's privatisation, a state-owned enterprise producing tyres for the Turkish army. Alarmed by this growing presence in strategic sectors, the military prepared a 'list of fundamentalist companies' considered as 'threats'. It denounced about 100 'suspicious' Islamist businessmen, for exploiting people's religious beliefs for the benefit of around thirty radical organisations. These companies were subject to extensive auditing by the Capital Markets Board, from where legal procedures were undertaken, and some of them made bankrupt. The military also denounced Islamic banks, accusing them of having funnelled some US$250 million into Islamist activities against the secularist state establishment. Finally, the Erbakan government was accused of having favoured Islamist companies in the privatisation process, a claim initiated by the secularist Turkish Industrialists and Businessmen's Association (TUSIAD) in collaboration with the military.[15]

The constituency of political Islam

The recent emergence of political Islam in Turkey is, in fact, an unintended consequence of the Kemalist project in Turkey. Authoritarian secularism and religion's exclusion from public life helped create a 'moral diaspora' effect, epitomised in the verse of Necip Fazil Kisakurek, the heroic poet of the Islamist circles: 'Stranger in his own home, slave in his own motherland', connoting that Islamists in Turkey were excluded and enslaved by Kemalist secularism. Such a sense of exclusion brought about an underlying motive of solidarity among Islamists.[16] As Casanova (1994) suggests, in Turkey the rise of political Islam was a reaction to the process of privatisation, with Islamist movements (re) appearing in the public sphere.

According to Öniş (1997), the rise of political Islam in Turkey can best be explained by reference to economic factors, especially those linked to the forces of globalisation. Coinciding with a vacuum caused by the absence of a solid alternative based on social democracy and the de facto convergence between left and right politics, he argues that the 'losers' of globalisation and neoliberalisation in Turkey supported political Islam. Öniş (1997: 748) suggests that '[political Islam] emerges as a political movement expressing the grievances of the poor and the disadvantages in both rural and urban areas'. Nevertheless, it was not only the poor who were drawn by the appeal of an alternative, finding refuge in political Islam. Many among the newly emerging middle class, people who had previously been excluded from the secularist state establishment along with secularist business circles, also found political refuge in it (Bugra 1999, 2003; Öniş 1997; Ugur and Alkan 2000). Another common argument explaining the emergence and flourishing of political Islam in Turkey is based on a core vs periphery explanation, i.e. the civil and military elite who champion strict secularism represent the former, while the conservatively religious masses, alienated by strict secularism, correspond to the latter. As a result, political Islam in Turkey stems from peripheral forces ranged against the (secular) political parties, representative of the established secular order (Demir *et al.* 2004; Yavuz 2006, Mardin 1983; Cizre-Sakallioglu 1996).

The crisis-prone economic and political context in Turkey in the 1990s paved the way for many people to seek an alternative in the political sphere. Consecutive stabilisation programmes implemented under the guidance of the IMF and successive economic crises, particularly those which broke out in 1994 and 2001, caused further deterioration of the living conditions of the poor. Political Islam provided a strong appeal for many among the poor, mostly in the urban areas, not only because of the discursive appeal of the 'just society' of the Islamist parties, but also because such parties' provided actual aid – both in kind and in cash.[17] Together, these instruments provided some degree of compensation for the losers of liberalisation, globalisation and parallel stabilisation programmes. In addition to such instruments used by the Welfare Party, the Virtue Party and the current AKP, particularly during the election periods, charity was promoted by the Islamic orders and communities, complementing or even substituting for the state's paltry social welfare instruments.

It would, however, be misleading to suggest that political Islam's constituency has been limited to the poor. Islamist parties, particularly the AKP, have also provided concrete appeal for the upwardly mobile, including educated professionals and urban businessmen (Öniş 2001, 2006; Yavuz 2006). The so-called rising Islamist bourgeoisie and the poor formed a 'coalition of the excluded', people who have largely supporting Islamist parties since the 1990s (Öniş 1997, 2001, 2006). This newly rising bourgeoisie mostly represents pious businessmen, mainly small and medium-sized entrepreneurs linked to the world markets and embracing neoliberalism that is highly congruent with the teaching of the Islamic orders to which many are affiliated. From the 1980s, this group has experienced significant growth, and the fact that such an entrepreneurial development has taken place, particularly among the most religiously conservative provinces in Turkey, has drawn considerable attention. Popularly referred to as 'Anatolian Tigers', a metaphor referring to the pre-existing 'Asian Tigers', these recently flourishing enterprises are mostly small and medium-sized (SMEs), mainly engaged in manufacturing oriented towards export markets (Bugra 1999). This recent phenomenon is noteworthy since such enterprises were never prioritised in Turkey within the context of development strategies that generally favoured Istanbul-based big business, closely allied with the strongly secularist state establishment. The import-substitution development strategy which prevailed for decades before the 1980s prioritised secularist big business by shielding it not only from international competition, but also from domestic competition. Highly politicised processes of rent distribution (such as provision of import permits and quota allocations) brought about by the implementation of this development strategy limited equal access to the market and, as a result, marginalised the SMEs. Islamist business groups were predominantly among this category of the SMEs which were excluded from major benefits. As a consequence of such setting, Islamist business was excluded in both economic and political spheres before the 1980s, a phenomenon which helped shape its identity and claims since then.

A common claim is that the SMEs were encouraged by the networks and institutions of so-called 'green capital' facilitated through Islamic financial institutions (Bulut 1999). Various arguments emphasise the importance of trust based on religious identity in Islamic capital networks, including (1) credit access through specific Islamic financial institutions; and (2) the ideational impact of so-called 'Islamic Calvinism' among the religiously conservative population.[18] Agreeing with Bugra (1999), I argue that Islamic financial institutions have played a minor role in the rise of the 'Tigers' and 'networks of social relations' have been more central in such rise. Islamist business networks and the ideas they helped spread have played a major role, along with the new space created by market liberalisation from the 1980s. These new ideas are strikingly congruent with neoliberal ideology and Islamist networks which have used the available new space after liberalisation to bolster Islamist businesses' fast integration with global markets. In the next section, we explore such links between Islamist networks, ideas and business.

Islamic capital/Islamist business networks

A new entrepreneurial profile emerged in Turkey in the late 1980s, the outcome of two major and interrelated processes: (1) economic liberalisation which started in the 1980s, and (2) expansion of Islamist business networks. Former prime minister and president, the late Turgut Ozal, key architect of liberal market reforms in Turkey in the 1980s, played a major role in both processes. I argue, however, that Ozal's role entailed more than opening the market, overseeing the state's retreat from the economy, and attempting to diminish the hegemony of the Istanbul-based big business. He called the latter 'the dukedom of Istanbul', claiming that 'he would abolish the sultanate of the Istanbul dukedom'.[19] The businesspeople grouped in this alleged 'dukedom' are overwhelmingly constituted by secularists, while Ozal was a disciple of a prominent Islamic order called the Iskenderpaşa Community,[20] an offspring of Naqshibandi.[21] The Iskenderpaşa Community, the most powerful Naqshi community in Turkey, is known for its pro-business stance, as well as its ambitions for political and bureaucratic posts in the state since the 1960s. For many, Ozal himself personified the compatibility between, on the one hand, being a devout Muslim and, on the other, eagerness to have access to worldly materialism and technology. A vivid description of Ozal's own persona epitomises such a role: 'holding a laptop in one hand, and a Koran in the other'.[22] The Ozal period created an opportunity space for Islamist businessmen. Two factors combined: the process of market liberalisation and the tolerance of Ozal and his cadre towards religious networks and accompanying Islamist companies, to provide substantial incentives for this novel entrepreneur class to flourish. Such incentives included access to credits provided by the state-owned banks; export subsidies; and production subsidies provided on a regional basis, particularly in the 'regions prioritised in development', such as central, eastern and southeastern Anatolia. Therefore, the end of the former development strategy, namely import substituting industrialisation, ended the rents associated with it, while market liberalisation created new ones from which Islamist business benefited considerably. Whenever the Ozal government had conflicts with big business represented by the secular Turkish Industrialists and Businessmen's Association (TUSIAD), mostly caused by the difficulties of adjustment to liberalisation and inherent uncertainties posed by the liberalisation process itself, it tried to carve new alliances with Islamist businesses, providing a wide range of incentives for sectors and regions where Islamist businessmen were concentrated, including tax cuts and substantial export subsidies.

Ozal and some others in his close bureaucratic/political circle were already part of various Islamist orders and communities. They not only provided an ideational base for the changing economic structure, but also offered business networks to help spread those ideas and develop trust-based relations between the members, as well as an arena to challenge the hegemony of secularist big business in the Turkish economy. Nevertheless, it would be misleading to treat these networks as monoliths. Mirroring the overall fragmentation of politics and society in Turkey, Islamist networks and business also present a highly disjointed structure. Currently, there are various business organisations which generate their own business networks, most of which are affiliated with religious orders, promoting distinct strategies, supporting distinct political parties, Islamist or centrist, and adhering to distinct versions of political Islam.

Islamic orders and the spread of ideas

Islamic orders and communities affiliated to them have increasingly played a major role in Turkey's economic and political spheres. Politically, it can be argued that some of these orders have been the key actors behind the project of political Islam since the 1950s. Economically, these orders have not only been active in the formation of business networks, but have also been substantially influential in the dissemination of ideas recently characterised as 'Islamic Calvinism'. Two orders have been particularly important in Turkey with respect to the recent growth of political Islam and Islamic capital: the Naqshibandi order, more specifically its Iskenderpaşa branch, and the Gülen Movement affiliated with the Nur order. These orders and communities have their own business networks and banks and they have followers who have occupied key posts in Turkish bureaucracy and politics. The following section will examine these two orders in terms of the ideas and networks they promote.

An ideational change in Islam: 'Islamic Calvinism'

Various academic and journalistic works have pointed out the ideational turn in 'Turkish Islam', coining a new term for this alleged phenomenon: 'Islamic reformation'.[23] This view argues that a 'quiet Muslim reformation movement'[24] has occurred in Turkey (Yavuz 2003), bringing about a hybrid: 'Islamic Calvinism'. The mayor of Kayseri, a town in central Anatolia, one of the so-called 'Anatolian Tigers', stated that to understand his town and its flourishing economy, one would have to read Max Weber![25]

The alleged reformation movement has emerged primarily as a result of ideas disseminated by certain Islamic orders and movements, bringing about worldly asceticism (as interpreted by Max Weber) into Islam akin to Protestantism, firmly encouraging business, and equating success in this regard with serving God. These ideas, promulgated by certain Islamic orders, have helped create a discourse on the congruence between Islamic ideals and pious Muslims' material interests. For example, the old Sufi belief in 'one bite, one coat', symbolising the minimised material aspirations of pious Muslims who would rather focus on their devotion to God through praying, has been converted to and promoted as 'one bite, one coat, one Mazda' by the Iskenderpaşa Community, a branch of Naqshibandi in Istanbul. This addition to the old belief signified a new aspiration for material wealth as well as a desire to acquire technology. Yavuz (2005: 192), states that Kotku, the leader of the Iskenderpaşa Community, claimed that 'Muslims having a good grasp of technology means that they shape their own fate. This is because if Turkish Islamists were incorporated into the middle class, then they would have the power to re-form their state and society from within.'[26] For that purpose, material aspirations and their promotion by religious networks has played a central role.

Identifying *homo Islamicus* as the key unit of analysis in a moral capitalist economy, Islamic orders and their extensive networks have helped establish a legitimate ground for furthering material interests of devout Muslim business-men. Following such an ideational foundation, these networks have served to aggregate the interests of these previously marginalised business groups, attempting to challenge the status quo in both economic and political spheres.

One of the largest Islamist business networks is organised around the Inde-pendent Industrialists' and Businessmen's Association (MUSIAD), a nation-wide business organisation known for its close ties with political Islam, particularly with the National View (*Milli Gorus*) of Erbakan. MUSIAD was established with an objective of breaking TUSIAD's hegemony in the business community as well as in state–business relations, as a response to the claimed exclusion of Islamist businessmen (Bugra 1999).

MUSIAD promotes ideas about the profit-maximising individual, which are not necessarily in contradiction with his or her moral and religious values. *Homo Islamicus*, the unit of analysis of the so-called Islamic economics which emerged in the mid-twentieth century, underlines the difference. S/he is claimed to be dif-ferent from *homo economicus* in his or her morality as s/he is situated somewhere spiritually beyond the limited [rational and secular] existence of *homo economi-cus*.[27] Trying to provide a legitimate ground for their economic ideology and interests, Islamist business networks base their discourses on the life of Moham-med, who was a merchant himself in the 'perfect' working market of Medina. The inference is that maximum trust between actors having appropriate morals and minimal state intervention is characteristic of *homo Islamicus*. According to the discourse favoured by MUSIAD, which sanctifies worldly activities:

> Commerce is part of the prayer. It also means devotion to God. As the Muslim businessman makes profit, he makes it for a spiritual goal, and is rewarded by the God for accomplishing such spiritual goal. *Homo Islamicus* increases his wealth because at the end of the day his wealth would serve to revive the Islamic civilization.[28]

Homo Islamicus, as the prototype promoted for the ideal Muslim businessman, is akin to *homo economicus* with respect to capitalism. He wholeheartedly supports free market capitalism and private initiative, following the example of the Prophet Mohammed.[29] *Homo Islamicus*'s major alleged difference compared to *homo economicus* is his or her intention to live in a so-called 'moral capitalist economy', which seems, however, a fuzzy concept. Such morality, as suggested by Islamist business circles in Turkey, would not stem from social welfare or a fairer income distribution. Indeed, the idea is that 'such instruments shall not be needed by good Muslims, because Islamic ethics will automatically resolve those problems'.[30] Here, what is striking is a discourse bringing together neoliberalism and an Islamic perspective on the economy. Both call for a minimal state, implying disengagement of the state from social welfare functions. According to this discourse:

> God-fearing pious employers would take care of their employees, and in turn, the employees would work with great enthusiasm knowing that they serve God as they do their work, and their work is part of their devotion. Both employer and employee would know that they work with the same objective of serving Islam.[31]

Indeed, such discourse contains most aspects proposed by the prevalent discourses of neoliberalism, indicating how congruent they are. Explaining free markets and minimum state, a former chair of MUSIAD stated that: 'The invisible hand of Adam Smith had characterised the Medina market, and Prophet Mohammad had said that it was Allah who determined the prices.'[32] Bugra (1999) suggests that MUSIAD's economic views come close to the neoliberal model, specifically in the focus on unfettered markets and rejection of unions in capital–labour relations, saying that labour unions are not 'necessary' because moral values of a pious business would resolve all potential conflicts peacefully.

I contend, however, that the 'moral' qualifier, popularly used to qualify the allegedly distinct perspective of these businessmen on the capitalist economy, does not, indeed, have any meaningful depth. However, it does provide a legitimate ground for interest maximising, while not granting their employees proper labour rights. One of the most widely suggested 'moral' duties of pious businessmen is being involved in charity, an instrumental realm through which moral duties would be fulfilled. The implication of such a suggestion, however, is broader, such that charity could easily substitute modern welfare instruments. Therefore, I suggest that most Islamist business networks Islamise neoliberalism by internalising its discourses and practices; and claiming unproblematic aptness between neoliberalism and Islamic principles. These networks justify the minimum state divorced from its social welfare functions, as charity ought to replace the state's social welfare instruments, while a 'morally grounded' interaction between employer and employee replaces modern labour rights in accordance with Islamic principles. Overall, this shows the high level of internalisation of the neoliberal turn and Turkish Islamist business networks' compatibility with global trends.

Some Islamist business networks in Turkey even justify interest or usury, despite the fact that interest and usury-based transactions are forbidden for devout Muslims.[33] Thus, it is deemed 'legitimate' either to use interest to achieve ultimate pious objectives (for example, the revival of Islamic civilisation) or to use the financial instruments of Islamic economics, which are disguised under different names but are in fact not substantially different from interest (Kuran 1993). Nevertheless, Islamic finance institutions are not used widely in the Turkish market, since their clientele is limited to a few individuals or firms (Bugra 1999: 29).

Such an ideational change has been taking place in Turkey for several decades, reflected by the rise of entrepreneurs all over Anatolia, but particularly in towns known for their religious conservatism, including Konya and Kayseri. These enterprises are mostly outward-oriented, exporting to markets worldwide, and technologically up to date, while the entrepreneurs are known by their attachments to communitarian and Islamic values. Some authors explain the success of these recently emerging entrepreneurs (the so-called 'Anatolian Tigers') through the impact of the changing ideational milieu. Yavuz (2003) suggests that as Turkish Muslims are going through a 'Protestantisation process', a particular form of conservatism has become conducive to the newly founded economic success in certain regions in Turkey.[34] Certain Islamic orders and communities have been instrumental in diffusing these ideas, and I suggest that the most important are Gülen and Iskenderpaşa. The business associations which are either affiliated or have shown a certain degree of allegiance to these specific Islamic orders have become the media for transmitting these ideas to devout businessmen. In addition, Islamist networks have expanded further through the activities of business organisations.

The Iskenderpaşa Community

The Iskenderpaşa Community, also known as Gümüşhanevi, is a group affiliated with the Naqshibandi order. It has played a very important role in recent Turkish political and socio-economic history. While contesting the strict secularism of the Turkish state establishment, the Iskenderpaşa Community has opted since the 1960s for penetration of that establishment, rather than isolation. As Mardin (2006: 15) notes, Kotku, leader of the community, 'took a personal interest in economic, political and cultural issues and encouraged his followers to do the same'. Since the 1960s, some of the most influential technocrats and politicians have been affiliated with this community. The Iskenderpaşa Community's stance has been very liberal in the economic realm, hence Turkey's neoliberal transition is in perfect congruence with the economic ideas promoted by this community.[35] Based on resentment towards state intervention in the economy, which, in the Turkish context, brought about a patronage-based alliance between the secular state elites and big business (also strictly secular), this community has encouraged a free market economy and a minimal state. Nevertheless, distribution of patronage has not declined, but has expanded further since the AKP came to power. The clientele of patronage distribution has changed: Islamist business is now the main recipient of such benefits.

The Iskenderpaşa Community has long promoted a mixture of ambitions for worldly success defined by economic well-being. The community has encouraged its followers not only to acquire more wealth but also to attain political and bureaucratic posts. It has also supported use of up-to-date technology and has advocated connecting with the global economy, both deemed to be perfectly compatible with Islamic moral values. Such objectives have been achieved by some followers of the community. For example, Turgut Ozal and his team were the first non-secular upper-level bureaucrats at the State Planning Organisation, the pinnacle of the economic bureaucracy in the 1960s. It was the Ozal brothers' core team at the State Planning Organisation which carried out the neoliberal transition in Turkey in the 1980s. The same group of people took the lead in legalising Islamic banking in Turkey, and showed unprecedented tolerance to the rise of Islamic movements in the 1980s.

In short, this Islamic community has worked towards two objectives: penetrating the bureaucracy, one of the main pillars of the secular republican elite of Turkey; and strengthening economically, while challenging the hegemony of the large conglomerates which used to be the closest allies of the secular republican elite. For the latter goal, the Iskenderpaşa Community gradually diffused the idea of correspondence between material interests and devotion. According to the late Cosan, leader of the Iskenderpaşa Community between 1980 and 1997, 'serving God could be realised in the market whose invisible hand is a reflection of God's will'. He claimed that

> [c]ommerce is a real and continuous activity in an individual's life. Other activities are imagined and virtual; whereas commerce is realistic. In my view, those who do not have commercial experience are not good persons either. The most pragmatic and realistic people are businessmen and merchants. If a businessman is a Muslim, he is the one who has reached the most harmonious state with his religious identity.[36]

The Gülen Movement

Another example of legitimating wealth and promotion of pursuit of material interests comes from the Gülen Movement, a branch of the so-called Nur order, organised around its most prominent thinker, Said-i Nursi. Yavuz (2003) and Demir *et al.* (2004) argue that the Nur order in general, and the Gülen Movement in particular, have been instrumental in legitimising aspirations for furthering material wealth. Fethullah Gülen, the founder and the leader of the movement, once suggested that:

> The ones who will first go the Heaven shall not be intellectuals, imams and hodjas, but merchants, artisans, businessmen who dedicate their property and life to the God (rightful), with the objective of seeking for the right and the truth.

The Gülen Movement originates from Said-i Nursi, helping it to spread through texts called *Risale-i Nur*, the writings of Said-i Nursi.[37] Although the Gülen Movement is only a branch of the Nur order, which split following the death of its leader Said-i Nursi, it is certainly the largest and the most influential one. It is an extensive network spreading through Africa, Central Asia, Europe and the US. It is claimed that the Gülen Movement has no conflict with the principle and practice of liberal democratic regime, since it is pro-democratic and against *shari'a* law. The central objective of the Gülen Movement is 'Islamising Turkish nationalism and Turkifying Islam'. It includes not only a wide network of businessmen, but also intellectuals, professionals and journalists. The Gülen community has founded twenty associations, 128 private schools (all over the world), 218 companies and 500 student residences, and owns companies covering a wide range of sectors, from media to finance, including: TV stations, daily newspapers, journals, news agencies and insurance companies. It also has major foundations, including the Turkish Foundation of Teachers and the Turkish Foundation of Journalists and Writers. The businesses affiliated with the Gülen Movement are not represented by MUSIAD, but they have their own business networks called ISHAD (Association of Solidarity in Business Life), at times in competition with MUSIAD, proving the presence of widespread fragmentation even within the supposedly cohesive Islamist business community.

Islamist business associations

MUSIAD (Independent Industrialists' and Businessmen's Association)

The Independent[38] Industrialists' and Businessmen's Association (MUSIAD) is the largest voluntary business association in Turkey. Founded in 1990 with a goal of breaking big business's hegemony in Turkish economy, MUSIAD mostly (although not exclusively) represents small and medium enterprises, identified with Islamist businessmen. Founded with the intention of constructing a large Islamist business network, MUSIAD has attempted to challenge TUSIAD's[39] dominance in the Turkish business community. The organisation currently has around 2,000 individual members and 7,500 affiliated companies, some of which are large conglomerates often accused of 'sponsoring political Islam'.[40] A membership requirement is being based in Turkey and recommended by two members, with an emphasis on creating and developing a close-knit community.

According to the founding members of MUSIAD, 'it is difficult to form an influential interest group through existing business organisations for the religiously conservative Anatolian business'.[41] MUSIAD was formed with such an objective, accusing the corporatist business representation and resulting chambers and federations of 'supporting the government, distant from the public, and pressured under the hegemony of large conglomerates'.[42] Based on such resentment, MUSIAD aimed to have a voice in these organisations and one of its former members, Murat Yalcintas, is the current (late 2008) chair of the Istanbul Chamber of Commerce.

According to Bugra, the main difficulty of forming such a community with established networks results from dispersed geographic locations and a broad range of economic activities. Founding of MUSIAD provided these businessmen with those networks and a consciousness of a shared class. Ever since its foundation, MUSIAD has worked on strengthening the solidarity and cohesion among its members, along with providing a broad range of services, such as organising committees, classes, conferences about economic and political subjects, help with technology and marketing, providing information about international markets, and promoting exporting (Bugra 1999).

MUSIAD members' pious identity and their common critique of the Turkish state establishment regarding secularism also played a unifying role, providing legitimacy for the claims and ambitious objectives of the association. MUSIAD aims to carry a previously silent and relatively excluded, but recently expanding group of businessmen from Islamist circles (mostly SMEs) into the public space, to aggregate the interests of these groups, and to access state actors (Ugur and Alkan 2000: 143). These recently flourishing groups of business and their association are eager to occupy both the economic and political spheres, attempting to challenge large and secular conglomerates' hegemony through their close ties with the state elites. Although MUSIAD had been critical of such clientelism between the secular conglomerates and state elites, the association and its individual members have replicated such clientelism since first the Welfare Party and then the AKP came to power. Benefiting from state contracts and privatisation bids, MUSIAD's privileged position, particularly during the Welfare Party's coalition government in the 1990, proves an internalised pattern of clientelism and state-sponsored business in Turkey. In an effort to compete with the large conglomerates in privatisation bids, MUSIAD pooled its members' resources, initiating shareholder companies such as Yatirim Holding (Ozcan and Cokgezen 2003).

MUSIAD has extensive access to a broad range of transnationalist Islamist business networks. The World Islamic Business Leaders' Summit, organised by the Organisation of the Islamic Conference, and the World Islamic Economic Forum, founded to establish global and regional forums to foster partnerships among Muslim entrepreneurs and between Muslim and non-Muslim businessmen, are the major transnational networks within which MUSIAD is engaged.[43] These networks aim to expand linkages between Muslim businessmen, attract investment into Muslim countries, promote technology transfer and develop trade and mutual projects between Muslim countries. Besides such active involvement in pre-existing transnational networks, MUSIAD has also tried to create new networks, including the International Business Forum (IBF), which was founded in Pakistan in 1995 with the objective of promoting the principles of Medina market (Islamic morality combined with liberal market principles) and which has been hosted by MUSIAD since 1997. The most recent meeting of the IBF was held in October 2008 in Istanbul and was attended by the representatives of major transnational Islamic networks such as the Organisation of the Islamic Conference, the World Islamic Economic Forum, the Islamic Development Bank and the Islamic Chamber of Commerce and Industry. 'Global business networking' has become the motto of MUSIAD's recent activities and signifies encouraging cooperation and creating linkages for the benefit of the Islamic world.[44]

MUSIAD has supported the goal of 're-Islamisation' of Turkish society in both private and public spheres and endorsed the political parties who pursue similar goals. When MUSIAD officials' public declarations and publications are analysed, a wide range of opinions can be observed with respect to political Islam. Although Islam is usually pointed out in terms of business ethics, one can also find writings of authors like Abdurrahman Dilipak defending the application of *shari'a* in individual and political life. In Dilipak's writings published by MUSIAD, Western influence in Turkey together with the military's hegemony and strict secularism are severely criticised, depicted as corrupt and immoral. However, such a reaction against the West does not necessarily close MUSIAD to Western capitalism or trade with Western countries. In fact, it is possible to argue that such a critical stance in MUSIAD's overall perspective is more rhetorical than practical. There is a clear admiration of East Asian-style capitalism in MUSIAD's perspective, as it is perceived as having both moral and religious values, as well as attachment to family and community.

MUSIAD's shift towards a moderate line

MUSIAD's stance has changed considerably in terms of its allegiances and economic ideas. Following the military intervention against the Erbakan government, the so-called February 28 Process, MUSIAD was pinpointed as an organisation representing the 'suspicious' companies and businessmen and as having gained considerable leverage through its allegiance with the Welfare Party.[45] Erol Yarar, the president of MUSIAD, was found guilty of suspicious activities but released later, and he was compelled to resign from MUSIAD's presidency. Following the February 28 Process, a survival strategy prevailed in the Islamist business circles. This included, for some, distancing from Erbakan and political Islam in the pro-*shari'a* line, and getting closer to a more centrist position, represented by Recep Tayyip Erdoğan (current prime minister) and Abdullah Gül (current president). MUSIAD followed Erdogan's moderate line, while loyal followers of Erbakan and a more conservative line left MUSIAD and founded the 700-member Anatolian Lions Businessmen's Association (ASKON), aligning with Erbakan's Felicity Party.[46]

Having become more 'moderate', the AKP line has changed drastically regarding Islamic capital. At a meeting of the Islamic Economic Forum in 2003, Tayyip Erdogan answered questions on an 'Islamic common market' by commenting: 'The economy has no religion. We will not establish our economic relations based on ethical, religious, and geographic concerns.'[47] MUSIAD's discourse mostly paralleled the AKP's, becoming more moderate. Omer Vardan, adviser to President Omer Bolat, claims that 'MUSIAD has nothing to do with Islamist economics'.[48] Initially, MUSIAD was against Turkey's bid to join the European Union and the Customs Union agreement, an essential step on that path. MUSIAD's perspective was parallel to that of the Welfare Party in the early 1990s. In the early to mid-1990s, MUSIAD promoted a project of a potential common market between the Muslim countries instead of Turkey's inclusion in the Customs Union (Öniş and Turem 2002). Erbakan's anti-Customs Union and pro-'East' or Muslim world perspective was wholeheartedly supported by MUSIAD. The Erbakan–MUSIAD alliance was further solidified when Erbakan treated MUSIAD as the representative of Turkish community in some of his official trips to foreign countries (Ugur and Alkan 2000). TUSIAD, a historical ally of the military, lobbied against MUSIAD and Islamist businesses, under the guise of a secularist point of view, while their economic interests were threatened by the newly emerging Islamist bourgeoisie.

While in government, Erbakan's Welfare Party promoted some of MUSIAD's projects such as the Silk Road Union, the Cotton Union (which would include Pakistan, Iran and the Central Asian Turkic Republics) and a Common Market of the Muslim world. Erbakan also developed an idea of D8, a potential grouping of developing countries in the region. In several trips, Erol Yarar, the MUSIAD chair, was appointed by Erbakan as the head of the Turkish business group. MUSIAD's vision emphasised 'Eastern' capitalism as an alternative to the Western model, which, in the Turkish case, would be solidified by potential accession to the European Union. According to the shared perspective between MUSIAD and the Refah Party, the Western model had been tried in Turkey since the mid-1800s, without much success, whereas the East Asian model had yielded very successive results in several regional countries.[49]

In terms of political Islam, MUSIAD's stance evolved from a pro-regime change standpoint to a more moderate one, paralleling the change of discourse from the Welfare Party to the AKP in the aftermath of the military intervention in 1997. MUSIAD's perspective also reflected that of the AKP with respect to prospective EU membership. The former opponent of such membership became a supporter of Turkey's cooperation with the 'West' in general, and Turkey's accession to the EU in particular. Erol Yarar, the former president of MUSIAD, asserts that the concerning change stemmed from the society and its demands within the context of democratisation and EU accession process.[50]

Economically, MUSIAD's focus is on a 'moral capitalist economy' constituted by actors called *homo Islamicus*. Discursively, however, the model promoted by MUSIAD has vacillated between a model *à la* Asian tigers (with a specific reference to traditionalism, social conservatism, community and family values as well as a certain level of state protectionism) and neoliberalism *par excellence* (minimum state, private sector dominance, no unions) (Yarar 1997). According to the association, the rules established by the prophet Mohammed in the Medina market are the fundamental guiding principles for MUSIAD's members, and these rules are minimum state intervention, liberal trade and minimum tax (*zakat* can substitute tax, as 2.5 per cent of total wealth is given to the poor). Despite such discourses widely used by MUSIAD, I suggest that the adjective 'moral' qualifying the capitalist economy is limited to a rhetorical stance.

Association of Solidarity in Business Life (ISHAD) and Confederation of Turkish Businessmen and Industrialists (TUSKON)

One of the misleading claims in the literature on Islamist business community in Turkey is that MUSIAD is usually considered as the only business organisation representing Islamist business (Bugra 1999; Öniş 2001; Ugur and Alkan 2000). In fact, this community is far from a cohesive unit and there is considerable fragmentation and power struggle between different business organisations over representation. Islamic orders and communities stemming from these orders constitute the basic divide between the Islamist business organisations. The Gülen Movement, for instance, established its own business organisations, the most important of which are the Association of Solidarity in Business Life (ISHAD), the Federation of Business Associations in Marmara Region (MARIFED) and Confederation of Turkish Businessmen and Industrialists (TUSKON). ISHAD was founded 1993 with rather vague objectives including improving Turkey's international business ties, strengthening the structure of affiliated companies, and promoting the dialogue between various economic actors. ISHAD initiated the first federations like MARIFED to which organisations like ISHAD belong, and then a confederation, TUSKON, to which federations are members. Founded in 2005 with the claim of becoming 'the umbrella business organisation in Turkey', TUSKON hosts 150 business organisations and 115,00 businesspeople. As 'global integration' is one of TUSKON's acclaimed objectives, it has opened offices abroad, including those in Europe, the USA, Russia, China and Africa. ISHAD and TUSKON have been engaged in various transnational networks and they have sister organisations particularly in the Middle East, Central Asia and Russia.[51] Therefore, in the overall picture, distinct Islamic orders seem to have not only their own nationwide business networks and organisations, but also transnational ones which are independent of each other.

Despite the claim that there is no competition between the various Islamist business associations, belonging to different religious communities and movements not only creates distinct business communities but also brings about allegiance to different currents of political Islam. For instance, contrary to MUSIAD's close alliance with the Refah Party, and now, partially, with the AKP, the Gülen Movement and its organisation ISHAD do not explicitly ally with a particular party, although many centre-right parties along with some on the centre-left have ties with the Gülen Movement.

Conclusion

This chapter has examined the impact of Islamic networks on the emergence of Islamic capital in connection with the resurgence of political Islam in Turkey. Attempting to 'deprivatise' Islam, some Islamic orders and communities have promoted penetration into the bureaucracy and democratic politics by means of Islamist parties. The same orders and communities also facilitated the creation of business networks and provided the ideational legitimacy for furthering material objectives. The ideas spread by some Islamic orders in Turkey converged with discourses and practices of neoliberalism and facilitated the rise of Islamist business. Processes of globalisation and liberalisation in general and Turkish neoliberal transition in particular empowered Islamist business networks by providing the space and incentives for their integration at the national and international levels.

I have argued that networks based on religious orders and communities have been and remain influential in an ideational transformation within the domain of religion, while facilitating expansion of business networks along with the growth of political Islam. In the Turkish case, these networks have attempted to challenge the status quo in the Turkish economy and politics, previously dominated by the hegemony of strictly secular big business in close cooperation with the Kemalist state establishment.

Notes

1 A speech delivered by Hasim Kılıç, the Chairman of the Constitutional Court (*Radikal*, 31 July 2008).
2 See Çarkoğlu and Rubin (2006) and Yavuz (2006).
3 In the Turkish context, I conceptualise Islamic capital based on networks of social relations and those close to the projects of political Islam (Bugra 1999). I avoid a definition based on Islamic financial institutions because of the limited reach of these institutions in the Turkish context, as I will explain in the respective sections in this chapter. My emphasis on social networks does not exclude the ideational sphere, as I conceptualise these networks as the media through which ideas are transmitted, and ideas related to the domain of religions are not exceptions to that.
4 For critiques of AKP, see Kuru (2006) and Taspinar (2005).
5 See Kuru (2006) for a more extensive account on these views. Kuru (2006: 140) suggests that the 'Islamist view', mainly represented by the National Outlook Movement initiated by Necmettin Erbakan, managed to avoid an explicit criticism of secularism, despite the use of Islamist rhetoric.
6 Mardin (1978: 186) asserts that CHP represented the 'bureaucratic centre', whereas the DP represented the 'democratic periphery'.
7 Mardin (2006: 15) suggests that the major expansion of various forms of media in Turkey in the 1950s and 1960s played an important role in enabling Islamic discourse to reach the public.
8 The I MSP was the successor of the MNP, as the latter was founded after the former had been banned by the 1971 coup. The MSP participated in coalition governments in the 1970s, but never came to power on its own.
9 Turgut Ozal became the chairman of the SPO, while his brother Korkut Ozal, and several other followers of the Iskenderpaşa Community, took key positions at the SPO.

10 Interviews with members of TUSIAD, a leading business organisation of big business, a close ally of the secularist state establishment Istanbul, August 2004.

11 *De jure* launching of this liberalisation programme preceded the military coup, but it
could not be implemented because of the then prevalent political chaos.

12 Although Imam Hatip schools are defined as vocational, their graduates also used to
go to college. However, the relevant law changed in 1999 to restrict Imam Hatip graduates' university education, so they could only attend faculties of divinity, disallow-
ing them the right to attend others. This change has led to much debate since 1999.
The current prime minister – Recep Tayyip Erdogan – is a graduate of these schools.

13 Turgut Ozal, founder of the Motherland Party, architect of the liberalisation programme that preceded the coup and a follower of the Iskenderpaşa Community from
the 1950s, represented the epitome of this amalgamation.

14 While there are no definitive estimates of the size of such capital and the accounts of
this are mostly limited to journalistic inquiries, there is general agreement that it was
large (see Bulut 1999).

15 See Ozcan and Cokgezen (2003) for a more extensive account of this.

16 See Demir *et al.* (2003) for a further analysis of such moral diaspora effect.

17 'Just society' was the popular slogan of the Islamist parties in Turkey, under the
leadership of Erbakan.

18 See European Stability Initiative, 'Islamic Calvinists, Change and Conservatism in
Central Anatolia', Istanbul: September 2005 (www.esiweb.org). Also see Bugra
(1999).

19 Interviews with anonymous former politicians from the Motherland Party (ANAP), of
which the late Ozal was the leader.

20 Initiated by Mehmet Zahit Kotku in affiliation with Gumushanevi Tekkesi. After
Kotku's death, Nurettin and Esad Cosan led the community.

21 Initiated by Mohammed Bahauddin Naqshibandi in the fourteenth century.

22 Interviews with anonymous former politicians from Ozal's inner circle.

23 See Bugra (1999); Yavuz (2003); Demir *et al.* (2004).

24 The implied reference here is specifically Max Weber's famous thesis in his 1958
book *The Protestant Ethic and the Spirit of Capitalism*, on the relationship between
the Protestant religious ethic and the spirit of capitalism.

25 See the European Stability Initiative, 'Islamic Calvinists, Change and Conservatism
in Central Anatolia', Istanbul: September 2005, available at www.esiweb.org

26 Based on an interview conducted by Hakan Yavuz with Lutfi Dogan, a disciple of
Kotku and a former politician. See Yavuz (2005: 192).

27 *Homo Islamicus* is free to acquire and increase his/her wealth as long as s/he abstains
from speculation, gambling and destructive competition.

28 *Homo-Islamicus*, a MUSIAD publication. See www.musiad.org.tr

29 Ibid.

30 Here, Islamic ethics has a specific reference, which is the rule of *zekat*, that each year
wealthy Muslims have to give away 2.5 per cent of their income to the poor.

31 *Moral Capitalist Economy*, a MUSIAD publication. See www.musiad.org.tr

32 From an interview conducted by Marie-Elisabeth Maigre (2005).

33 'Those who devour usury will not stand ... Allah has permitted trade and forbidden
usury ... Allah will deprive usury of all blessing, but will give increase for deeds of
charity' (Qur'an 2: 275–6) 'O you who believe! Devour not usury, doubled and multi-
plied. But fear Allah, that you may really prosper' (3: 130). It is widely believed that
the Prophet Muhammad cursed those who pay interest, those who receive it, those
who write a contract based on it, and those who witness such a contract.

34 See 'Islamic Calvinists' at www.esiweb.org

35 The founder of the community, Mehmet Zahit Kotku, was prosecuted when the religious orders and Sufi brotherhoods were banned by the new republican regime in
1926.

36 See www.iskenderpasa.com
37 Like Mehmet Zahit Kotku, Said-i Nursi was also prosecuted by the Turkish state, spending his life in exile (within Turkey), and becoming a hero in Islamist circles.
38 Independent: *Mustakil*. In the business and political circles, the first letter M is widely interpreted as the first letter of Muslim, rather than Mustakil, reading MUSIAD as Muslim Businessmen's Association.
39 TUSIAD has always had a predominantly secular stance, often aligning with the military, and its member companies make up of 45 per cent of Turkey's GDP.
40 Such as Ulker Holdings and Kombassan Holdings. See Bulut (1999).
41 Based on interviews in Maigre (2005).
42 See *MUSIAD Bulten*, Year 3, 9 (1995), pp. 8–9.
43 Ibid., and see www.wief.org.my and www.oic.org
44 Interviews with anonymous MUSIAD officials, Istanbul, 2003.
45 As pointed out earlier, the February 28 Process was a thorough challenge to Islamist business. While some MUSIAD members like Kombassan and Yimpas were accused of financing Islamist activities, companies like Ulker lost their contracts with the military as suppliers.
46 Currently, the Felicity Party is fairly marginalised with less than 3 per cent of the votes and it now represents a more conservative line than the AKP.
47 See www.webislam.com, no. 240, 22 January 2003.
48 Maigre (2005: 127).
49 See www.musiad.org.tr.
50 Yarar (1997).
51 See www.tuskon.org/

Bibliography

Akdogan, Y. (2006) 'The Meaning of Conservative Democratic Political Identity', in Y. Hakan (ed.), *The Emergence of a New Turkey, Democracy and the AK Party*, Salt Lake City: University of Utah Press, pp. 49–65.
Bugra, A. (1997) 'The Claws of the Tigers', *Private View* (TUSIAD), 1, 2, pp. 1–8.
Bugra, A. (1999) *Islam in Economic Organizations*, Istanbul: Turkish Economic and Social Studies Foundation and Friedrich Ebert Stiftung.
Bulut, F. (1999) *Yesil Sermaye Nereye* [Where is the green capital heading to?], Istanbul: Su Yayınevi.
Çarkoğlu, A. and Rubin, B. (eds) (2006) *Religion and Politics in Turkey*, London: Routledge.
Casanova, J. (1994) *Public Religions in the Modern World*, Chicago: University of Chicago Press.
Cizre-Sakallioglu, U. (1996) 'Parameters and Strategies of Islam–State Interaction in Turkey', *International Journal of Middle East Studies*, 18, pp. 231–51.
Demir, O., Acar, M. and Toprak, M. (2004) 'Anatolian Tigers or Islamic Capital: Prospects and Challenges', *Middle Eastern Studies*, 40, 6, pp. 166–88.
Fuller, G. (2003) *The Future of Political Islam*, New York: Palgrave Macmillan.
Haynes, J. (1993) *Democracy and the Political Change in the Third World*, London: Routledge.
Haynes, J. (ed.) (2006) *The Politics of Religion*, London: Routledge.
Ji-Hyang Jang (2005) 'Taming Political Islamists by Islamic Capital: The Passions and Interests in Turkish Islamic Society,' unpublished dissertation, University of Texas, Austin.
Keddie, N. (2003) 'Secularism and Its Discontents', *Daedalus*, 132, 3, pp. 14–30.

Kuran, Timur (1993) 'The Economic Impact of Islamic Fundamentalism', in M. Martin and R. Scott Appleby (eds), *Fundamentalisms and the State: Remaking Polities, Economies, and Militance*, Chicago: Chicago University Press.

Kuru, A. (2005) 'Globalization and Diversification of Islamic Movements: Three Turkish Cases', *Political Science Quarterly*, 120, 2, pp. 253–74.

Kuru, A. (2006) 'Reinterpretation of Secularism in Turkey: The Case of the Justice and Development Party', in H. Yavuz (ed.), *The Emergence of a New Turkey, Democracy and the AK Party*, Salt Lake City: University of Utah Press, pp. 136–59.

Kurtz, L. (1995) *Gods in the Global Village*, Pine Forge: Sage.

Maigre, M.-E. (2005) 'Formacion y evolucion de los negocios Islamicos, el caso del MUSIAD en Turquia', unpublished Master's thesis, Fundacio CIDOB and Universitat Autonoma de Barcelona.

Mardin, Ş. (1983) 'Religion and Politics in Turkey', in J. Piscatori (ed.), *Islam in the Political Process*, New York: Cambridge University Press, pp. 138–59.

Mardin, Ş. (2006) 'Turkish Islamic Exceptionalism Yesterday and Today: Continuity, Rupture and Reconstruction in Operational Codes', in A. Çarkoğlu and B. Rubin (eds), *Religion and Politics in Turkey*, London: Routledge, pp. 3–24.

Norris, P. and Inglehart, R. (2004) *Sacred and Secular: Religion and Politics Worldwide*, Cambridge: Cambridge University Press.

Öniş, Z. (1997) 'The Political Economy of Islamic Resurgence in Turkey: The Rise of the Welfare Party in Perspective', *Third World Quarterly*, 18, 4, pp. 743–66.

Öniş, Z. (2006) 'The Political Economy of Turkey's Justice and Development Party', in H. Yavuz (ed.), *The Emergence of a New Turkey, Democracy and the AK Party*, Salt Lake City: University of Utah Press, pp. 207–34.

Öniş, Z. and Turem, U. (2002) 'Entrepreneurs, Democracy and Citizenship in Turkey', *Comparative Politics*, 34, 4, pp. 439–56.

Ozcan, G. Berna and Cokgezen, M. (2003) 'Limitations of Alternative Capital Formations: The Case of Anatolian Holding Companies', *World Development*, 31, 12, pp. 2061–84.

Taspinar, O. (2005) *Kurdish Nationalism and Political Islam in Turkey, Kemalist Identity in Transition*, London: Routledge.

Tepe, S. (2006) 'A Pro-Islamic Party? Promises and Limits of Turkey's Justice and Development Party', in H. Yavuz (ed.), *The Emergence of a New Turkey, Democracy and the AK Party*, Salt Lake City: University of Utah Press, pp. 107–35.

Thomas, S. (2005) *The Global Transformation of Religion and the Transformation of International Relations: The Struggle for the Soul of the Twenty-First Century*, New York: Palgrave Macmillan.

Tugal, Cihan (2002) 'Islamism in Turkey: Beyond Instrument and Meaning', *Economy and Society*, 31, 1, pp. 85–111.

Ugur, A. and Alkan, H. (2000) 'Turkiye' de Isadami-Devlet Iliskileri Perspektifinden MUSIAD', *Toplum ve Bilim*, 85, pp. 133–55.

Yarar, Erol (1997) *Is Hayatinda Islam Inancı*, Istanbul: Zaman Yayınlari.

Yavuz, H. (2003) *Islamic Political Identity in Turkey*, Oxford and New York: Oxford University Press.

Yavuz, H. (2005) *Modernlesen Muslumanlar* [Modernizing Muslims], Istanbul: Kitap Yayınevi.

Yavuz, H. (ed.) (2006) *The Emergence of a New Turkey, Democracy and the AK Party*, Salt Lake City: University of Utah Press.

8 The Jamiat al-Adl wal-Ihsan

Religion, political opposition and stalled democratisation in Morocco[1]

Francesco Cavatorta

Introduction

In an article published in 1991, Henry Munson Jr analysed the stability of the Moroccan monarchy and argued that the country was not following the same trend as its Arab neighbours where political Islam was on the rise. Munson explained that Morocco was immune from the dangers of religious fundamentalism and that the monarchy was still very much able to use its religious legitimacy to marginalise religion-based contestation of its power. Two decades later, such an analysis seems only partially correct. While the monarchy has indeed been able to remain in control despite the death of King Hassan II in 1999, the ruling elites of Morocco have joined Arab counterparts elsewhere in attempting to stem the rising tide of Islamism. The answer of the monarchy to the challenge of opposition political Islam has rested for a number of years on the dual strategy of co-optation and repression. Hassan II, unlike Algerian and Tunisian rulers, had decided in the mid-1990s that dealing with opposition Islamists solely through repression would not secure the stability of the Kingdom and, employing some of the same strategies that he had used in the past to co-opt sectors of the secular leftist opposition, he attempted to bring Islamists into the political system. While he was only partially successful for reasons explained below, we do have today (late 2008) in Morocco an established Islamist party, the Party for Justice and Development (PJD), legally allowed to run for office in both local and legislative elections. So far, much scholarly attention has been devoted to accounting for the rise of the PJD, explaining and highlighting its support base, assessing how it fares in elections and generally attempting to analyse the impact of the emergence of a legal Islamist party into a nominally democratising polity (Albrecht and Wegner 2006).

The participation of an Islamist party in legal political and electoral processes is particularly significant in Morocco because of the monarchy's attempt to present the country as both modernising and democratising. This, however, should not lead one to assume that the PJD represents the whole spectrum of political Islam in Morocco. There are in fact two other Islamist tendencies in the Kingdom that also have an impact on how political and social life is shaped (Laskier 2003).On the one hand, there are a number of small extremist groups imbued with a violent *jihadi* ideology – that is, based on the assumption of the existence of a cosmic struggle between Islam and the infidels, including all Muslims who do not share this view. Such groups are responsible for a number of recent terrorist attacks both in Morocco and outside the country's borders However, following the Casablanca and Madrid bombings of 2003 and 2004, they were severely weakened through both mass arrests of activists and better control by the security services. In addition, owing to their extremist positions and violent tactics, they enjoy very little popular support. On the other hand, there is the very popular but semi-legal Jamiat al-Adl wal-Ihsan (Justice and Charity Group) led by a long-time opponent of the monarchy, Sheikh Abdessalam Yassine. This organisation is a significant actor on the Moroccan political scene because of its extensive welfare network and its radical political positions on social, constitutional and foreign policy matters, which pit it against the monarchy, the secular parties and even other Islamist formations. Thus, Islamism in Morocco is quite a complex phenomenon, highlighting the plural nature of political Islam, which gives rise to movements that may have very different ideological tenets and radically different strategies of behaviour.

This chapter, through an analysis of al-Adl, contributes in two ways to a more general understanding of the relationship between democratisation, religion and politics in the regions examined in this book. First of all, the chapter highlights how certain Islamist actors operate within rationalistic parameters in Morocco, and how they are able to exploit the available structure of opportunities in order to increase their legitimacy and popularity. Far from simply being highly ideological actors, Islamist movements are capable of adapting to changing circumstances in their surrounding institutional environment and in the process they also re-interpret some of their ideological tenets in order to gain political advantages. Thus, Islamist movements should be considered rational actors in the same manner with which the wider literature of comparative politics treats political actors in other regions of the world. This is a rather novel approach to the study of Islamist groups, which are usually examined by attempting to identify whether they are by nature 'pro-democracy' or 'anti-democracy'. Following Brumberg's work (2002a, 2002b), this chapter argues that attempting to find the 'true nature' of Islamist organisations is problematic and probably doomed to failure. The chapter demonstrates that in Morocco Islamist actors tend to be very pragmatic, adapting to a changing political environment and institutions. Second, the chapter contributes more generally to an understanding of Moroccan politics. That is, rather than being a country on the path towards democratisation, the Moroccan political system is actually constantly renewing itself, especially its authoritarian nature, in order to foster both own internal and international legitimacy. The uncompromising position of al-Adl with respect to the legitimacy of the King to rule challenges the stability of the system, and this chapter contends that scholars should pay much closer attention to what happens in Moroccan society outside of stage-managed elections and the associated debates of an increasingly discredited political class. Such an analysis helps explain why the 2007 legislative elections were not the turning point that some policy-makers, including King Mohammad VI, and many scholars believed they would be.

The next part of the chapter briefly outlines how the Moroccan political system operates, and describes the position of al-Adl within the system. The chapter then analyses al-Adl's structure and what it does. Finally, it outlines the institutional constraints which help explain why al-Adl has chosen a 'third way' to seek to effect political, social and economic change in Morocco.

Morocco as a 'liberalised autocracy'

Rémy Leveau (1997: 95) contends that Morocco has a 'political system based on authoritarian pluralism'. In fact, since independence in 1956 the royal family, and more specifically King Hassan II (d. 1999), have ruled the country with a tight rein and, at times, with an iron fist. At the same time, however, rulers have always permitted a degree of political pluralism, especially competing political parties and civil society organisations. They have played their part in a political system designed to give the impression that Morocco is gradually moving towards a recognisably democratic political system. Howe (2001: 59) highlights how 'Morocco [is] generally respected by world powers as a stable constitutional monarchy engaged in the democratic process and as an Islamic voice of moderation'. In reality, however, such democratisation has never actually materialised, although King Hassan II did begin a more convincing move towards political change in 1997/8 known as *l'alternance* (changeover of political power), when he offered the Socialist Party, usually kept in opposition, the opportunity to head the government. This change seemed to signal a genuine intention both to move the country away from authoritarianism at a time of increasing international pressure in favour of democratisation and to prepare the terrain for his son, Mohammed VI, who would succeed him upon his death in 1999 with the proclaimed objective of further modernising Morocco. The early days of Mohammed's VI reign were euphoric, both for ordinary Moroccans and for political actors who had for a considerable amount of time called for increased liberalisation that the new King was indeed promoting (Howe 2005; El Ghissassi 2006). While maintaining a solid grip on policy-making power through his constitutional prerogatives, Mohammed VI set about liberalising society, allowing increased individual freedoms while restraining the country's coercive apparatuses. There were quick signs of progress to the extent that, as Howe (2001: 60) noted, 'nowhere else in the Arab world has the public mood of fear changed so dramatically in so little time, nor have citizens acquired such extensive freedom of press, speech and assembly'. In addition, as Tozy (2008: 36) argues, 'the leadership around the King now seeks the support of public opinion and encourages political participation'. Ultimately, however, the programme of democratic reforms was both politically and institutionally disappointing. For instance, an intense debate about modifying the Constitution in order to limit the prerogatives of the monarch did not in the end lead to any substantive change.

Mohammed VI did, however, continue the integration of the PJD into parliament by permitting the party to run in the legislative elections of 2002, and this was a considerable novelty in the Arab world – where opposition Islamists are usually not allowed open access to the political system. In addition, while there were in the past severe limitations and constraints placed on the party itself in terms of its ability to run candidates at elections (Willis 2004), the 2007 elections saw a radical shift in so far as the King and his advisers not only underscored the importance for ordinary citizens to turn out to vote, but also permitted the PJD to run in all constituencies.

As Hamzawy (2007: 4) noted, 'prior to the elections expectations were high regarding the Islamists' potential gains, especially against the background of Western and domestic polls', and while a landslide victory for PJD may not have mattered much in terms of policy-making autonomy, it would have nevertheless had enormous symbolic significance. In the end the results were rather disappointing for the PJD: it only came second in the poll behind the Independence Party. The elections were also very disappointing for the monarchy as turn-out was very low, with little more than a third – 37 per cent – of voters bothering to cast their ballot (Storm 2008b). King Mohammad, his advisers and leading politicians had been quite vocal in encouraging ordinary citizens to vote, and while opinion polls prior to the election indicated that a lot of Moroccans would not bother voting, the low figure represented a serious setback for the King and his regime as it tried to deepen its legitimacy.

The disaffection with the political system – despite its relative openness – represented a failure of the policies that the King and successive governments had implemented since the late 1990s. Despite strong economic growth peaking in 2006 with GDP growth of 8 per cent, with an increase in current US dollars from 37.06 billions in 2000 to 65.40 billions in 2006 (World Bank data),[2] the country was still largely mired in poverty, illiteracy and corruption. The Human Development Index placed Morocco in 126th position in the world in 2005, between Namibia and Equatorial Guinea.[3] It may be that lack of genuine political change is largely responsible for this state of affairs, as the King continues to dominate policy-making yet without increasing his accountability. In particular, it should be emphasised, as does Tozy (2008), that there is no clear relationship between, on the one hand, the vote and, on the other, policies that are then implemented. This is largely because policy-making power is still in the hands of unelected yet powerful figures, such as André Azoulay, which in turn leads to further discrediting of both the elected and the King-appointed political class (Willis 2002). Initially, it seemed that this strategy of 'enlightened despotism' would last until Mohammed VI's power base was consolidated and he could then move towards a new strategy based on a new ruling bargain with citizens (Maghroui 2001). However, there was not the necessary political willingness to deliver genuine reforms that would necessarily limit his own power. King Mohammed VI did bring a new generation of technocrats to power and delivered on his promise to reform the family code which had been a two-decade-long controversial issue for a Moroccan public characterised by both 'tradition' and 'modernity'. Yet the necessarily radical, political transformations that would be needed in order truly to place citizens at the heart of decision-making never occurred. Thus, by the time of the 2007 elections many ordinary Moroccans viewed even the PJD with a degree of suspicion because, it was widely believed, whoever was elected would be implementing the King's social, economic and political programme (Tozy 2008: 39).

Thus, while the space for civil society that Mohammed VI opened up was not closed down and remains the only context where genuine opposition politics can take place (Cavatorta 2006; Khrouz 2008), significant institutional reforms in favour of accountability have not occurred and, according to Moroccan constitutionalist Bendorou (2005: 28) 'all power is really in the hands of the King'. It is therefore not a surprise that the 'de-politicisation' of the population that Maghroui highlighted in 2001 is today clearly evident and it may eventually pose a significant problem for the monarchy's survival (Beau and Graciet 2006).

In conclusion, the Moroccan political system, based on both co-optation and intimidation of dissidents and opponents since the days of independence half a century ago, still functions today. Yet its stability is much more uncertain because of the social changes within the country and the challenging international situation. While the co-optation of the PJD represents a victory in the short term for the King, the presence of a plurality of Islamist actors in the Kingdom means that there are important Islamist political actors such as al-Adl that remain outside the control of the monarchy. While in the past, the religious legitimacy of the royal family seemed to insulate it from criticisms from the Islamists, its religious legitimacy has now declined, less able to deflect such criticism. This is due for the most part not to real differences about the interpretation of religious texts, but to the inability and ineffectiveness of the monarchy to deliver its historical promise of sustained economic and social progress. It follows that the immunity from criticism of the Commander of the Faithful (that is, the King) has largely disappeared, as other political actors, especially the Islamists, have appropriated the language and symbolism of religion to question his claim to rule because of his lineage with the Prophet (Mohsen-Finan and Zeghal 2006).

The challenge to the monarchy from the militants of the violent group Salafist Jihad – responsible for the attacks in Casablanca in May 2003 – has, however, been dealt with quite successfully at the time of writing (late 2008). After the attack, the King reshuffled the security apparatus and granted the security services both necessary resources and power to undertake a severe crackdown on all suspected militants. This had the support of most domestic and international political actors, and by doing so the King forcefully signalled that violence to attain political objectives was not going to be tolerated under any circumstances.

Al-Adl: organisational structure and political programme

Apart from the violent radicals, a further significant challenge for the King has come from the organisation Jamiat al-Adl wal-Ihsan, a social movement with a pronounced oppositional political agenda. Al-Adl denies the King's religious legitimacy to rule, and offers a policy of radical transformation of the society to be achieved through Islamisation of politics, economics and social life. The King has allowed the leader of al-Adl, Sheikh Abdessalam Yassine, to act in the open, although the association per se was in legal limbo in late 2008. The choice to allow the movement to operate with only a modicum of interference is not only explained by the popularity of the movement. It is also due to the King's unwillingness to end the relatively benign relationship with al-Adl. He may also be hoping for a new leader of the movement whom he may be able to co-opt into the existing political system. Analysing how al-Adl operates within the constraints of the existing political institutions and how it exploits the opportunities that arise is crucial in understanding both how it survives politically and attempts to take advantage of the current failing political system.

There is very little doubt that in the face of the current social and economic crisis, the monarch is not able to provide a programme of transformation that might mobilise ordinary Moroccans, who, like many of their Arab counterparts, are increasingly attracted by the solutions that Islamist groups offer, as recent Palestinian and Egyptian elections have shown. While it is true that when offered the chance in 2007 Moroccans did not massively vote for an Islamist party (McFaul and Cofman Wittes 2008), it should be emphasised that staying away from the polls might have been a vote of confidence for the only popular organisation – al-Adl – that can justifiably claim to offer a real alternative to the programme of social, political and economic development that the monarch presented and that all legal political parties subscribed to. This is a view held by influential commentators such as Hamzawy (2007).

Jamiat al-Adl wal-Ihsan: background and history

The Jamiat al-Adl wal-Ihsan or Justice and Charity Group was officially founded in 1981 by Sheikh Abdessalam Yassine, an Islamic thinker and school inspector, who had risen to prominence in 1974 because of his open criticism of the policies of King Hassan II. At this time the monarchy was under sustained criticism from large sectors of society, particularly the secular left, while the King had personally survived two military coups. One of the only remaining pillars of his legitimacy was his role as Commander of the Faithful, and it was precisely against the notion that the royal family had links to the Prophet and that therefore it had some sort of entitlement to rule Morocco that Sheikh Yassine criticised the King. In an open letter titled 'Islam or the Deluge', the Sheikh 'admonish[ed] him to hold firmly to the teachings of Islam and forsake the un-Islamic policies he had been pursuing' (Laskier 2003: 4). Such an open challenge to the monarch led to Yassine's imprisonment, although Islamists were not particularly strong at the time and the monarch was more preoccupied with the challenge coming from the secular left.

Al-Adl, from its foundation, was the target of the repressive apparatus of the state and Yassine was placed under house arrest in 1989 for ten years. In the meantime, Islamism had become a much more important political force in

Morocco and al-Adl benefited quite strongly from this, partly because of the inflexibility of the Sheikh, a man not easily co-opted. Despite remaining only a semi-legal organisation al-Adl was able to expand its activities and membership to such a degree that, according to John Entelis (2002: 21), it was 'by far the most popular Islamist group' in the country. Since then, if anything the reputation of al-Adl has grown, partly as a consequence of the well-received the range of social services it offers to many ordinary Moroccans, its high media profile, and the boldness of some of the statements of its most prominent leaders, including Sheikh Yassine and, even more so, of his daughter Nadia.

The association was first founded with the intention of disseminating the Sheikh's thoughts and writings and did not initially have a clear organisational structure. However, with the growth over time of the numbers of militants[4] and the vast expansion of its social services it became necessary to provide its component groups with a much clearer structure. This has been done over the years and now the group has national, regional and local entities, often dominated by militants. Both militants and sympathisers work together to establish charitable associations and/or cultural groups organically linked to al-Adl. The objective is to provide specific services such as literacy classes or public conferences on various issues of popular interest. At the national level there is a political group that guides the strategic choices of the group in line with the Sheikh's teachings, which are partly informed by *sufi* mysticism (Lauzière 2005). The political circle has three different sections: trade union affairs, women's affairs and youth affairs. Women in fact make up almost half the membership of al-Adl and are extremely active in all areas of its work (Graciet 2006). The 'poster girl' of the group is none other than the Sheikh's daughter, Nadia. The political circle is at the heart of the organisation, in charge of 'assuring the links with the other political actors on the Moroccan scene as well as defining the societal project and the political programme of the association' (Graciet 2006: 17). The main spokesperson of the group is Fatlallah Arsalane, who is rumoured to be a likely future leader of al-Adl once the Sheikh passes away.

While the political programme of al-Adl is far from detailed, it emerges quite clearly from the writings of the Sheikh and the pronouncements of the leading members that its objective is a radical transformation of the social, economic, political and cultural arrangements in Morocco. The aim of such a transformation is an Islamic state. In this respect, the programme for change is 'revolutionary.' From an institutional point of view al-Adl favours the establishment of procedural democracy whereby accountability of elected officials is guaranteed by the periodic holding of elections. In addition, this should take place within the context of a new constitution, which would greatly reduce the powers of the monarch. In fact, more recently, the association, via Nadia Yassine, has even flirted with republicanism, which in Morocco is tantamount to treason. From an economic point of view, the economy should be completely reformed and Islamicised with a return to a more competitive market economy and not one dominated by corruption, oligarchical agreements and an overall lack of meritocracy. On the issue of free trade, there is a considerable degree of criticism for

the way that the free trade agreements with the US and the EU have been negotiated. While quite conservative on social issues, al-Adl is quite favourable to the
idea of equality of sexes within an Islamic legal framework, and the association
performed quite a spectacular turnaround on the reform of the family code,
switching from opposition to acceptance under the internal pressure of the
women's affairs section (Cavatorta 2006). Foreign policy is both anti-Western
and anti-Israel, but this is not something that makes the association stand out
with respect to other Islamist and left-wing political actors on the Moroccan
scene.

No revolution and no participation: the rationale

Having briefly detailed the structure and the main ideological tenets of al-Adl
organisation, it is now time to look in more detail at the strategies that it utilises to
try to achieve its goals of transformation of both society and the political system.
Morocco has been 'in transition to democracy' since the mid-1990s and the
problem of genuine democratisation is inevitably bound up, as in the rest of the
Arab world, with the role of political Islam. It is no surprise, therefore, that both
the policy-making and the scholarly debates are preoccupied with the presence of
Islamist actors whose purpose is to make religion the guiding principle of public
policy-making. In most cases, processes of democratisation in the Arab world
would hinge on the role and beliefs of Islamist parties and movements. In particular, the debate always focuses on the nature of Islamist parties and their rationality.
When it comes to the ethos of Islamist parties, many studies argue that Islam and
Islamism are inherently democratic (El Ghobashy 2005; Goddard 2002), while
other studies find the same movements to be inherently authoritarian (Ben
Mansour 2002). When it comes to the rationality of Islamist parties, this is a trait
that is largely neglected in favour of an analysis that examines parties exclusively
through the prism of religion as the defining characteristic of the organisation. This
leaves out the possibility that religious actors might be both flexible and rational –
because it is assumed that unbending religious views dictate behaviour (Khalil
2006). Most studies on al-Adl (see, for example, Maddy-Weitzmann 2003; Zeghal
2005) are therefore preoccupied with identifying the religious sources of the
Sheikh's thinking and writing in order to determine the nature of the movement
and explain behaviour accordingly. Through these sources, scholars then usually
derive an understanding and an explanation for how the association operates, what
it believes in and what role it might have in a process of democratisation.

Such theoretical discussions about the ideology underpinning the activities of
the organisations are very useful in so far as they trace the quite unusual brand
of Islamism that characterises the movement, combining an innovative interpretation of traditional legal sources discourse with sufi mysticism: that is, focusing
on the spiritual value of Islam. However, these discussions are not as helpful in
analysing how al-Adl operates as a political actor per se with objectives it wishes
to achieve and constraints it seeks to overcome, deriving from the presence of
other political actors with whom it competes for popular support and resources.

The creation of a political grouping within the organisation emphasises that beside its spiritual dimension and charity activities, al-Adl is very much involved in political issues. In the context of what Brumberg calls Morocco's 'liberalised autocracy' (Brumberg 2002b), it is useful to try to understand how the organisation 'plays the game' of politics. Unlike some other Islamist organisations across the Muslim world and in Morocco itself, such as the Boutchichia, which is linked to the King, al-Adl is not seeking acceptance from the regime in order to participate in the political institutions of the country. This choice is not simply the product of 'religious' beliefs that would see such political participation as 'wrong'. It also does not have much to do with the very real religious disagreement about the interpretation that has to be given to the figure of Commander of the Faithful. In fact, there is much rational thinking behind the decision not to participate directly in elections and to the institutions that the regime has set up over the course of the years with all other political actors and NGOs, including the Moroccan Organisation for Human Rights and Amnesty International–Morocco. Al-Adl's reading of the liberalising reforms and the changes that Morocco has experienced since Mohammed VI's accession to the throne in 1999 deviates from how other political parties and social movements interpret the situation. Its choice of non-participation certainly has an ideological religious base, inextricably linked with the interpretation that direct lineage to the Prophet should not guarantee legitimacy to rule. At the same time, it is also bound up with the necessity to deny the monarchy legitimacy, because the policies it implements are failing and a different set of policies should therefore be implemented.

Civil society actors, in particular the largely secular NGOs, including the Moroccan Organisation for Human Rights and Springtime for Equality linked to the human rights movement and to the women's movement, have praised the liberal reforms introduced by the King, and they have willingly participated in the different fora organised by the regime to discuss issues of relevance to the country, such as the reform of the family code and a new human development programme to fight poverty. While al-Adl might usefully contribute to such debates, it has refused to take part. All political parties, including the PJD, legitimise the current system by participating in the elections, subject to the conditions laid out by the palace. All this is presented by the King and his advisors as steps towards full democratisation, but al-Adl's interpretation is quite different. This is a crucial point. The disagreement with the other political actors rests on two quite separate political visions for the future of Morocco and, while such disagreements also depend on the role that religion should have in public policy, they are also due to fundamental differences that exist in terms of policy choices related to, for instance, free trade, foreign policy and privatisation of state-owned assets. While many political parties, NGOS and the monarch would describe Morocco as a country that is both modernising and democratising, according to Mr Arsalane, the spokesperson of al-Adl, 'in Morocco there is no democracy, we just have the names people associate with democracy (parties, parliament and human rights)'.[5] It follows that participation in such a system for al-Adl is not an option, but not because it lacks democratic ethos. The choice of non-participation is currently a rational move, and al-Adl calculates that such a stance will be more beneficial to the movement in the long run, for a number of reasons.

First, there is great dissatisfaction with political parties among ordinary citizens, as parties are largely discredited, and therefore being associated with them in different forums and even in parliament might be a cost rather than an asset. Given their lack of credibility, it is better for al-Adl to exploit its role as the outsider that does not compromise. This line of thinking applies also with respect to the PJD, which, in theory, could represent a potential ally in the struggle to Islamicise Morocco. However, the relationship between the two actors is fraught with difficulties. The PJD, in order to participate and 'enter' the political system, had to proclaim its allegiance to the King, and also had to restrain its electoral ambitions. While the PJD was able to secure the agreement of the King in running candidates in all constituencies in the 2007 elections, it did so after 'ditching' some of its most controversial figures and agreeing in principle to the policy framework that the King has presented the country with. This is quite unacceptable to al-Adl, which would participate only on the condition that the role of the King is constitutionally diminished before the setting up of new rules of the game, and on the condition that there would be no obstacles to the free will of the people when it comes to choice of government. This means that voters' decisions and public policy-making should be more closely linked. On the al-Jazeera television network, Nadia Yassine stated that:

> our movement is one of *da'wa*, which enjoins on us not to fish in troubled waters, nor fall into the traps of political scheming. The movement will not participate unless it has guarantees that it will participate in a real political process, not in a comedy, and that it will not be imprisoned in the vicious circle of carrying out instructions from the high echelons of power.[6]

Given that policy-making power is in the hands of the King, al-Adl calculates that it would lose support if it worked with institutions that are believed to be unable to affect desirable and progressive changes. Mr Arsalane had this to say about the other political actors that have decided to enter the state's institutions: 'theirs is a hypocritical stance because they participate in government. They are just pretending to be in opposition to the ruler; in reality they are fully part of the Makhzen.'[7] The call to stay away from meaningless elections appears to have been successful in 2007 and this may further confirm that al-Adl leadership is currently adopting a successful political strategy.

A second reason for the rationality of non-participation lies in the diminishing popular support for both secular left-wing parties and for civil society organisations associated to the left and run by former leftist political dissidents. Electoral results (Storm 2008a, 2008b) point to the significant decline of the left over the last decade, and civil society groups are by their own admission on the retreat in wider society owing to the expanding support for Islamism (Cavatorta 2006). Diminishing support forces such organisations, in order to achieve some of their objectives, to rely on the King for support when it comes to modifying legislation or obtaining funding. Consequently, the King becomes the all-important arbiter, tying his political fate to that of liberal reformers who are aware of the growing impact of Islamism and are keen to stop it. As Brumberg (2003: 111) notes, 'in the Middle East … fear of Islamist victories has produced "autocracy with democrats", as key groups that might choose democracy, absent an Islamist threat, now actively support or at least tolerate autocrats'. While there are certainly many points of disagreement between Islamist groups and such civil society organisations, on some themes they actually have room for co-operation. For instance, there is a commonality of interests in the respect for the rights of prisoners, on the right not to be tortured and on a number of socio-economic rights such as the sexual exploitation of children. Despite such coincidence of interests, the level of co-operation between al-Adl and the secular sectors of civil society is almost non-existent. In this respect the organisation is keen to distance itself from what it perceives to be an 'unholy' alliance with groups that not only differ ideologically from al-Adl, but also tend to be seen by many ordinary Moroccans as the representatives of post-colonial elites disconnected with citizens' objective needs.

A third reason for non-participation lies in the complicated relationship with the palace. The King is not in principle against the direct participation of al-Adl and there have been extensive contacts between the two actors to try to strike a deal that would suit both. This should not come as a surprise given the tradition of co-optation of the Moroccan monarchy. Nadia Yassine states that 'the regime tried more than once to negotiate with the movement', but al-Adl has so far refused because it would be obliged to recognise the religious primacy of the King. Aside from being a highly contested theological point, such recognition is perceived within the organisation to be the beginning of a co-optation that would result in the nonattainment of its key objectives. Unlike other social movements, al-Adl's agenda for change is wide-ranging. The organisation believes that the degree and nature of changes it seeks cannot be obtained through co-optation. In addition, al-Adl is very sceptical of the intentions of the monarch to democratise meaningfully, and is also convinced that the institutions set up by the monarchy cannot be easily reformed. The attitude of all of the other players in the system is that recognition of the primacy of the monarchy in the public space is the price to be paid for entering institutional politics and attempting to then impose democratisation on the monarchy. For al-Adl, however, the strategy of the other players is fundamentally flawed because it believes that by participating they then give up the right to deny legitimacy to the monarchy and to criticise it. Such denial of legitimacy is what, according to al-Adl, would trigger a transformation of the political system. This is the reason why the organisation calls for a constitutional assembly that would discuss such matters without the interference of the King. While it is widely believed that the monarchy as an institution is both popular among ordinary Moroccans and necessary for political stability, al-Adl banks on the fact that such popularity appears to be declining consequential to growing economic and social difficulties. Thus, being seen to have legitimised the policy-making role of the monarchy for such a long time is not likely to prove to be popular. However, if al-Adl keeps its distance from the monarchy, criticises it from the outside and pours scorn on those political actors that have been co-opted in exchange for some privileges, it believes that in the longer run it will be the main beneficiary of the disillusionment of ordinary citizens with their system of government. Such a negative view of the monarchy's performance and the potential danger it runs is also shared by many well-informed scholars (see, for example, Tuquoi 2001; Beau and Graciet 2006).

However, remaining outside institutional politics has costs. The first cost is that by choosing to stay out of politics, the organisation misses out on the opportunity to influence the direction of the country if, for instance, the King decides that full democratisation is the solution to Morocco's problems. In that case the parties already occupying the institutions would likely benefit from having been there for some time. The al-Adl leadership is, however, very sceptical of this possible change of heart of the King and this is the reason they choose to 'provoke' him through trying to play the 'republican card'. The second cost is that by not engaging directly in politics and with a deteriorating situation, al-Adl might find itself out-flanked by more radical and violent elements. Al-Adl recognises this danger. As Arsalane notes, 'we believe that democracy is the solution … the alternative is radical violence', implying that such an alternative would be a terrible development for Morocco. The attacks in Casablanca and elsewhere since 2003 seem to confirm such fears. Al-Adl has a very long tradition of condemning violence to achieve political objectives, but such a choice is not simply determined by the type of ideological Islamism to which they subscribe. It is also partly the product of experience. The *salafi* groups are not popular and are perceived to be dangerous by the vast majority of ordinary citizens, as recent 'anti-terror marches' indicate. Violence is therefore not an option for the organisation because it would likely lead to state repression and therefore the inability to achieve other important goals. It is also not an option because it would alienate a great number of members who are attracted by its spiritual dimension and who would almost certainly not be keen on the use of violence. Finally, the leadership is very well aware of the fact that violence has not led to the achievement of political objectives in any other Arab society, where *salafi* groups have all failed.

Conclusion

The literature on opposition movements in the Middle East and North Africa, and particularly that dealing with Islamist movements, tends overwhelmingly to focus on attempts to discover the true ethos of such movements in order to make claims about their democratic credentials, or their lack of them. This often leads, however, to a rather sterile approach because the surrounding environment is not taken into due consideration and the rational calculations that such movements might make are neglected when it comes to explaining why they operate the way they do and the choices they make. This occurs because of the highly controversial conflation of religion and ideology that Islamist groups embody. This research does not underestimate the relevance of the ideological tenet derived from religion and how it affects the decision-making process of such groups. However, it is also important to underline that there might be a neglected component to their decision-making, which is the institutional environment around them. This environment offers different courses of action subject to certain constraints and subject to the choices that other players in the system make.

The case of al-Adl in Morocco is particularly significant because the movement rejects both participation and violence to achieve its objectives. This is not simply the product of its ideological allegiance to *dawa* and social activism, but is also the product of Moroccan liberalised autocracy, where the King plays a complex game of 'divide and conquer' in order to remain the exclusive decision-maker (Cavatorta 2007). Al-Adl calculates its costs and benefits through its reading of the relationships that it has with the monarchy, with other political parties and with civil society actors. Ideology certainly influences the way the association reads the 'vision' that the King has for Morocco, but al-Adl is also keenly aware that multiple failings are undermining the legitimacy of the monarchy and of the political class that is closely linked to the King's 'programme for change'. Al-Adl has come to the conclusion that democracy is the way forward, but wishes to change the rules of the game before engaging directly in politics, while banking on the continued dissatisfaction of the public with the monarchy. These 'subtle calculations' are meant to strengthen the bargaining position of the association and lead it in the future to achieve political power on its own terms, with the prospect of radically transforming society. Given the popularity of Islamism in Morocco, the rather spectacular failure of the 2007 elections to inject legitimacy into the system, the marginalisation of the PJD as an Islamist rival, and the deteriorating political, economic and international situation, the calculations of the al-Adl leadership might be correct.

The main finding of this chapter is that while Islam as an ideology is important in giving a direction and a theoretical 'policy' framework to movements in Morocco that define themselves as Islamic, such movements are also rational political actors whose objectives are shaped both by ideology and political realities.

Notes

1 This chapter originates from a paper presented at the ECPR Joint Sessions Workshop 22, 'Religion and Politics', Helsinki, Finland, May 2007. An earlier version of this chapter was published in *Mediterranean Politics*, 12, 3 (2007), pp. 379–95. I am grateful to Jeff Haynes for his helpful comments. Finally, I would like to acknowledge the excellent hospitality and stimulating intellectual atmosphere of the Centre for Contemporary Middle East Studies at the University of Southern Denmark. The Centre hosted my sabbatical for the academic year 2008/9.
2 The summary of the data regarding the Moroccan economy is available at http://ddp-ext.worldbank.org/ext/ddpreports/ViewSharedReport?&CF=&REPORT_ID=9147&REQUEST_TYPE=VIEWADVANCED&HF=N/CPProfile.asp&WSP=N (accessed 15 September 2008).

3 UN Human Development Report, 2007. The ranking can be found at http://hdr.undp. org/en/statistics/ (accessed 15 September 2008).
4 The spokesperson of the organisation refused to say how many members the group has and thus it is impossible to have a definite figure. By most accounts the organisation seems to be able to count on at least 50,000 committed militants and up to 500,000 sympathisers. At demonstrations on Palestine and Iraq or against the reform of the family code, al-Adl was able to mobilise over a million people each time.
5 Interview with author, Sale, August 2005.
6 Transcripts of the interview are available at www.nadiayassine.net (accessed 12 April 2007).
7 Interview with author, Sale, August 2005.

Bibliography

Albrecht, H. and Wegner, E. (2006) 'Autocrats and Islamists: Contenders and Containment in Egypt and Morocco', *Journal of North African Studies*, 11, 2, pp. 123–41.

Beau, N. and Graciet, C. (2006) *Quand le Maroc sera islamiste*, Paris: La Découverte.

Ben Mansour, L. (2002) *Frères musulmans, frères féroces. Voyage dans l'enfer du discours Islamiste*, Paris: Éditions Ramsay.

Bendorou, O. (2005) Interview, *Le Journal Hebdomadaire*, 23–29 April, p. 28.

Brumberg, D. (2002a) 'Islamists and the Politics of consensus', *Journal of Democracy*, 13, 3, pp. 109–15.

Brumberg, D. (2002b) 'The Trap of Liberalized Autocracy', *Journal of Democracy*, 13, 4, pp. 56–68.

Brumberg, D. (2003) 'Liberalisation versus Democracy: Understanding Arab Political Reform', *Carnegie Papers*, 37, pp. 3–20.

Cavatorta, F. (2006) 'Civil Society, Islamism and Democratisation. The Case of Morocco', *Journal of Modern African Studies*, 44, 2, pp. 203–22.

Cavatorta, F. (2007) 'More than Repression; Strategies of Regime Survival. The Significance of *Divide et Impera* in Morocco', *Journal of Contemporary African Studies*, 25, 2, pp. 187–203.

El Ghissassi, H. (2006) *Regard sur le Maroc de Mohammed VI*, Neuilly-sur-Seine: Michel Lafon Editions.

El-Ghobashy, M. (2005) 'The Metamorphosis of the Egyptian Muslim Brotherhood', *International Journal of Middle East Studies*, 37, 3, pp. 368–79.

Entelis, John (2002) 'Un courant populaire mis à l'ecart', *Le Monde Diplomatique*, 589, pp. 22–3.

Goddard, H. (2002) 'Islam and Democracy', *Political Science Quarterly*, 73, 1, pp. 3–9.

Graciet, C. (2006) 'Les Suffragettes du Cheikh', *Le Journal Hebdomadaire*, 263, pp. 16–21.

Hamzawy, A. (2007) 'The 2007 Moroccan Parliamentary Elections. Results and Implications'; available at www.carnegieendowment.org/files/moroccan_parliamentary_elections_final.pdf (accessed 20 August 2008).

Howe, M. (2001) 'Fresh Start for Morocco', *Middle East Policy*, 8, 2, pp. 59–65.

Howe, M. (2005) *Morocco. The Islamist Awakening and Other Challenges*, Oxford: Oxford University Press.

Khalil, M. (2006) 'Egypt's Muslim Brotherhood and Political Power: Would Democracy Survive?', *Middle East Review of International Affairs*, 10, 1, pp. 44–52.

Khrouz, D. (2008) 'A Dynamic Civil Society', *Journal of Democracy*, 19, 1, pp. 42–9.

Laskier, M. (2003) 'A Difficult Inheritance: Moroccan Society under King Mohammed VI', *Middle East Review of International Affairs*, 7, 3, pp. 1–20.

Lauzière, H. (2005) 'Post-Islamism and the Religious Discourse of Abd Al Salam Yasin', *International Journal of Middle Eastern Studies*, 37, 2, pp. 241–61.

Leveau, R. (1997) 'Morocco at the Crossroads', *Mediterranean Politics*, 2, 2, pp. 95–113.

McFaul, M. and Cofman Wittes, T. (2008) 'The Limits of Limited Reforms', *Journal of Democracy*, 19, 1, pp. 19–33.

Maddy-Weitzman, B. (2003) 'Islamism, Moroccan-Style: The Ideas of Sheikh Yassine', *Middle East Studies Quarterly*, 10, 1; available at www.meforum.org/article/519 (accessed 20 August 2008).

Maghraoui, A. (2001) 'Monarchy and Political Reform in Morocco', *Journal of Democracy*, 12, 1, pp. 73–86.

Maghraoui, A. (2002) 'Depoliticization in Morocco', *Journal of Democracy*, 13, 4, pp. 24–32.

Mohsen-Finan, K. and Zeghal, M. (2006) 'Opposition Islamiste et pouvoir monarchique au Maroc', *Revue française de science politique*, 56, 1, pp. 79–119.

Munson, H. Jr (1991) 'Morocco's Fundamentalists', *Government and Opposition*, 26, 3, pp. 331–44.

Storm, L. (2008a) 'Testing Morocco: The Parliamentary Elections of September 2007', *Journal of North African Studies*, 13, 1, pp. 37–54.

Storm, L. (2008b) 'The Parliamentary Elections in Morocco, September 2007', *Electoral Studies*, 27, 3, pp. 359–64.

Tozy, M. (2008) 'Islamists, Technocrats and the Palace', *Journal of Democracy*, 19, 1, pp. 34–41.

Tuquoi, J. P. (2001) *Le Dernier Roi*, Paris: Éditions Grasset.

Willis, M. (2002) 'Political Parties in the Maghrib: The Illusion of Significance', *Journal of North African Studies*, 7, 2, pp. 1–22.

Willis, M. (2004) 'Morocco's Islamists and the Legislative Elections of 2002: The Strange Case of the Party that Did Not Want to Win', *Mediterranean Politics*, 9, 1, pp. 53–81.

Zeghal, M. (2005) *Les Islamistes Marocains*, Paris: La Découverte.

9 The church in opposition
Religious actors, lobbying and Catholic voters in Italy

Luigi Ceccarini

Introduction

The Catholic Church today plays a quite different role in the Italian political system compared to the past. For roughly half a century, from shortly after the Second World War, the church was represented politically by the Christian Democratic Party (DC). This phase was characterised by delegation and 'collateralism', which is to say close collaboration, with the DC. In the early 1990s, however, with the demise of the First Republic and the collapse of the DC, the Catholic Church revised its strategy for political representation and began to establish a new public presence.

Once the Catholic Church moved beyond its long-standing policy of collateralism, it became an 'extra-parliamentary' actor. Through the Italian Episcopal Conference (CEI) and its president, Cardinal Ruini, the Catholic Church has followed a strategy of *neutrality* from political parties and from political alliances, playing a role in the political scene directly as a lobby without any intermediaries. In other words, its political representation has moved 'from the party to the pulpit'.

Over the last few years the political scene in Italy has been complicated by increasing importance in public debate of various ethical issues. In particular, *biopolitics* – whereby ethical questions of life enter into the political decision-making processes – has become an important topic in political debate in Italy. Various issues, including stem cell research, medically assisted fertilisation, abortion, the RU486 pill, 'biological' or 'living' wills, euthanasia and cloning, together with other social issues including, first and foremost, 'the family', have become legislative issues for politicians – and Catholic MPs in particular.

Ethical bipolarism and political bipolarism have become interlinked in public debate. The confrontation between political and religious actors has become very heated.

Over the last few years, the Catholic Church has played a direct and resolute role, taking a public stand, trying to influence political decisions. It has acted in the socio-political scene as a *political entrepreneur*, mobilising resources and taking advantage of the context and the (open) windows of opportunity in the political structure.

Moreover, during this phase, especially from the general elections of April 2006, it has been possible to observe the Catholic Church (as well as the Catholic universe) draw closer to the centre-right coalition, the House of Liberty, or alternatively the House of Freedoms (Casa delle Libertà, CdL). The April 2006 election was won by the centre-left coalition (the Union), with the Catholic Church provocatively labelled an *opposition church.*

However, this categorisation over-simplifies a complex situation that we will examine in this chapter. In short, it seems that the Catholic Church may have gone beyond the 'neutrality phase' and, in the meantime, exacerbated the differences between the two political coalitions, and the Catholic MPs belonging to the two coalitions. Furthermore, we can observe a significant cleavage within the centre-left coalition, and a bipartisan Catholic front emerging on so-called ethical issues.

This chapter will concentrate on the period between 2005 and 2007. It will examine events that took place under the rule of the centre-left government led by Romano Prodi. This government fell at the beginning of 2008 and early elections were held shortly thereafter. The elections brought to power a new government headed by the media magnate, owner of Milan football club and current prime minister, Silvio Berlusconi.

Catholic voters, religious actors and (bio)politics

Catholics and politics: a question from the past

While the 'Catholic question', dating back to Italy's unification in 1870, has evolved over time, it has nevertheless remained a fixture in Italian politics. A key turning point was the founding of the Christian Democracy Party (DC) by Alcide De Gasperi and other Catholic figures in 1942. With the DC, the relationship Catholics had with politics took the form of *political unity,* which is to say the almost exclusive orientation of Catholic voters towards the DC (Mannheimer and Sani 1987; Cappello and Diamanti 1995).

Until the early 1990s, political unity was a defining characteristic of the social and political history of the post-war period in Italy. However, in 1994 the DC collapsed and from it emerged new political actors: the Popular Party, CCD, CDU, then UDC, Udeur. Subsequently, the Popular Party, along with other moderate parties, gave rise to a new political entity: the Margherita (English: Daisy).[1] The fragmentation of Catholic-inspired parties and the resultant fragmentation of Catholics – including, MPs, electors, political and association leaders – between the two coalitions (whether in Catholic-inspired parties or in other parties like Forza Italia) complicated the framework wherein takes place the relationship between Catholics and politics (Diamanti and Ceccarini 2007: 43–6).

With the demise of the DC and the collapse of the First Republic, the political unity phase also came to an end. According to surveys conducted in 2007, a mere 7 per cent of Italian electors are in favour of Catholics' political unity, and among practising Catholic voters this percentage is only slightly higher at 9 per cent. If we add to this number those voters who think that Catholics should vote for parties that express a Christian identity (23 per cent), the percentage reaches almost a third of regularly practising Catholics, who, however, represent only a quarter of Italians: which is to say, they are in the minority. According to public opinion, Catholic voters should be free to vote for any party (41 per cent of the overall population and 29 per cent among practising Catholics: see Table 9.1).

In fact, over time, the religious meaning of voting for the DC has weakened. The governmental role of the DC and growing popular secularisation led scholars to refer to the DC as a 'state-sponsored party' rather than a 'church-sponsored party' (Allum 1984). The majority of Italians belongs to the 'majority religion' (Garelli 1991), a term used to describe the phenomenon whereby most citizens identify themselves as Catholic, yet many do not have a deeply devout relationship outlook. Rather, they live according to a sense of morality, a style of attitudes and behaviours, which differs, at times quite sharply, from the ecclesiastical hierarchy's instructions and recommendations.

Moreover, political unity has been defined as a 'myth' (Pace 1995), since this unity progressively weakened to the point of becoming minor, to the extent that only a sort of collective belief in it has survived. While politicians and others continue to refer to 'Catholic political unity', the concept increasingly exists only in theory, not reality; the term has outlived its actual political incarnation. Now, many Catholics look beyond the DC, seeking different political orientations, particularly at election time. Indeed, long before the collapse of the DC, it was emphasised that the party was 'a' – not 'the' – party of Catholic voters, no longer 'the' party of the Catholic electorate (Arturo Parisi 1979: 85; see also Cappello and Diamanti 1995; Scoppola 1997, 2006; Galli 1968, 1993; Franco 2000; Diamanti and Riccamboni 1992; Segatti and Vezzoni 2008).

In short, the demise of the DC eliminated any lingering doubts about the fate of Catholic political unity. Its demise unequivocally signalled the end of the

Table 9.1 The political unity of Catholics is often discussed. What solution do you think is right today?

	Practising Catholics	Overall population
Catholics should vote for a single party of Christian inspiration	9.0	7.0
Catholics should vote for the parties that chiefly express Christian values	23.0	11.6
Catholics can vote for different parties, of any ideology, while seeking to assert in these parties Christian values	29.5	31.3
Catholics can vote for any party without posing particular problems of their conscience	29.1	41.0
Don't know/not indicated	9.4	9.1
Total	100	100
N	*257*	*641*

Source: Demos-Eurisko for *La Repubblica*, 19–20 February 2007 (*N* = 641).

period of Catholic concentration (and the idea of concentration itself) within a single party.

From the party to the pulpit: an extra-parliamentary church

The end of the First Republic coincided with the related demise not only of Catholic political unity – never truly achieved – but also of the prevalence among Catholics of voting for only one single party or alignment. Instead, Catholics distributed their votes among different alignments and parties in the 1994 elections, without shifting the political equilibrium in any specific direction (Diamanti 1997: 336). And, the same thing happened in subsequent elections (1996 and 2001) (Diamanti 1997: 347; Cartocci 2002: 191–2), despite sharply differing outcomes: the centre-left won power in 1996 and the centre-right in 2001. This shift in the electoral orientation of Italian Catholics reflected and accompanied other shifts. Together they characterised the political choices offered and the strategies of the church and the Catholic universe (Diamanti and Ceccarini 2007).

The church had considered the crisis of the former political representation model long before the traditional Italian political system collapsed. Clergy high in the hierarchy kept away from the DC and, in general, from political parties. The Catholic Church started to act autonomously and assumed a critical stance towards the parties, both because they were discredited in the eyes of many voters and because they often seemed far removed from society and its concerns. The risk was that the Catholic Church would also be considered in the same light as the political party, the DC.

During the 1980s, the role of Cardinal Ruini grew to be very important. Ruini became CEI general secretary in 1986, and was president of the same institution from 1991 to 2007. His project affirmed the church's autonomy in the realm of politics – all collateralism aside. Ruini theorised and implemented an 'extra-parliamentary Church', as Sandro Magister (2001) has defined it.

Over the course of the post-war period, the church had entrusted the representation of Catholics to the party. In the 1990s, following the crisis of the First Republic and the DC, this approach was reversed. The church decided not to encourage new Catholic parties or move to support any of the existing Catholic parties. Instead it transferred the task of Catholic representation 'from the party to the pulpit' (Kalyvas 1996).

This process dates back to the second half of the 1980s. Cardinal Ruini, following the second Ecclesial Convention of Loreto, held in April of 1985, set out a plan for the church's new public presence, in agreement with the Vatican (especially in the wake of the social encyclicals issued by Pope John Paul II) (Brunelli 1995; Melloni 2007). Over time, the bishops became aware of the disintegration of the Italian political system, and by 1991, during the 35th General Assembly of the CEI, it had become clear that political unity had lost much of its former importance. Moral questions and ethical issues were brought to the attention of the greater public. They became the key elements which, on the one hand, sought to reinforce the relationship between Catholics in society and, on the other hand, to stimulate political actors to act.

Soon afterwards Cardinal Ruini's Cultural Project (oriented in a Christian sense) took shape. The aim was to imprint its views on Italian cultural life, making the presence of the church and its ethical perspective stronger.

Consequently, the church increasingly acted more independently in support of its own values and interests, by exerting 'pressure' on parties and institutions, taking advantage of its own diffuse territorial organisation and relying on the public credibility it possessed both nationally in Italy and worldwide (Casanova 1994; Garelli 2007). This stance was strengthened by the great power of social attraction exerted by Pope John Paul II, who was Polish and only marginally interested in Italian politics. Instead, the Pope devoted his efforts, his commitment and his overall mission to global problems, including poverty and international politics.

Recently, specifically between 2005 and 2007, the 'Catholic question' was affected by certain events linked to ethical issues. These events encouraged the relationship between the church and Italian political actors and politics to be redrawn, offering some useful clues towards understanding how this relationship had changed from the late 1990s.

The events in question inform this study of how the church acts politically today; which windows of opportunity are now open in the socio-political context; which alliances take shape in the political arena; which political cleavages have become crucial; and which resources are used by religious actors. Specific events include:

- the election of Cardinal Ratzinger to Pope, April 2005;
- the referendum on medically assisted fertilisation and stem cells, June 2005;
- the general election, April 2006;
- the DICO draft law, February 2007.

Biopolitics: elements and events from the Italian scenario

The church and society

The election of Cardinal Joseph Ratzinger (Benedict XVI) as Pope in April 2005 was an important turning point in the relationship between the church and Italian politics. The new Pope was particularly interested in Italian domestic affairs, whereas his predecessor, Pope John Paul II, was not. The conflictual relationship between politics and religious actors may well be a consequence of his interest. Moreover, issues on the political agenda that can be considered to be of an ethical nature are very important for religious actors and their pronounced political controversies. In addition, some political actors seek to use these issues to help shape their identity, build alliances and attempt to gain societal consensus.

If Pope John Paul II was a 'pastor', Benedict is a 'theologian'. John Paul II named Ratzinger Prefect of the Congregation for the Doctrine of the Faith in

1981. Originally this institution was called the Sacred Congregation of the Universal Inquisition, as its duty was to defend the church from heresy. Today the aim of this institution is to promote and safeguard the doctrine of faith and morals throughout the Catholic world.

Cardinal Ratzinger left this role when he was nominated to be Pope, at the same time that Italian public debate became centred on issues concerning bio-politics. The election of Pope Benedict reinforced the already strong continuity and agreement that characterised the relationship between the Holy See and the Italian bishops (CEI). This happened for two main reasons: (1) the attention which the new ope gives to the Italian case, and (2) the common vision that Cardinal Ruini and Pope Benedict shared in this regard.

In fact, an expert observer (Magister 2007) emphasises that Benedict and Ruini are both working towards making the Italian case a sort of 'export model', a reference point for other Catholic churches in the Western secularised world. The Pope himself, in his speech at the Fourth Ecclesial Convention (held in October 2006 in Verona), said about the peculiarity of the Italian Church:

> Here, in fact, the Church is a lively reality – and we see it! – which conserves a capillary presence in the midst of people of every age and level. Christian traditions often continue to be rooted and to produce fruit.
> (Address of Pope Benedict XVI to the participants of the Fourth National Ecclesial Convention, Verona, 19 October 2006)

This particular presence aids the church in reaching the greatest possible public, and thus in spreading and propagating Christian traditions.

Opinion polls in Italy continually show that the Catholic Church is among the institutions that enjoy the highest level of social trust, as Figure 9.1 indicates.

Table 9.2 shows that more than a quarter (about 27 per cent) of Italians are regular church-goers, and nine out of ten define themselves as Catholics, even

Table 9.2 Citizens who define themselves as Catholics and the main reason they define themselves as such (percentages among those who declare themselves Catholic)

Those who define themselves Catholic	*86.4*
Because I was born into a Catholic family	49.0
Because I believe in this faith	30.3
Because I am devoted to Catholic values	11.1
Because it is part of the history and culture of my country	9.5
Not indicated	0.2
Total	100
N	1445

Source: Demos-Eurisko for *La Repubblica*, 19–20 February/12–13 March 2007 (*N* = 1,445).

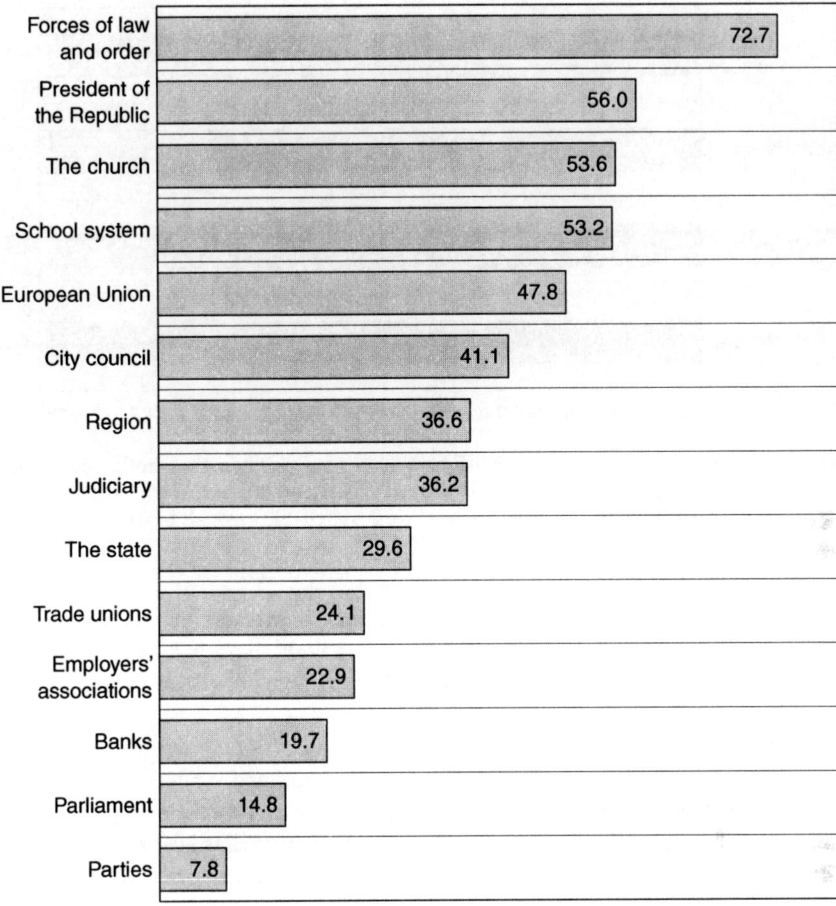

Figure 9.1 How much trust do you have in the following organisations, associations, social groups, and institutions? (percentages of those who stated having much or very much trust) (source: Demos for *La Repubblica*, 26–30 November 2007 ($N = 1,300$)).

though among them half (49 per cent) say that they are Catholic just for family reasons, and 10 per cent give traditional and cultural motivations for their faith.

Religious actors are fully aware that Italy is a deeply secular country, but the higher-level clergy are also conscious that the Catholic Church still has a strong normative role in the society itself (Cesareo *et al.* 1995; Garelli 1991; 1996, 2007; Pace 2007). The role extends beyond practising believers, as Figure 9.2 demonstrates, since the relevance of a Catholic upbringing is widespread among Italians independent of their level of religiosity.

In other words, Italy is seen by the church as a 'laboratory', characterised by ideal conditions, where it is possible to try to galvanise and build opposition to

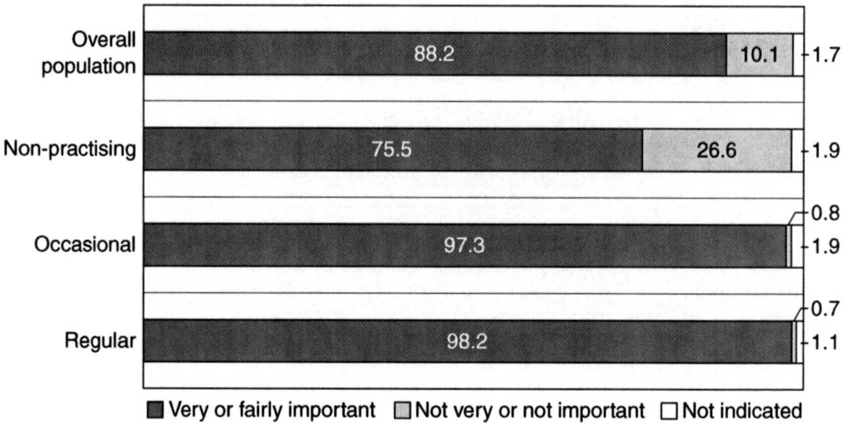

Figure 9.2 How important do you consider giving your children a Catholic education? (percentage values based on religious practice) (source: Demos-Eurisko for *La Repubblica*, 19–20 February/12–13 March 2007 (*N* = 1,445)).

the de-Christianisation – that is, secularisation – process, involving both a *laicism* and *rationalism* that the church claims with some justification deeply affects all Western societies. Summing up, Italy is a sort of export model, as one can read in the Pope's words:

> The Italy of today presents itself to us as a profoundly needy Land and at the same time a very favourable place for such a witness. It is profoundly needy because it participates in the culture that predominates in the West and seeks to present itself as universal and self-sufficient, generating a new custom of life. From this a new wave of illuminism and laicism is derived, by which only what is experiential and calculable would be rationally valid, while on the level of praxis, individual freedom is held as a fundamental value to which all others must be subject. Therefore, God remains excluded from culture and from public life, and faith in him becomes more difficult … If we can do it, the Church in Italy will render a great service not only to this Nation, but also to Europe and to the world, because the trap of secularism is present everywhere and the need for a faith lived in relation to the challenges of our time is likewise universal.
>
> (Address of Pope Benedict XVI to the participants of the Fourth National Ecclesial Convention, Verona, 19 October 2006)

Scholars, including Magister (2006, 2007), have noticed that in countries like Portugal and Spain, there is now, compared to the past, a stronger response from their domestic churches to the debate on ethical issues. In other words, the Italian model may be influential: it may have stimulated other European Catholic churches to oppose political decisions concerning ethical values, such as abortion, homosexual marriage, euthanasia, and so on, in a more determined way.

In Portugal, for instance, the church forcefully opposed the referendum on the liberalisation of abortion (11 February 2007), and owing to the limited voter turnout the referendum was invalidated. The same thing had happened in 2005 in Italy with the referendum on medically assisted fertilisation.[2]

When draft laws on ethically sensitive issues were being proposed in Spain during the second term of José María Aznar's government (2000–4), the reaction from the church in Spain was weak. However, with the successive government of Zapatero and the approval of these laws, the reaction of the Episcopate was much stronger. The Spanish bishops organised an initiative on 30 December 2007 in Madrid in support of the traditional family. An enormous number of people participated in the rally, and the Pope addressed the event live from Rome.

The rally in Madrid was actually a repeat performance of Italy's Family Day, held in Rome on 12 May of the same year. Reading the official documents of the Spanish Episcopate, specifically the 'pastoral instructions' issued on 30 March and 23 November 2006, one understands the extent to which the Italian model, personified by Cardinal Ruini,[3] represented an important reference (Magister 2006). The documents represent a turning point for the Spanish Episcopate. The 23 November instruction is modelled on the speech given by Pope Benedict XVI at the Fourth National Ecclesial Convention in Verona (October 2006). The two documents respectively refer to (1) the doctrinal and moral deviations present in the Spanish Church that impede successfully meeting the challenge of secularisation; (2) the changes that had occurred in Spanish society and politics, appealing to the Catholics to take up their religious and civil responsibilities in effective response.

In sum, the widespread Catholic presence in Italian society, the spatial proximity of the Holy See to the Italian political scene, the strong link between the Vatican and the Italian bishops,[4] ensuring continuity among the universal, national and local churches and, as we will see, resources to mobilise, as well as a particular political structure, make the Italian case a favourable 'laboratory' in which to experiment (and from which to then export) this model of political representation and the public presence of the church.

The failed referendum: strategies for mobilisation and de-mobilisation

On 12 and 13 June 2005, a referendum was held in Italy on the issue of medically assisted fertilisation and stem cells (L.40/2004). In the spring of 2004, the Radicals had presented the request for the referendum to abrogate the existing law. Subsequently, the Organising Committee was formed: the Referendum on Assisted Fertilisation and Freedom of Scientific Research, supported by people from the lay world and from the traditional political left. That summer the DS party and the CGIL union mobilised to collect the 500,000 signatures needed by

30 September for the proposed referendum to appear on the ballot. The aim of the referendum movement was to modify some parts of the law in order to make it less restrictive.

Even though this law was not completely accepted by the church hierarchy, it was nonetheless considered an important law because it safeguarded certain principles concerning the defence of life. First, there was the issue of equalising the mother's life to the life of the embryo. This was an important juridical principle that was necessary to re-open the debate on the abortion law and its legitimacy[5] (which has actually happened). It is easy to imagine how much was at stake in this referendum; it became a sort of vendetta for the Catholic movement after it had lost the 1981 referendum on abortion. However, more than that, the referendum was also an important occasion to affirm the fundamental principles of Ruini's cultural project. The CEI immediately started working towards invalidating the referendum. The church mobilised its resources – above all Catholic associations and the media – and became active in a campaign to de-mobilise the electorate, finally achieving the goal of not meeting the referendum quorum.

The association network

The Catholic universe – comprising a plurality of groups, associations and movements widely spread throughout the country – appeared strongly united on this occasion. The church had sought the active involvement of these associations and their militant supporters, who formed an extensive and widespread network throughout the country. In various ways – including, organisation of public meetings and debates, public and private discussions, and through various media – the message and reasoning of the Catholic world was communicated to society. In addition to the message that arrived from the highest church officials, the invitation to abstain from voting was sent out. The goal was to invalidate the results of the referendum through the lack of a quorum.[6] Mobilisation in order to de-mobilise the electorate was an extremely important component of failing to meet the referendum quorum. A large number of Science and Life Committees were strategically organised for this purpose. They included not just the bigger and traditional Catholic associations but also many smaller religious groups.[7] Paola Binetti – a doctor and member of a bio-ethical committee – was the leader of this network, coordinating a number of initiatives (seminars, meetings, demonstrations, etc.) on the ground. In the 2006 general elections, she was elected as a member of parliament for the centre-left coalition (Daisy Party).

The media

Taking advantage of communication resources and the different kinds of media was a fundamental strategy of the church. On the one hand, religious actors have their own media structure at their disposal (Ceccarini 2001): such as 'new media' (on-line forums, hundreds of websites, blogs, etc.), satellite television and traditional media outlets such as radio broadcasting, daily newspapers (*Avvenire* and

L'Osservatore Romano, respectively the CEI's and the Holy See's organs), a network of 140 diocesan weeklies, press agencies like SIR, widely circulated magazines like *Famiglia Cristiana*, and some niche journals for Catholic elites and intelligentsia. On the other hand, in reference to the media, the higher clergy, Catholic figures (politicians and public personalities) and those referred to by current affairs journalists as the 'faithful atheists'[8] played an important role in the 'lay' media: making statements, releasing interviews or taking part in talk-shows and television programmes as guests or opinion leaders.

Religious actors and Catholic personalities made great use of the media resources at their disposal, promoting the church's point of view in the public sphere. This kind of presence from the 'top', together with the associations' diffuse work from the 'bottom', contributed to transmitting the Catholic message to society. In the end, the referendum movement's arguments passed into the background (Ceccarini 2005: 862; Manconi 2005: 993–6). Only 25.9 per cent of electors voted, the quorum was not reached, and the referendum was invalidated.

Election 2006: a window of opportunity

The centre-left coalition won the general elections held in 2006, and Romano Prodi became prime minister. Three things from this election are particularly interesting for our discussion:

1   the voting behaviour of practising Catholics, which moved towards the centre-right coalition (the House of Liberty led by Berlusconi);
2   the distribution of seats in parliament, which revealed concrete problems in the Senate chamber for the majority;
3   a transverse presence in both political coalitions, majority and opposition, of Catholic MPs.

These elements contributed to putting the centre-left government in a weak position. This meant that windows were opened in the political opportunity structure for the lobbying action of religious actors.

Voters and the political offering

In recent years the public debate has revolved around ethical issues. These issues, among others, also characterised the 2006 electoral campaign (Segatti 2006a). Voting behaviour analysis shows that a higher percentage of practising Catholics voted for the centre-right coalition compared to the previous election. This same trend repeated itself in the 2008 elections (Ceccarini 2008).

It is likely that the presence of radical–libertarian parties in the centre-left coalition intimidated some moderate practising Catholics with respect to economic and ethical issues (Segatti 2006b). The electoral campaign was particularly heated on biopolitics issues, and a sort of continuity between the church and the centre-right coalition was established in the public debate. In fact, the

Table 9.3 In your opinion, the Church today is closer ... (percentage values)

...to the centre-right/to Casa delle Libertà (House of Liberty)	26.4
...to the centre-left/to L'Unione	4.1
...to neither of the two sides: the church is outside of the political debate	37.1
...depends on the issues in question	10.5
Doesn't know/no response	21.9
Total	100
N	*1445*

Source: Demos-Eurisko for *La Repubblica*, 19–20 February/12–13 March 2007 (*N* = 1,445).

Catholic Church was seen by public opinion as being much closer to the centre-right than the centre-left (Table 9.3).

A weak and unstable majority

The social and political cleavage mentioned above could also be seen at the institutional level (Diamanti 2007). The situations of the majority in the two parliamentary chambers were quite different (Italy uses a perfect bicameral system). The distribution of seats produced a stable majority in the Chamber of Deputies, but in the Senate the government coalition had just two seats more than the opposition. This led to a condition of ungovernability. The decisional process was continually uncertain, especially on issues concerning biopolitics, where Catholic senators were present in both coalitions.

A bipartisan and influential minority

The demise of the DC and the fragmentation of Catholic political representation led to the fragmentation of Catholics engaged in politics. This modality of political presence for the church has become very important and efficient over time. Catholics involved in politics, in both coalitions, are an *influential minority* (Diamanti and Ceccarini 2007). They have gained an important role in the public debate, in particular some Catholic figures who take an 'intransigent' position and are strongly oriented towards defending moral values in the political process. The current affairs press has termed them *teodem* (to address certain MPs of the centre-left) and *teocon* (for those of the centre-right). These two parliamentarian components have been united when the political debate takes on ethical issues, emerging as a sort of transverse axis. This situation, in other terms, represents a window of opportunity for the church to protect its interests.

The draft law on de facto couples and the parliamentary quagmire

The civil union: from the electoral programme to the Senate seats

The electoral programme of the centre-left coalition in 2006 included the juridical recognition of certain rights for de facto couples, the term used to refer to committed couples who were not married. This issue soon became a delicate topic and a political battleground. The church took part in the debate, defending the concept of the traditional family. This reaction was due, first and foremost, to the fact that gender was not a discriminating element in the legitimisation of de facto couples. For this reason the issue was seen as a Trojan horse from the Catholic perspective: homosexual marriage would be legitimised, which would then also extend to these couples the legal right to adopt children.

Legitimisation of de facto couples actually is not a new issue, but during the 2006 electoral campaign this policy – known as PACS (Patto Civile di Solidarietà; Civil Solidarity Pact) – was widely discussed among electoral competitors. Once the centre-left coalition was in office, two ministers – Rosy Bindi (minister for family policies) and Barbara Pollastrini (minister for equal opportunities), the first a Catholic and the second a secular leftist – proposed a draft law named DICO (Diritti e doveri dei conviventi – Cohabitants' rights and obligations).

It is manifest that these two figures were chosen not just for their institutional roles, but also for the associated mediation between – in electoral terms – the two main political cultures which are present in the centre-left coalition: reformist left and democratic Catholic traditions. There were, in any case, those who made objections to the draft law presented, from leaders of the radical left to Catholics leaders (e.g. ex-DC politicians like Clemente Mastella, minister of justice from 2006 to 2008, but also *teodem* MPs).

Considering the framework described in the first part of this chapter, it becomes easy to understand that it would be very difficult for this specific law to be approved in the parliament, and in particular in the Senate chamber.

In sum, from the brief reconstruction outlined above, it clearly emerges that the idea of the *influential minority* is an important factor in the Italian political scenario. The division *between* the coalitions and especially *within* the government alliance is particularly crucial, and in the meantime the cross-party presence of Catholic MPs makes the decisional process about ethical issues uncertain.

The church, politics and the 'binding' pastoral note

We have seen so far that the lobbying action of the church has passed through resource mobilisation – above all through associations and the media – while also taking advantage of the open socio-political opportunity windows. By means of this strategy, religious actors intervene in the political scenario and in the public debate, including important Catholic figures such as the Pope, higher clergymen like the CEI president or general secretary, and well-known bishops or cardinals. The mobilisation of Catholic groups or movements on the ground emerges as a complementary action in a multi-pronged lobbying strategy.

In 2007, public demonstrations took place, for example, in favour of DICO,[9] in which some government ministers physically participated (including the above-mentioned Barbara Pollastrini, minister for equal opportunities, who was on the stage). Others took part through the media, making statements broadcast on mega-screens set up at the rally site, including Rosy Bindi, minister for family policies). Other ministers, including Clemente Mastella (minister of Justice), did not participate at all, adopting a polemical stance and skipping the march. It was clear that the confrontation on this issue had become heated among different members of the majority. The debate on this issue brought about a confrontation not only between the centre-right and centre-left, but also within the majority government between the Catholic and lay constituencies.

On the other side, Catholic actors and those in the opposition prepared counter-demonstrations, like Family Day.[10] Minister Mastella and certain majority MPs announced that they would instead participate in this public march, and proceeded to do so. It must be taken into consideration that such initiatives received wide media coverage and became part of the public debate, following a sort of circular logic. Furthermore, such events are also good occasions for the actors involved to demonstrate their political identities.

The strategy followed by the church seems to have been particularly successful. The church entered into the conflictive lines which characterise the Italian political system, taking advantage of the open windows of opportunity mentioned above. Ethical questions seemed to divide primarily the centre-left from the centre-right coalitions, but secondarily (though not less importantly) the cleavage also ran inside the centre-left, within the different political cultures that composed the unstable alliance.

An important move made by the CEI was the pastoral note, 'binding' for Catholic MPs, as it was defined by the church hierarchies. This document was discussed on 26 March 2007 at the CEI Permanent Commission.[11] It was an explicit message to Catholics involved in politics to defend 'non-negotiable' moral values, such as life and the family. The document was written by the Italian bishops taking into strict consideration what the Pope, just some days earlier (13 March), had said about these values in the Apostolic Exhortation entitled *Sacramentum Caritatis*. Paragraph 83 of this document states

> Here it is important to consider what the Synod Fathers described as *eucharistic consistency*, a quality which our lives are objectively called to embody. Worship pleasing to God can never be a purely private matter, without consequences for our relationships with others: it demands a public witness to our faith. Evidently, this is true for all the baptized, yet it is especially incumbent upon those who, by virtue of their social or political position, must make decisions regarding fundamental values, such as respect for human life, its defence from conception to natural death, the family built

upon marriage between a man and a woman, the freedom to educate one's children and the promotion of the common good in all its forms. These values are not negotiable. Consequently, Catholic politicians and legislators, conscious of their grave responsibility before society, must feel particularly bound, on the basis of a properly formed conscience, to introduce and support laws inspired by values grounded in human nature. There is an objective connection here with the Eucharist. Bishops are bound to reaffirm constantly these values as part of their responsibility to the flock entrusted to them.

(Post-Synodal exhortation *Sacramentum Caritatis* of Pope Benedict XVI)

This exhortation of the Vatican was a very important document, since it was widely interpreted as a pontificate programme, in which the Pope reminded Catholic MPs in particular of their responsibility to propose and to vote in favour of certain policies. This document, together with the CEI's pastoral 'binding' note, gave the idea of a unitary and consistent communication strategy and plan enacted by these two important religious actors. It also directly told Catholic MPs to vote against the DICO legitimating project.

The church strategy went beyond the action of institutional pressure on decisional processes, places and actors, which was an 'invisible' activity. The strategy also extended to the local dimension, into communities and the parish churches. These actions were per se very important in spreading the message, but especially so when they were able to take advantage of wide media coverage.

Religion, public opinion and the DICO draft law

At this point in our discussion, it would be useful to pose and answer the following question: What was the response of public opinion to this continued public presence of the church and its lobbying action?

The public stance of the church on biopolitics issues, and more specifically its mobilisation against the DICO, produced interesting changes in attitudes and in public opinion, as demonstrated by recent longitudinal surveys.[12] In particular, the trend of attitudes regarding the hypothesis of legitimisation of de facto couples reflected this change, as Figure 9.3 shows.

The Demos-Eurisko opinion poll, February–March 2007, showed that half of Italians were in favour of the DICO law: that is, in favour of the legitimisation of de facto couples. But this position scored higher during the period October 2004 to June 2006, about 60 per cent, or about 10 per cent more than the most recent percentage (Figure 9.3).

This trend could probably be explained by the heated public and political debate on these kinds of issues, in which religious actors have recently played a central role. Consequently, the draft law may have come to be seen by many voters as more of a threat to a traditional family institution – the family – than many considered it to be in the recent past. Among practising Catholics, one out

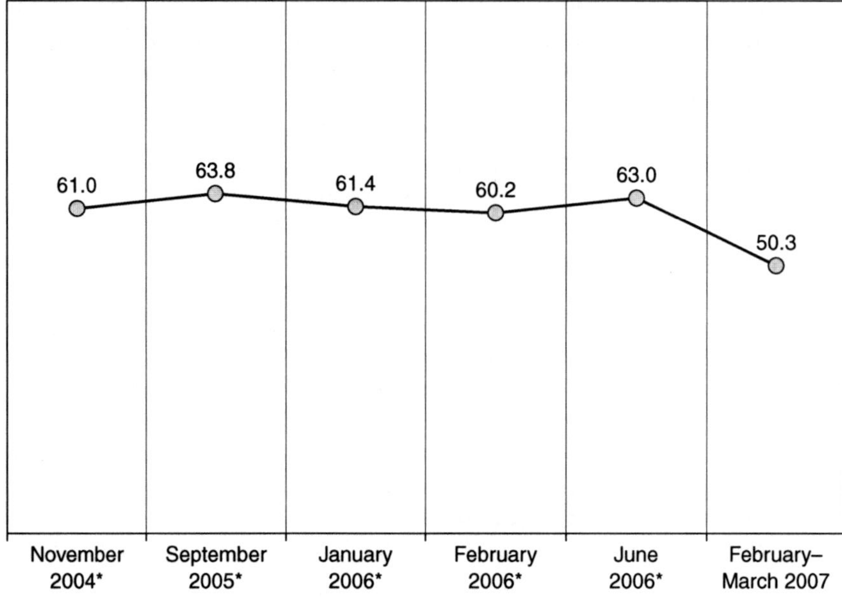

Figure 9.3 The centre-left government has recently proposed a law on DICO, that is regarding de facto couples who live together stably outside of marriage. The law provides for extending the rights that married couples enjoy to these couples. Would you say you were in favour of or opposed to a law of this type? (percentage values of those who responded "in favour") (sources: Demos-Eurisko for *La Repubblica*, 2–4 November, 2004 ($N = 1{,}000$); Demos-Eurisko for *La Repubblica*, 13–15 September, 2005 ($N = 1{,}542$); Demos-Eurisko for *La Repubblica*, 16–18 Juanuary 2006 ($N = 1{,}508$); Demos-Eurisko for *La Repubblica*, 14–15 February 2006 ($N = 1{,}556$); LaPolis, *Post-electoral survey*, 15–21 June 2006 ($N = 1{,}200$); Demos-Eurisko for *La Repubblica*, 19–20 February/12–13 March 2007 ($N = 1{,}445$)).

Note
* For the findings prior to February–March 2007, a different question was used: '*More and more couples decide not to marry and to live together stably outside of marriage. For some time law proposals have been discussed to extend to these couples the same rights that married couples enjoy. Would you be in favour or opposed to a law of this type?*'

of three (33 per cent) reported to be in favour of the policy, while among non-practising citizens the percentage was nearly double (60 per cent).

This indicates that when religious attitudes and political orientation combine, opinions are likely to become more radical, and it is possible to observe significant differences between the two electorates (see Table 9.4).

The politicisation effect which characterised this issue was quite evident: Over two-thirds (68 per cent) of practising Catholics among centre-left voters reported to be in favour of DICO, while less than a quarter (23 per cent) of practising Catholics who vote centre-right alignment claimed to support the DICO

Table 9.4 The orientation of those in favour of the DICO law among the different seg-
　　　　　ments of voters

Centre-left voters	81.3
Practising Catholics centre-left voters	67.9
Non-practising	60.0
Overall population	50.3
Centre-right voters	39.0
Practising Catholic voters	32.8
Practising Catholic centre-right voters	22.9

Source: Demos-Eurisko for *La Repubblica*, 19–20 February/12–13 March 2007 ($N = 1,445$).

law. In other words, at the same level of religious involvement, political orientation contributed to radicalising opinion on the DICO issue.

The trend noted above, which highlights a considerable reduction in public
favour towards the legitimisation of de facto couples, is consistent with other
attitudes detected by the Demos-Eurisko survey. In fact it is possible to see, in
terms of social–moral acceptability, that certain behaviours or personal choices
– concerning family, sexuality, life, and so on – are less tolerated socially compared to the past, as shown in Figure 9.4.

As might have been predicted, there was a sharp difference in the attitudes
demonstrated by practising Catholics and non-practising citizens in Italy. This
reflected perspectives that religious actors had strongly advanced publicly in
recent years, which were explicitly addressed to the 'defence of life' and in
defence of moral values and the traditional family, certain kinds of sexuality
only, and so on.

It is interesting to note that the concept of family is for the most part seen by
Italians as the union between a man and a woman, by means of a marriage ceremony – regardless of whether the ceremony is religious or civil (56 per cent, as
demonstrated in Figure 9.5, 30.1 per cent plus 25.9 per cent). Support for the
role of a formal ritual, civil or religious, increased by 8 per cent in three years,
and the idea that 'family equals cohabitation' slightly declined (–3 per cent), as
shown in Figure 9.5.

It must also be said that what we have sought to illustrate above are perceptions only. However, it is widely believed that the traditional family in Italy is
facing a deep crisis, and new kinds of families and young couples who live
together without getting married are increasing in numbers. But the opinion
climate we have attempted to delineate is relevant to our discussion. In fact, it
reflects the ethical admonishment issued by the church after a phase in which religious actors were very active publicly. In sum, it appears that Italians now pay
more attention to the church's moral recommendations as compared to the past,
although this consideration is not actually as linear and direct as it first seems.

In fact, our data do not offer evidence in favour of increasing religious awareness among Italians. Some indicators collected in the same survey reveal that the

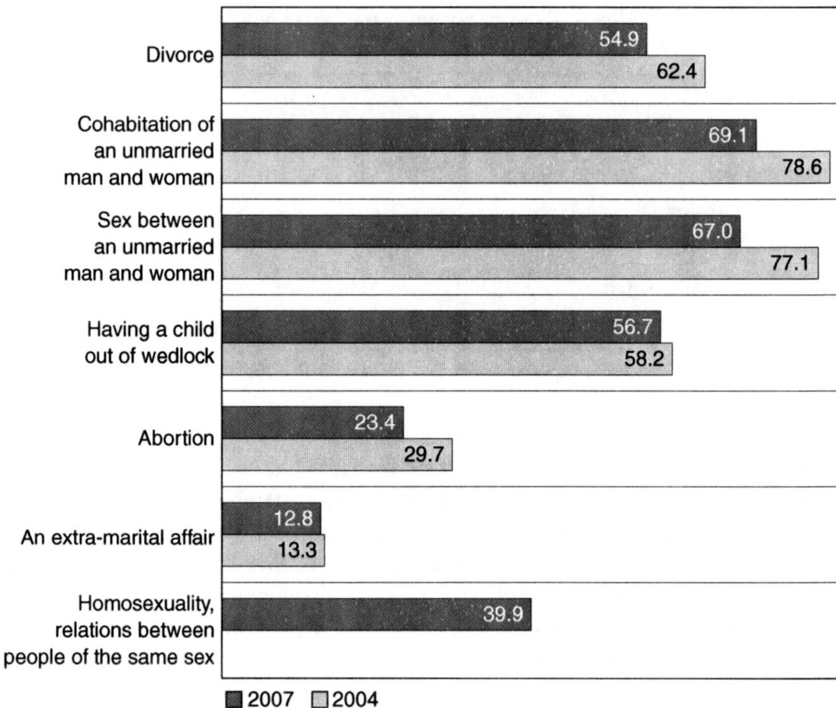

Figure 9.4 Now I will read you a series of behaviours. According to your moral point of view, are they acceptable or wrong? (data by percentage of those who feel that the behaviour proposed is acceptable) (sources Demos-Eurisko for *La Repubblica*, 2–4 November 2004 (*N* = 1,000); Demos-Eurisko for *La Repubblica*, 19–20 February/12–13 March 2007 (*N* = 1,445)).

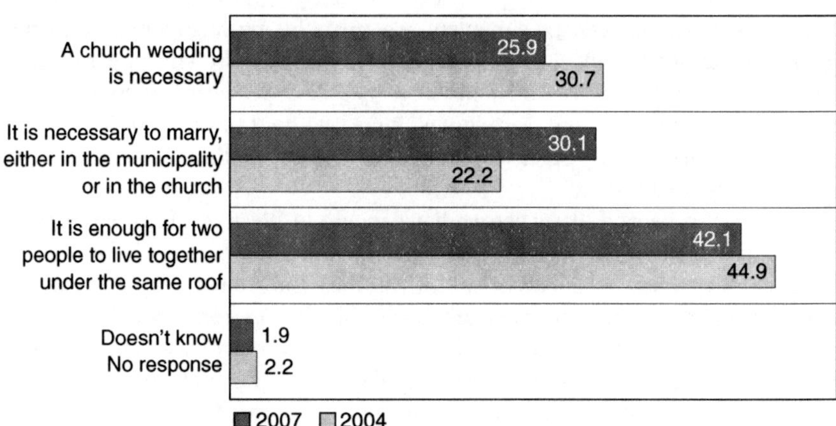

Figure 9.5 Without considering what the law says, what does being a family mean for you? To be a family ... (percentage values) (sources: Demos-Eurisko for *La Repubblica*, 2–4 November 2004 (*N* = 1,000); Demos-Eurisko for *La Repubblica*, 19–20 February/12–13 March 2007 (*N* = 1,445)).

percentage of Italians who say that religion occupies a *fundamental* or *important* place in their life perspective decreased from 62 per cent to 55 per cent during 2003–7 (Table 9.5). In the meantime, the church's exhortation concerning moral issues and people's life behaviour is today considered 'very important to follow' at the same level as in the past: 25 per cent. Moreover, most Italians interviewed say that the church's recommendations are important but that people should behave according to their own consciences (57 per cent; Table 9.6). This perspective is also shared by nearly half (49 per cent) of regularly practising Catholics. These data suggest that there is ample space for the *privatisation* of the church's exhortations, which leads to a lifestyle that is autonomous and individualised in respect to religious rules.

Table 9.5 What position does religion occupy in your life?

	2007	*2003*
Fundamental	19.6	23.3
Important	35.4	38.4
Relatively important	28.9	22.8
Not very important	9.3	10.2
Completely irrelevant	6.5	4.5
Not indicated	0.3	0.8
Total	100	100

Sources: Demos-Eurisko for *La Repubblica*, 17–19 June 2003 (*N* = 1,000); Demos-Eurisko for *La Repubblica*, 19–20 February/12–13 March 2007 (*N* = 1,445).

Table 9.6 How do you consider the teaching of the church in respect to people's morality and life (values, family, sexuality)?

	2007	*2003*
Very important, should be followed	24.6	24.7
Useful, but each person should behave according to his/her conscience	56.8	57.8
Indifferent	3.9	4.6
Improper, the Church should concern itself with other things, above all faith	10.9	6.6
Negatively, should never be followed	2.7	1.5
Doesn't know, no response	1.0	4.7
Total	100	100

Source: Demos-Eurisko for *La Repubblica*, 17–19 June 2003 (*N* = 1,000); Demos-Eurisko for *La Repubblica*, 19–20 February/12–13 March 2007 (*N* = 1,445).

In conclusion, what emerges is a sort of contradiction at the social level: on one hand, there is increasing attention to morality that is consistent with the recommendations of the church. On the other hand, religious attitudes are not more widespread now in comparison to the past and the attention paid to church exhortations is also at the same level as formerly. This framework supports and strengthens the idea that public opinion on biopolitics and ethical issues is established first on political grounds and in the current public debate, and only reflects religious attitudes on a secondary level.

Ethical or political bipolarism?

The social orientations illustrated above probably depend to a significant extent on the debates that have taken place in the public sphere, and particularly on the heated tones of political confrontations. In our interpretation, the political cleavage is more important than the ethical one. In other words, political actors have appropriated moral value topics and inserted these issues into the political debate (Fiorina 2005), in order to delineate their identities during this current confused phase. The subject of biopolitics is used to build political alliances and create difficulties for antagonistic political counterparts (between and within the coalitions) with the aim of political positioning in the context of public opinion and in the political market (see also Ricolfi 2001; Quagliariello 2006).

Ethical bipolarism, as the expression of divergent value systems, ends up intertwining political meanings (Bobba 2007). This interweaving becomes particularly significant for the political actors who use it to distinguish themselves in the age of the 'permanent campaign'. This is particularly true for those issues that are deeply politicised, like the PACS/DICO issue. In fact, in the period examined in this chapter, 2004–7, social orientation is less 'explained' by political variables than by religious ones for other ethical issues, such as abortion or euthanasia.

The church's attempts to pressurise politicians are not widely accepted among ordinary Italians. Most of those interviewed (61 per cent) do not agree with the church's attempts to encourage Catholics MPs to vote against the de facto couple law. This means that they do not approve of the pastoral 'binding' note. This position is also widespread among practising Catholics: 44 per cent. Among occasional church-goers this opinion is held by 62 per cent, and unsurprisingly it is even higher among non-practising voters (73 per cent). Among practising Catholics, 61 per cent of centre-left voters do not agree with the CEI's pastoral 'binding' note, and on the other side, 35 per cent of practising centre-right voters also do not agree (81 per cent of all centre-left voters; 53 per cent of all centre-right voters). Overall, it is *political inclination* that seems to explain these orientations.

This gap is wider if practising Catholics are taken into consideration. A large portion of Italian voters seems to have a clear idea of the line that separates religion and politics. In other words, they appear to have a well-defined idea of laity, defending the autonomy of the MPs' task from the pressure of the church and its

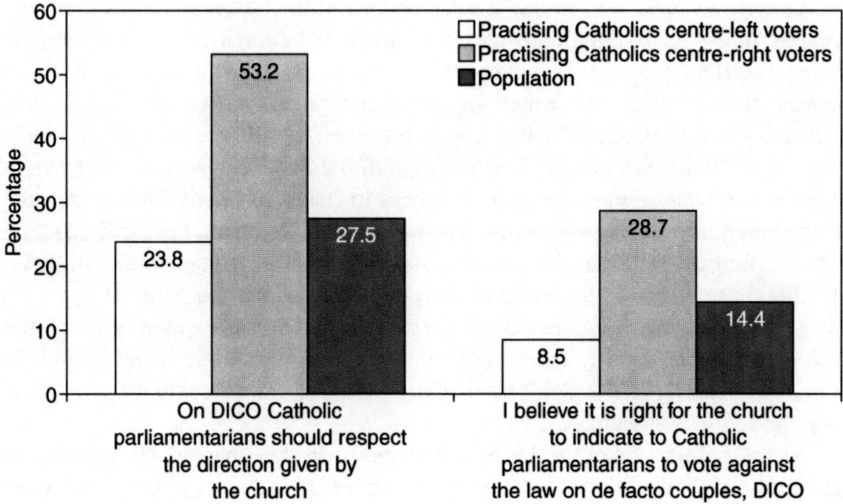

Figure. 9.6 The Church, Catholic parliamentarians and politics according to practising centre-right and centre-left voters (percentage values) (source: Demos-Eurisko for *La Repubblica*, 19–20 February/12–13 March 2007 (*N* = 1,445)).

exhortations (Figure 9.6), even though they recognise the right of the church to intervene in the public sphere.

In conclusion, with particular regard to the DICO question, the Catholic clergy's action finds favour in only one section of political society – that is, among centre-right party leaders. At the level of society, however, these actions are not widely welcomed. A lay orientation seems to be widespread among citizens in general and also among practising Catholics, which underscores first and foremost the autonomy of parliamentarians.

Conclusion

We have outlined above some events that demonstrate the presence of a political conflict between religious and secular political actors, on issues regarding ethical questions. Politics and religion take shape as a sort of interweaving which also involves an important theme for democracy: the laicisation or secularisation of the state.

In fact, this topic has been publicly addressed very often, in particular in the political debate. The strident confrontation among the various party actors involved in these topics is also a way to define their political identities, in a phase where traditional left–right secular ideologies are weaker than in the past.

Obviously, Catholic voters also play a role, as they represent an important segment of the electorate despite the fact that regularly practising Catholics are actually a minority of Italian citizens. The number of non-practising or 'secular

Catholics' is much larger. Indeed, in Italy an ethno-cultural interpretation of religiosity is widespread among a large portion of the citizens, who exhibit their relationship with religion and the teachings of the church in a privatised (and secularised) manner. But it is interesting to note how the politicisation of certain issues, such as those of a sensitive ethical nature, has enlivened recent public debates. Cleavages opened which seem, however, to reflect more citizens' ideological, not religious, nature. This is a sign of the relatively weak importance of faith in political orientations and in respect to issues of public interest in Italy. The church, mobilising opportune resources (communication/the media, associations, political subjects, the Catholic identity of citizens), succeeded in maintaining these issues at the centre of the public debate and the political dynamic. Together with other religious actors, the church assumed an explicit, even central role in the public sphere. The fact that the church enjoys broad social consideration, even among subjects not particularly involved from a religious viewpoint, was certainly an advantage.

At the political level, in the period analysed in this chapter, the church and the centre-right coalition seemed to share a bond on the basis of their respective (and different) interests. An interesting trend in this regard is the shift towards the centre-right coalition of the practising Catholic electorate's vote over the course of the 2006 electoral campaign, which continued in the 2008 elections.

The church itself took part in the public debates and in the media frequently and directly, utilising different outlets and resources. It also took advantage of the context, in particular, of the (open) windows of opportunity in the Italian political situation. The church took steps to mobilise multiple resources on the ground that were essential to the defence of its interests, adopting a lobby strategy.

As a result, the church entered into the political and therefore democratic process, thus provoking harsh criticism by those who consider the secular nature of the state under threat.

This scenario makes the Italian case a sort of ideal 'laboratory' where the church can experiment its strategy against the privatisation of religion, and also against laicism and rationalism, which have touched Western societies in late modernity, as has been stressed by the highest members of the clergy.

In this perspective Italy has become a sort of 'export model' in order to stimulate other national Catholic churches, with the basic aim of reinforcing Western societies' Christian values. However, this stance goes beyond the Catholic milieu, enjoying support among (secular) centre-right leaders and intellectuals, and is intertwined with the continuing political debate on the preamble of the European Constitution, concerning the recognition of Europe's 'Christian roots' (see Madeley's chapter in this collection).

Notes

1 The Margherita and the Democratici di Sinistra (Ds), or Democrats of the Left, joined together in October 2007 to form the Partito Democratico (Democratic Party).

2 On this argument see next section.
3 Under Wojtyla, Cardinal Ruini was the Pope's Vicar for the Diocese of Rome, a position he still holds under Ratzinger.
4 In Italy there are 222 bishops who lead the same number of dioceses.
5 The law on abortion was approved in 1978 and in 1981 a referendum to restrict the terms of this law was held, but the referendum question proposed by the Catholic life movement was rejected by the majority of the Italian voters (68 per cent).
6 The outcome of an abrogative referendum is valid only if at least 50 per cent plus one of the electorate vote.
7 Thirty associations were charter members of this committee: Azione Cattolica, Forum delle Associazioni Familiari, Movimento per la Vita, Rinnovamento dello Spirito, Comunione e Liberazione, Compagnia delle Opere, Cammino Neocatecumenale, Focolari, Comunita' di Sant'Egidio, Centro Sportivo Italiano, Farmacisti Cattolici, Federazione Mondiale Associazioni Medici Cattolici, Acli, Agesci, Cisl, Coldiretti, Cif, Fuci, Movimento Cristiani Lavoratori, Meic, Misericordie, Movimento dei Genitori Cattolici, Confederazione Italiana Centri Regolazione Naturale Fertilita', ARIS (Istituti socio-sanitari), Forum Nazionale Associazioni Trapiantati, Associazione Talassemici della Liguria, Confederazione Italiana Consultori Familiari di Ispirazione Cristiana, Coordinamento delle Associazioni per la Comunicazione (CoPerCom), Associazione Cattolica Operatori Sanitari (ACOS), Associazione Medici Cattolici Italiani.
8 'Faithful atheists' are defined as those lay public figures who do not have a tradition of social or political involvement in the Catholic arena – because they are ex-communists, liberals, conservatives, etc. – but who distinguish themselves for their public support of positions very close to church principles, in particular those linked to the Christian roots of European cultural identity as well as biopolitics issues.
9 This demonstration, which could be called 'DICO Day', was held on 10 March 2007 in Rome.
10 This demonstration, Family Day, was held on 12 May 2007 in Rome.
11 The CEI Permanent Commission, which has about thirty members, is the governing leadership of the CEI and is composed of the president, vice-presidents, secretary, regional president and president of the commissions. It meets three times a year, at the beginning of autumn, winter and summer. In the spring the general assembly of the CEI meets.
12 Cf. the dossier Demos-Eurisko issued in the newspaper *La Repubblica*, 18 March 2007. Articles written by Ilvo Diamanti, Fabio Bordignon and Luigi Ceccarini are available at www.demos.it/2007/pdf/eurisko_03_2007.pdf

Bibliography

Allum, P. (1984) 'La DC vicentina nel secondo dopoguerra. Appunti per una ricostruzione', *Strumenti*, 3–4, pp. 19–35.

Bobba, L. (2007) *Il posto dei cattolici*, Torino: Einaudi.

Brunelli, G. (1995) 'La scommessa perduta sul partito cattolico', *il Mulino*, 2, pp. 237–43.

Cappello, F. S. and Diamanti, I. (1995) 'Appartenenza religiosa, secolarizzazione, preferenze politiche', in A. Parisi and H. Schadee (eds), *Sulla soglia del cambiamento*, Bologna: il Mulino, pp. 139–84.

Cartocci, R. (2002) 'Voto, valori e religione', in M. Caciagli and P. Corbetta (eds), *Le ragioni dell'elettore*, Bologna: il Mulino, pp. 165–201.

Casanova, J. (1994) *Public Religion in the Modern World*, Chicago: University of Chicago Press.

Ceccarini, L. (2001) *Le voci di dio. Stampa cattolica e politica in Italia*, Naples: L'ancora del mediterraneo.

Ceccarini, L. (2005) 'Fedeli, secolarizzati, irregolari. I cattolici italiani', *il Mulino*, 5: 852–62.

Ceccarini. L. (2008) 'La fine della questione cattolica?', in Itanes (Italian National Elections Studies) (ed.) *Il ritorno di Berlusconi. Vincitori e vinti nelle elezioni del 2008*, Bologna: il Mulino, pp. 123–35.

Cesareo, V., Cipriani, R., Garelli, F., Lanzetti, C. and Rovati, G. (1995) *La religiosità in Italia*, Milan: Mondadori.

Corbetta, P. and Parisi, A. (ed.) (1997) *A domanda risponde*, Bologna: il Mulino.

Diamanti, I. (1997) 'Identità cattolica e comportamento di voto. L'unità e la fedeltà non sono più una virtù', in P. Corbetta and A. Parisi (eds), *A domanda risponde*, Bologna: il Mulino.

Diamanti, I. (2007) 'The Italian Centre-Right and Centre-Left: Between Parties and "the Party"', *West European Politics*, 30, pp. 733–62.

Diamanti, I. and Ceccarini, L. (2007) 'Catholics and Politics after the Christian Democrats: The Influential Minority', *Journal of Modern Italian Studies*, 1, pp. 37–59.

Diamanti, I. and Riccamboni, G. (1992) *La parabola del voto bianco*, Vicenza: Neri Pozza.

Fiorina, M. (2005) *Culture War? The Myth of a Polarized America*, New York: Pearson Longman.

Franco, M. (2000) *I voti del cielo*, Milan: Baldini e Castoldi.

Galli, G. (ed.) (1968) *Il comportamento elettorale in Italia*, Bologna: il Mulino.

Galli, G. (1993) *Mezzo secolo di Dc: 1943–1993. Da De Gasperi a Mario Segni*, Milan: Rizzoli.

Garelli, F. (1991) *Religione e Chiesa in Italia*, Bologna: il Mulino.

Garelli, F. (1996) *Forza della religione e debolezza della fede*, Bologna: il Mulino.

Garelli, F. (2006) *L'Italia cattolica nell'epoca del pluralismo*, Bologna: il Mulino.

Garelli, F. (2007) 'The Public relevance of the Church and Catholicism in Italy', *Journal of Modern Italian Studies*, 1, pp. 8–36.

Itanes (Italian National Elections Studies) (ed.) (2006) *Dov'è la vittoria? Il voto del 2006 raccontato dagli italiani*, Bologna: il Mulino.

Itanes (Italian National Elections Studies) (ed.) (2008) *Il ritorno di Berlusconi. Vincitori e vinti nelle elezioni del 2008*, Bologna: il Mulino.

Kalyvas, S. (1996) 'La formazione dei partiti confessionali in Europa', *Rivista Italiana di Scienza Politica*, 2, pp. 317–63.

Magister, S. (2001) *Chiesa extraparlamentare*, Naples: L'ancora del mediterraneo.

Magister, S. (2006) 'The Church in Spain, but It's Not Zapatero's Fault', 28 July; available at http://chiesa.espresso.repubblica.it/articolo/74326?eng=y

Magister, S. (2007) 'The Italian Church Exports Its Model to Spain', 23 February; available at http://chiesa.espresso.repubblica.it/articolo/122761?&eng=y

Manconi, L. (2005) 'Referendum e conflitti morali. Che vinca il migliore', *il Mulino*, 5, pp. 993–6.

Mannheimer, R. and Sani, G. (1987) *Il mercato elettorale*, Bologna: il Mulino.

Melloni, A. (2007) 'The Politics of the "Church" in the Italy of Pope Wojtyla', *Journal of Modern Italian Studies*, 1, pp. 60–85.

Milani, L. (1965) *L'obbedienza non è più una virtù*, Florence: Libreria editrice fiorentina.

Pace, E. (1995) *L'unità dei cattolici in Italia*, Milan: Guerini e Associati.

Pace, E. (2007) 'A Peculiar Pluralism', *Journal of Modern Italian Studies* 1, pp. 86–100.

Parisi, A. (ed.) (1979) *Democristiani*, Quaderni dell'Istituto Cattaneo, Bologna: il Mulino.

Parisi, A. and Schadee, H. (eds) (1995) *Sulla soglia del cambiamento*, Bologna: il Mulino.

Pope Benedict XVI, address to the participants of the Fourth National Ecclesial Convention, Verona (19 October 2006); available at www.vatican.va/holy_father/benedict_xvi/speeches/2006/october/documents/hf_ben-xvi_spe_20061019_convegno-verona_en.html

Pope Benedict XVI, Post-Synodal exhortation *Sacramentum Caritatis* (13 March 2007); available at www.vatican.va/holy_father/benedict_xvi/apost_exhortations/documents/hf_ben-xvi_exh_20070222_sacramentum-caritatis_en.html

Quagliariello, G. (2006) *Cattolici, pacifisti, teocon. Chiesa e politica in Italia dopo la caduta del muro*, Milan: Mondadori.

Ricolfi, L. (2001) *Frattura etica, Saggio sulle basi etiche dei poli elettorali*, Turin: Trauben.

Scoppola, P. (1997) *La repubblica dei partiti*, Bologna: il Mulino.

Scoppola, P. (2006) *La democrazia dei cristiani*, Bari: Laterza.

Segatti, P. (2006a) 'Cattolici e voto', in R. Mannheimer and P. Natale (eds), *L'Italia a metà*, Milan: Cairo Editore, pp. 86–96.

Segatti, P. (2006b) 'I cattolici al voto, tra valori e politiche dei valori', in Itanes (Italian National Elections Studies) (ed.) *Dov'è la vittoria? Il voto del 2006 raccontato dagli italiani*, Bologna: il Mulino, pp. 109–26.

Segatti, P. and Vezzoni, C. (2008) 'Religion and Politics in Italian Electoral Choice. Which Comes First in the New Century Electoral Divisions?' *Polena: Political and Electoral Navigations*, 2, pp. 9–28.

10 Morality politics in a Catholic democracy

A hard road towards liberalisation of gay rights in Poland

Anja Hennig

Introduction

In Western democracies during the last two decades, the quest to legalise same-sex partnerships has led to a new wave of liberalisation (Kollman 2007). The arguments promoted by the European Union (EU)[1] in favour of a partnership-law are based on the claim to guarantee non-discrimination and human rights as fundamental norms of liberal democracies. According to recent teaching of the Catholic Church, however, legalising same-sex partnerships would fundamentally undermine divine law and lead to the irrevocable decay of desirable cultural values (Ratzinger and Amato 2003). What does this imply for the outcome of such a sensitive policy issue in the Catholic democracies of contemporary Europe?

Recent studies reveal that in many liberal democracies, Catholicism still impacts to a certain extent on gender-related policy outcomes (Castles 1994). However, if we look at the abortion law or the legal status of same-sex partnerships, the picture of the Catholic landscape in Europe is not homogeneous. For example, in Spain in 2005, the newly inaugurated left-wing government implemented one of the most liberal laws allowing homosexual marriage and conjunctional adoption of children – against the protests of the Catholic Church (Twiston Davies 2005). In Poland and Italy, on the other hand, there was in late 2008 still no status regulation for homosexual couples, with the Catholic Church in both countries strongly opposed to any moves towards legalisation.

Poland is considered to be the Catholic 'under-secularised exception' in contemporary 'over-secularised Europe' (Casanova 2003). Poland has one of the highest church-going rates in Europe, with as many as 95 per cent of Poles declaring themselves to be Catholic. Historically, in addition, the cultural impact of Catholicism and the political role of the Catholic Church have always been strongly aligned with Polish national identity and nationalism (Bruce 2003). With the beginning of fundamental political change after 1989, as in most post-communist countries, there was open competition between church and state for political control in Poland, in particular over morality policy issues such as abortion, marriage and divorce (Teitel 1999).

A closer look indicates, however, that the high church-going rate in Poland has to be seen alongside a low public acceptance of interference in moral questions or political engagement by the Catholic Church (Grabowska 2004). At the same time, pluralisation of lifestyles in the country has become a matter of fact. In recent years, Polish gay and lesbian as well as feminist interest groups have been claiming equal rights with increasing fervour, including the legalisation of same-sex partnerships. At the societal level, their public appearance has helped slightly to improve the negative public view of homosexuals. However, the recent attempt to implement a same-sex partnership law failed. How can we explain that?

Studies in recent years emphasise the extent to which the Catholic Church has sought new political power in post-communist Poland. The paradigmatic example is the restrictive abortion law, the outcome of bargaining between representatives from the government and Episcopate. On the other hand, the Polish Catholic Church and many Catholic intellectuals embody the religious force that supported the anti-communist movement and helped pave the way for democracy (Casanova 1994).[2] This twofold political role of the Polish Catholic Church as both being supportive towards democratisation and restrictive towards liberalisation seems contradictory.

There is, however, no contradiction if we consider that moral issues make a difference to such outcomes (Mooney 2001; Gutmann and Thompson 1997). This is a domain where religions are still seeking political influence, even if it implies violating the norms of liberal democracies. It would, however, be misleading to focus solely on the agency of the Catholic Church. Analysis of contemporary moral conflicts in Poland rather demonstrates that various religious and political actors concur or co-operate in the course of the decision-making processes over morally sensitive policies.

With reference to the overarching issue of this section of the book, my basic assumption is that the impact of religion on democratisation in terms of liberalising morality policy issues depends not only on the strength of the Catholic Church. It also depends to a great extent on how political and religious actors mutually behave, and under which political conditions efforts towards liberalisation are made. With regard to the conflict about legalising same-sex partnerships, the key question of this chapter is: to what extent did specific patterns of the interaction of religion and politics constrain the success of implementing gay rights in contemporary Poland?

Recognising that religion continues to have a public dimension (Casanova 1994: 66), I propose an analysis of three different levels as the loci where religion and politics interact: the *institutional level*, the *level of behaviour* and the level of *political and religious actors' ideology* (Heclo 2001: 4–7). Their interaction is analysed in three contexts: the state, political society and civil society (Casanova 2008). I identify this particular conflict as a *morality policy*, introduced and discussed in the first part of the chapter. The purpose is to distinguish a particular value-based public policy and its process from other policy fields (Mooney 2001; Smith and Tatalovich 2003).

After that, I discuss from a gender perspective why it is so difficult for the Catholic Church to accept legalisation of homosexual partnerships as a democratic right. This is followed by an empirical study focused on the impact of religion and politics on the abovementioned policy process in Poland. I conclude by weighing up the factors and making a judgement on the hypotheses discussed here.

Implementing gay rights and the concept of morality politics

The political claim of homosexual interest groups in Poland and elsewhere concerns equal treatment for gays and lesbians in terms of legalising same-sex partnerships and the protection against discrimination and homophobia. This claim has often provoked unwelcome counter-reactions from individuals and groups from within both political and civil society.

Moony *et al.* argue that this type of conflict can be classified as morality policy, a type of public policy that differs from others in at least three points (Mooney 2001; Mooney and Schuldt 2006). First, morality policy is – in line with Lowi (1964) – seen primarily as shaped by value-based and not economy-oriented reasoning. In this sense, morality policy and its politics 'are characterised by debates over first principles', in which 'at least one advocacy coalition portray[s] the issues as one of morality or sin' and, second, it 'use[s] moral arguments in its policy advocacy' (Haider-Markel and Meier 1996; Mooney 2001: 3–4). Third, morality policy exists, when it is based 'on the perception of the actors involved and the terms of the debate among them' (Mooney 2001: 3–4). These characteristics impact on the process of morality policy. This is a process where societal and religious actors, in particular, are more deeply involved than in other policy fields (Mooney 2001; Smith and Tatalovich 2003).[3]

Seeking to understand the conflict about implementing gay rights as morality policy in Poland, I analyse both the political process and the actors involved (Anderson 2000). The analysis concentrates on three stages of the political process: *agenda setting, policy formulation* and *adopting a policy with concrete policy output* (Anderson 2000: 31–2).

To understand the success of social actors calling for a liberal policy of gay rights in the course of the political process, success can be understood in a threefold manner which, for Lochon and Mazmanian (1993), correspond to the already mentioned stages. Thus, social movement actors may be successful in terms of *agenda setting*, if they are able to redefine the political agenda. Success in *policy formulation* implies acceptance of the social group as having legitimate interests, a process that precedes the formulation of policy. Success in *terms of policy output* means that they are able successfully to promote policy change (Lochon and Mazmanian 1993).

With this conceptual understanding of the morality policy process and dimensions of success as the dependent variable, the next section locates the intersections of religious and political actors as independent variables in the context of morality politics.

Religion and public policy

Mapping religion in the public

Casanova argued fifteen years ago that religious actors in modern societies seek political influence by working within civil society (Casanova 1994). Now, however, he adopts a more global and less 'Catholic' perspective, arguing that public religion in modern societies also seeks to influence political society (for example, political parties) at the state level.[4] Taking this assumption of *public religion* into consideration, I will next analyse the process of interaction between religious and political actors in all three public contexts. Then I explain how to locate the points of interaction between religion and public policy. Following Hugh Heclo, I suggest three analytical levels: the institutional, the behavioural and the philosophical (Heclo 2001). (See Table 10.1.)

The institutional level – the pattern of church–state relations

This focuses on the way organised structures of religion and government impinge on each other and together on society (Heclo 2001: 4–5). Referring to the literature on church–state relations, I regard the institutional level of religion and public policy as patterns of church–state relations. The three public contexts come into focus when we seek to operationalise these patterns as the *structural context* between church and state organised at state level in terms of legal arrangements, as de facto *structures of communication* between Episcopate and government. This occurs mainly in the state arena as particular *modes of cooperation* between religious and state actors across the arenas of both political and civil society.

Minkenberg argues that the public policy impact of religion is most evident where churches are partially established and Catholicism prevails (Minkenberg

Table 10.1 The elements of the analytical concept

Stages of the policy Process	*Level of analysis*		
	Institutional level	*Behavioural level*	*Ideological level*
	(Church–state relations	*(Voting behaviour and political strategies)*	*(World views)*
Agenda setting			
Policy formulation			
Policy adoption	State arena	State arena	State arena
Policy output	Political society	Political society	Political society
⇒ Focus of analysis	Civil society	Civil society	Civil society

2002). We will see that in Poland the partial establishment of the Catholic Church is a possible reason for the relative lack of success of homosexual interest groups. The institutional level in terms of communication structures shows that in Poland the success of gay rights is constrained by the extent to which Catholic clergy find better conditions for political lobbying in political society. Considering the institutional level as mode of cooperation, Htun contends that conflicts between church and state open a window of opportunity for liberalisation (Htun 2003). The Polish case shows, however, that conflicts between church and state over issues to do with the EU have led to cooperation. As a consequence of the compromise with the church over the EU, the government did not implement the partnership bill.

The behavioural level – political strategies and Catholic voting

The 'behavioural' is the second level of interconnectedness between religion and public policy (Heclo 2001: 5). With reference to the political culture literature (Almond and Verba 1965), it follows the idea that religious attachments may to a certain extent influence a person's voting behaviour (Calvo *et al.* 2006, Chan 2000, Norris and Inglehart 2004). Politicians, on the other hand, may choose a political strategy that corresponds with particular voting preferences (Anderson 2000). I focus on the intertwining of the behaviour of political leadership and the electorate in both political and civil society. In this regard, the Polish case shows that homosexuality is politically instrumentalised to try to mobilise a minority section of society – namely, the Catholic nationalist and Eurosceptic voters – which has hindered implementation of gay rights.

The 'philosophical' level – ideology

Heclo calls the third level of the relationship between religion and politics, 'philosophical'. In the case of Poland, this term is better expressed as the 'level of ideology', as it emphasises the 'substructure of ideas'. Here 'one is trying to capture the intersections of religion and policy-making that involves ideas and modes of thought bearing on a fundamental ordering of society's public life' (Heclo 2001: 6).

The focus is on right-wing extremist leadership and the radical Catholic right in Poland. Here, we can also see that interaction of politics and religion takes place in both political and civil society. As to the 'behavioural level', homosexuality is politically instrumentalised to try to mobilise the section of the electorate that is both 'Catholic nationalist' and Eurosceptic.

Liberalisation, (homo)sexuality and the Roman Catholic Church

Morality policy typically considers world views in general and those of religious actors in particular as important. This section examines the normative perspective of liberalism and the view of the Roman Catholic Church towards homosexuality and same-sex partnerships in Poland.

Equal rights as norm for liberal democracies

Issues concerning family, marriage or life and death matters are fundamental for the authority of most religious institutions (Minkenberg 2002; Norris and Inglehart 2004). From that perspective, the claims of liberalisation might be problematic. From a normative–secularist stance, however, liberalism in democratic policy must guarantee the choice between a religious and a non-religious position. It is what Stepan, within a multicultural setting, calls the *twin toleration* (Stepan 2000). In addition, sexual minorities should not be discriminated legally against the norm of a heterosexual married majority. This is an understanding which the Roman Catholic Church opposes.

The position of the Vatican and the Polish Catholic Church

The Roman Catholic Church addressed the broader issue of the morality of homosexuality in a series of documents in the 1980s and 1990s. Nowadays, Catholic moral teaching acknowledges the existence of a homosexual orientation but evaluates it as an 'objective disorder' (Kalbian 2005), which should be accepted 'with compassion' and 'unjust discrimination' condemned. However, the homosexual act is still regarded as sin, and chastity is the only way to proceed (Ratzinger and Amato 2003).

In reaction to some European states' political initiatives to legalise homosexual partnerships and to provide gay and lesbian couples with the same or similar rights as heterosexual ones,[5] in 2003 the Congregation for the Doctrine of Faith published an important document. Its authors confirmed that the traditional point of view of the Catholic Church was still relevant today:

> Legal recognition of homosexual unions or placing them on the same level as marriage would mean not only the approval of deviant behaviours, with the consequence of making it a model in the present-day, but would also obscure basic values which belong to the common inheritance of humanity.
>
> (Ratzinger and Amato 2003)

The document justifies this point of view, referring to core religious values and interpretations. These encompass the complementarity of man and woman as God's will, the sacramental value of heterosexual marriage, the norm of procreative family life, and the interpretation that homosexuality is against natural law. In this vein, homosexual unions are regarded as a threat to human values.

The document ends with a call to Catholic politicians to vote against any projects in favour of legalising homosexual unions: the 'Catholic law-maker has a moral duty to express his opposition clearly and publicly ... To vote in favour of a law so harmful to the common good is gravely immoral.' When such legislation is already in force, 'the Catholic politician must oppose it in the ways that are possible for him' (Ratzinger and Amato 2003).

In moral issues, the Polish Catholic Church strictly follows the line of the Vatican. Although the Episcopate unites conservative as well as more liberal and dialogue-orientated points of view, the group of traditionalist bishops is the most influential (Gowin 1999, Hierlemann 2005: 92). Consequently, the clergy teach that homosexuality is a deviation and illness, upholding the idea, expressed in particular by Cardinal Glemp, the conservative former president of the Bishops' Conference, that a homosexual can be healed from his 'state of disorder' (Biedroń 2004: 206). There are, however, some rare exceptions to this line, including priests who have recently worked as non-official custodians of gay and lesbian Catholics (Biedroń 2004: 211).[6]

Owing to the hierarchical structure of the Roman Catholic Church, the national churches are obliged to follow the line of the Vatican (Martin 1978). In addition, the position of the Polish Catholic Church is also closely linked to the continuing tremendous moral authority of the late Polish Pope John Paul II, an avid proponent of a strict moral line.[7]

Sexual ethics and Catholic authority

Casanova states that while modern Catholicism recognises the autonomy of the secular sphere, it 'does not accept the claims of these spheres to have detached themselves completely from morality. Consequently, it does not accept the relegation of religion and morality to the private sphere, insisting on the links between private and public morality' (Casanova 1994: 104).

Why, however, does the Catholic Church care so much about the political project of legalising same-sex partnerships? Here, the study by the political theologian Aline Kalbian of the abovementioned congregational document offers an explanation. Her first argument refers to the sexual ethic as a core element of Catholic teachings, an institution for which the sacramental significance of marriage, the norm of gender complementarity and the norm of procreative sexuality are fundamental. Therefore, 'the possibility of legally sanctioned same-sex-marriage poses a serious threat to Catholic sexual ethics' (Kalbian 2005: 138).

Second, Kalbian argues that the authority of the Catholic Church relies on a twofold sense of order: on 'interpreting right order' by describing the relationship of 'order to purpose' and on 'the order of giving orders' by regulating and enforcing (Kalbian 2005: 4–5). In this vein, 'the documents interpret what God intends for the human sexual act and they also prescribe specific action guides (norms of behaviour)'. An example of this twofold order is the prescription of sexual abstinence for all homosexuals. 'By disciplining these desires, the Church believes that it maintains the natural order of procreative sex and gender complementarity' (Kalbian 2005: 141–2). In sum, she argues that

> [S]exual doctrines and attitudes about gender are intimately connected to
> church authority in a way that ensures the Church's power both to interpret

and to enforce order in the lives of all Catholics. [Taking that into considera-
tion] [T]he prospect of legitimate same-sex unions poses a serious challenge
to the Catholic theology of marriage.

(Kalbian 2005:140)

We may conclude that recent political developments to provide equal rights for
gays and lesbians threaten not only the church's authority and the value-based
fundament of its teachings. If we regard changes in gender roles as a central
indicator for value change in modern societies (Norris and Inglehart 2004), these
structural changes may also affect the societal acceptance of the church and challenge its (already contested) place in the society.

We have seen to what extent and for what reason the position of the Catholic
Church concerning the implementation of gay rights is contrary to the liberal
position. Does this, however, allow the conclusion of a solely Catholic effect on
morality policy decisions in Poland?

Morality policy and the Polish conflict concerning equal rights for homosexuals

Historical legacies, post-communist transformation and EU integration

In communist Poland homosexuality was an invisible and publicly untouched
issue. Furthermore, in the mid-1980s homosexuality was politically used in order
to persecute and put pressure on certain people (Warkocki 2006: 1).

After 1989, in the course of societal, political and economical transformations
a sub-cultural homosexual infrastructure began to develop, with semi-public
magazines, radio stations, clubs, informal networks and registered organisations.
While, until the late 1990s, the first wave of emancipation was mainly driven by
the need to establish structures for identity and network building as well as emer-
gency help in cases of homophobic assaults (Warkocki 2006: 14), the second
wave since then can be characterised by increasingly public emergence of homosexuals and formulation of their political claims (Majka-Rostek 2002).

In Western Europe the process of homosexual emancipation lasted about 30
years, beginning in the 1960s. National discussions since the end of the 1980s
have been about legalising homosexual partnerships,[8] followed by the formulation of a European anti-discrimination policy in the late 1990s. In Poland,
however, these issues emerged after 1989 in the context of both democratisation
and joining the EU.

In 2008, there were two main representative organisations for gays and lesbians in Poland: the Campaign against Homophobia (KPH)[9] and Lambda.[10] Both
are small but also well connected internationally, receiving financial support for
civil society-building projects from Western European governments and non-
state actors.

Successes and failed successes: analysing the policy process

Entering the mass agenda

Despite the fact that since 1996 single personalities from culture and the media 'came out of the closet', such as the writer Izabela Filipiak (Graff 2006: 434), the existence of a sexual minority in Polish society and the increasing problem of homophobia until 2003 remained publicly invisible (Warkocki 2006). In 2001 and 2002, the first demonstrations were held, addressing the importance of tolerance towards sexual minorities in terms of human rights protection. Unlike the carnival-like gay pride manifestations in many Western European cities, the so-called Equality Parade in Warsaw (*Parada Równości*) and the Marches of Tolerance (*Marsz Toleranci*) in Poznań[11] were primarily political events, during which gays and lesbians were able to see how many they were. There was, however, no discernible public reaction (Graff 2006: 438).

A public agenda did not surface until March 2003, when the KPH provoked societal turmoil by staging a nation-wide public exhibition, where homosexuality appeared in public for the first time. This exhibition consisted of thirty photographs featuring fifteen male and fifteen female ordinary-looking same-sex couples, mostly young and urban, holding hands.[12] Huge billboards with photographs, each stamped with the words 'Let Them See Us', were openly displayed in public places in the centres of many Polish cities. The project was funded by the office of the government plenipotentiary for equal status of men and women and by the Dutch Embassy (Ramet 2006: 127).

Within a few days, however, most billboards were damaged. While politicians remained silent, the media kept showing the destroyed pictures, 'if only to express outrage at the "ostentatious" nature of the material' (Graff 2006: 438). The homophobic attack against the exhibition provoked, for the first time in Poland, a controversial debate about homosexuality in the leading newspapers. Over the next four months, representatives from non-governmental organisations, the media, political society, the Catholic Church and newspaper readers hotly debated a core question: can a democracy tolerate the public expression of the interests of a sexual minority? This was an issue which many considered offensive in public (Semka 2003).

Once homosexuality became public, the Equality Parades in Poznań and Krakow were attacked. While the nationalistic All-Polish Youth Organisation assaulted the participants, Lech Kaszyński, currently (late 2008) the Polish president but at the time mayor of Warsaw, in 2004 and 2005 banned the Equality Parades in the city. Some clerics strongly criticised the parade in 2005, while a few liberal priests argued that the church should learn to accept, if not respect, homosexuals (Pater Kozuch 2005).

At the same time, these manifestations became a focal point for a wider defence of democratic and human rights. People suddenly took part 'who always thought that sex is a private thing' (Graff 2006: 6). Evaluating the effects of the public appearance of homosexuals from 2003, Robert Biedroń and Marta

Abramowicz from the KPH point to a rather positive changing awareness within both society and the media.[13]

Successful policy formulation, failed policy output

In 2002, the issue of a partnership law first entered the political agenda, although it was not then pursued. An important step was the establishment of an advisory board for the protection of sexual minorities against discrimination, launched by the leftist premier Leszek Miller from the post-communist Democratic Left Alliance (SLD). In reaction to the EU requirements concerning gender equality policy, it was meant to be a starting point for further steps towards an anti-discrimination policy;[14] however, it was a project that still lacked complete implementation in late 2008.

In terms of successful policy formulation, in August 2003 a same-sex partnership bill was presented in the Senate. The author of the project was Maria Szyszkowska, a philosophy of law professor and left-wing senator, who formulated the proposal without consulting her party, the SLD. Instead she discussed the text with legal experts from the KPH. The law aimed to secure the legal and political status of non-married hetero- and homosexual couples, guaranteeing the same economic and tax rights, and the right of succession after the partner's death. The options of marriage and of adopting children were excluded.[15]

In autumn 2003, Szyszkowska and Biedroń, chairman of the KPH, started a nation-wide campaign, promoting the legislative project to the public, and collecting signatures both nationally and internationally. The Polish Episcopate carefully monitored the process. In February 2004 it published a letter, advising the government and the public not to support the campaign.[16] As right-wing, pro-life organisations and ultra-Catholic actors got involved, the conflict became more intense and Szyszkowska received threats on her life and was for half a year under police protection.[17]

After seventeen months of debate in the Senate, in December 2004 the senators decided to forward the law proposal to the Sejm (*Gazeta Wyborcza*, 3 December 2004); the vote was thirty-eight in favour, twenty-three against and fifteen abstentions. However, within this legislation period no Sejm commission further dealt with the project.[18] Then, in June 2005, a conservative coalition under Jarosław and Lech Kaszyński came to power and launched an anti-liberal agenda. Later, in November 2007, an economically liberal government, the Civic Platform (PO), took power under the leadership of Donald Tusk. However, it failed to take concrete steps towards legalising same-sex partnerships.[19]

New government, new alliances

In autumn 2005, a new right-wing conservative–radical Catholic coalition was established, involving Law and Justice (PiS), the League of Polish Families (LPR) and the right-wing Self-defence (Samoobrona). It promoted a programme based on the idea of the 'traditional Polish family' as the core value of the

Catholic nation (Blumberg-Stankiewiz 2008). In June 2006, the LPR leader Roman Giertych became the new minister of education. Claiming to defend Catholic values, he followed both a strict anti-abortion policy and a decisively homophobic agenda.

During 2006–7 a new alliance against Giertych's policy emerged, involving a teachers' association, KPH and Lambda. Furthermore, the liberal newspaper *Gazeta Wyborcza* covered the issue with previously unknown openness, for example publishing an interview with an anonymous gay teacher at the protest demonstration (Czeładko 2007).

With the issue now getting international coverage, the KPH continued informing international human rights officials about the situation in Poland, provoking only diplomatic notes from the EU, however. After the European Parliament published a general resolution against homophobia in Europe, in May 2006 the EU advised Poland (as well as Malta and Italy) to legalise homosexual partnerships.[20] The Polish Bishops' Conference reacted immediately. Acknowledging the attempt to take action against the discrimination of gays and lesbians, their letter argued that to put same-sex partnerships on the legal level as married couples would be against 'natural law'. Furthermore, the bishops made an appeal to stop the 'dictatorship of relativism' and the 'restriction of religious freedom of the citizens of the European member countries'.[21] In this way, the issue was framed as a question of religious faith and not as a question of human rights.

Conclusion: three dimensions of success

The two main homosexual interest groups, KPH and Lambda, were most successful in terms of getting the issue of equal rights for homosexuals on the *political and mass agenda*.[22] As a consequence, the media began to address the topic more openly, while more Poles began to talk freely about their homosexuality.

Nonetheless, homophobic assaults remained a salient problem.[23] Furthermore, society was still divided concerning its attitude towards homosexuality (Table 10.2), and the public acceptance of registered partnerships remained negative, despite slight changes in 2005 (Table 10.3). A negative view correlates with a high church-going frequency and – this is a crucial point – with not knowing any gay or lesbian person, which in 2008 was still the case for 85 per cent of the population. A positive attitude is linked to better education, younger age and having contact with homosexuals (CBOS 2008: 1–2).

In terms of *successful policy formulation*, a partnership bill was published and gay and lesbian representatives were recognised politically as important civil society actors. However, for the government between 2005 and 2007, homophobic politics dominated the agenda and a slight negative turn concerning the acceptance of a partnership law might be a consequence (Table 10.3). At the same time, from 2005 onwards, new alliances emerged with media and social actors, such as teachers or mine-workers, who stood for a liberal understanding of democracy in terms of guaranteeing equal rights.[24] Concerning the *policy output*, social actors were not successful since the partnership bill was not approved.

Table 10.2 Attitudes towards homosexuality in Poland

	Is something normal (%)	Is a deviation that should be tolerated (%)	Is a deviation that should not be tolerated (%)	Difficult to say (%)
2001	5	47	41	7
2005	5	55	34	6
2008	8	52	31	9

Source: CBOS (2008: 8).

Table 10.3 Attitudes towards the implementation of registered partnerships (marriage) in Poland

	In favour (%)	Against (%)	Difficult to say (%)
2003	34 [24]	56 [69]	11 [7]
2005	46 [22]	44 [72]	10 [7]
2008	41 [18]	48 [76]	11 [6]

Source: (CBOS, 2008:6).

In conclusion, I contend that the lack of legal status for homosexual couples is best explained by the low public support that is partly connected with religiosity. I argue that these factors definitely impact on the decision-making process. However, this does not help to explain the way political decisions are taken. Therefore, I will look at three levels where religious and political actors intertwine, asking to what extent they constrain the success of implementing gay rights in Poland.

Religion and morality policy in Poland

As explained previously, the intertwining of religious and political actors can be located if we look at the institutional (church–state relations), behavioural (voting behaviour and political strategies) and ideological (world view) levels.

The institutional level: church–state interaction at the state level

Legal relationship

In post-socialist Poland, the regulation of church–state relations is a story of initial mistrust and bargaining between the left-wing government and the Episcopate. According to the Constitution from 1992, church and state in Poland are separate, while Art. 11 declares Poland as a non-confessional secular state (Anderson 2003) From 1997 onwards, as in other Catholic states, a concordat with the Vatican has regulated particularities of the relationship between the church and the state. In Poland, both documents put the relationship on a twofold basis: 'on the principle of respect for the autonomy and the mutual independence of each in its own sphere' and on the 'principle of cooperation for the individual and the common good' (Anderson 2003: 83; Steger 2001: 45).

Table 10.4 shows core indicators of formal arrangements within the church–state relationship (Chaves and Cann 1992). We see that the Polish Catholic Church is only privileged through the concordat and in terms of state-funded Catholic universities.[25, 26]

Concerning the hostile attitudes in society towards homosexuality one may argue that the new Catholic domain on religious education is crucial. However, with regard to the failed policy output it is worth asking how state and church effectively interact on the basis of constitutional separation, particularly when it comes to moral issues. This leads to the next two aspects of the institutional level.

The struggle at the state level: the constitutional norm of heterosexual marriage

In Poland, a result of the competitive cooperation between state and church in morality policy issues was the Constitution itself. In 1997, after a long process of controversial discussion concerning the concept of nation and the role of Catholicism (Anderson 2003), the new Constitution was adopted, replacing the transitional 'Little Constitution' from 1992.

With regard to the issue of equal rights for gays and lesbians, Art. 18 is a fundamental result of bargaining between the left government and the church. It

Table 10.4 The regulation of church–state relations in Poland

Church status in Constitution	State–church separation, Poland as a secular, neutral state
	Catholic Church privileged by concordat
Relationship to other denominations	Equal before the law, agreements between the state and fourteen denominations
Existence of taxes and tax reductions	No church tax
	Tax reduction for the church as for other societal institutions
Other subventions	No
Religion as obligatory subject in public schools	No but de facto the norm
State funding of Catholic schools	No
State funding of Catholic universities	Four state funded Catholic Universities

Source: Rynkowski 2005.

prescribes marriage as a 'relationship between woman and man', putting motherhood and parenthood under the particular protection of the Polish Republic (Mieżelińska 2001: 287). A particular protection because of sexual orientation is not foreseen. It could, however, be understood as covered by Art. 32, which guarantees equality before the law. Furthermore, the concordat makes Catholic marriages legally binding (Anderson 2003: 84).

Since the already mentioned partnership bill excluded marriage as an option, there is no constitutional restriction against such a legal project. However, a norm privileging heterosexuality was formulated and any further attempts to legalise same-sex partnerships could be considered as a potential act against the Polish Constitution (Mieżelińska 2001). The question arises of why the Catholic Church can successfully influence state policies.

Structures of communication: the state and political society

Recent studies show a developing a web of formal and informal communication structures involving the political establishment and the clergy in Poland (Steger 2001; Hierlemann 2005; Drzonek 2006).

A particularity is the Common Commission between government and the Episcopate at the level of the state. It is an official board, where six representatives from state and church respectively meet two or three times a year. It dates back to the year 1948, formalised by law in May 1989. The aim was to discuss issues related to church-relevant questions as the implementation of religious education at public schools, sexual education or abortion (Hierlemann 2005: 95–7).

In political society, such formal communication structures do not exist. There are, however, informal contacts between political parties and the Episcopate (Hierlemann 2005: 247). Hierlemann's interview-based analysis shows that the Episcopate has informal connections directly to the Sejm. The contact between the political right (post-Solidarity camp) and the Episcopate is traditionally more cordial. However, although more pragmatic, communication with left-wing politicians is stable, too (Hierlemann 2005: 246). In sum, there are structural advantages fostering a close co-operation between church and state on moral issues. The last institutional aspect refers to the character of church–state relationship, focusing on the morality policy process itself.

Modes of cooperation in the arena of political society

EU integration and moral conflicts between church and state

The failure of the formulated partnership bill should be seen together with a conflict between state, church and society in the context of Poland's approaching EU accession. A crucial point was the Polish EU referendum in May 2003. Although polls predicted increasing public support for Poland's EU integration,[27] the government feared that the Catholic Church would have a great impact on public opinion (Drzonek 2006: 218). Since the mainstream position of the Episcopate was decisively Eurosceptic, the left-wing government was keen on enrolling the Catholic Church as a supporter of Poland's EU accession.

The most powerful group of traditionalist bishops strongly opposed Poland's EU membership (Jackowska 2003), considering the European Union to be a secularising force, threatening Polish values (Gowin 1999). A key fear was that Poland would be forced to implement regulations concerning national policies on abortion, euthanasia and homosexuality (Biedroń 2004: 218; Hierlemann 2005: 212–14). As mentioned previously, homosexuals were seen as the incorporation of Western values, threatening both Polish Catholic and national identity. Graff and others argue that since there was no public discourse about Poland's place in Europe and the EU, these negative images, promoted during holy masses and in the media from 2000, replaced open debate (Graff 2007).

Hierlemann and Drzonek document the year-long process during which Polish Church representatives at both national and EU levels lobbied for recognition of 'the particular protection of life' and of 'marriage and family' as fundamental European values. As a result, in April 2003, two month before the EU referendum, the Polish Sejm approved and published a declaration, which guaranteed the superiority of Polish over EU law in moral issues (Hierlemann 2005: 222).

Interestingly, before the partnership bill was published, the left-wing government under premier Leszek Miller (SLD) had supported from 1997 the attempt to liberalise the strict abortion law, an initiative of particular concern for the Episcopate. However, this liberalisation initiative stopped suddenly in 2003 just before the EU referendum. The Polish Catholic Church in turn started publicly supporting Poland's accession to the EU.

One can assume that the pro-European position of Pope John Paul II influenced the position of the Polish Episcopate (Jackowska 2003). However, the 'abortion deal' and the 'silent agreement'[28] between government and church representatives, guaranteeing further the church's influence on moral issues, were decisive (Eberts 2003; Hierlemann 2005).

Analysing the intertwining of religion and politics at the institutional level of the relationship between church and state, I have shown that this relationship has different facets if we consider the dimension of communication structures and particular modes of co-operation. The church successfully lobbied its restrictive approach to moral issues in the state arena and was partly backed by the political establishment. The next two sections focus on the role of the political culture and political and societal actors as factors constraining the implementation of gay rights.

Behavioural level: politicisation of homophobia

The point of departure for analysing the impact of the behaviour of politicians and voters in the arena of political society is the assumption that the public emergence of gays and lesbians in 2002–3 helped conservative and right-wing political and societal actors to define a 'new evil' for the Polish nation as a mobilising force during an election.[29]

At the end of the 2001–5 legislature, the post-communist government under premier Leszek Miller and President Aleksander Kwaśniewski (both SLD) was undermined by several serious corruption scandals and its popularity decreased dramatically. Thus, the parliamentary and presidential elections in 2005 implied a real chance for the post-Solidarity camp and for new opposition parties, such as the Civic Platform (PO).

However, political culture in Poland is marked by a low level of party attachment and by extremely low electoral turnout[30] (Markowski 2006: 827–9; Bachmann 2006). Data show that those who are likely to vote are the educated, elderly and/or practising religious people. Since 1989 religious praxis has been correlated in Poland with voting activity (Grabowska 2004: 310). Furthermore, there is a strong correlation between religious praxis or church affiliation and the vote for non-communist and post-Solidarity parties (Grabowska 2004: 320). However, this is only in relation to a minority of about 15 per cent.

Taking into account the 'uncertainties' in terms of voter instability and low electoral frequency, a reliable factor for the competing parties was the ultra-Catholic electorate. An analysis of the election in 2005 shows that PiS, once it departed from a classical conservative programme, became 'a party that appeals to people whose populist-, nationalist-, and religion-based expectations might change its programmatic profile for good' (Markowski 2006: 827). At the same time, the competition became more issue-orientated and PiS, the Civic Platform (PO) and the fundamentalist Catholic LPR particularly tried to compete on moral questions, including abortion, euthanasia and homosexuality (Markowski 2006: 828).

Focusing upon the relevance of the behavioural level during the election campaign in 2005, we can note the actions of the presidential candidate Lech Kaszyński. While homosexuality until 2003 was not an issue on his agenda, in 2004 and 2005 he banned Equality Parades in Warsaw; these were 'well-planned moves in his career' (Graff 2006: 436). In autumn 2005 the question of the legality of gay marches became one of the key themes in the presidential elections. According to Graff, 'a candidate's attitude towards sexual minorities served as a litmus test for her or his views on modern democracy, Poland's westernization, freedom of speech, and traditional Catholicism' (Graff 2006: 436).

Also, the failure of the partnership bill has to be seen in the context of election strategies and the politicisation of homosexuality. According to Szyszkowska, most liberal and left-wing senators voted in the deciding round in the Senate against the bill. Strong opposition came from Włodzimierz Cimoszewicz, who was preparing for his presidential candidacy and did not want to be associated with someone who paved the way for the legalisation of homosexual partnership.[31]

Although the politicisation of homophobia is not exclusively a Polish phenomenon, this perspective moves the focus from the church's influence to political activities in the course of the morality policy process. The last section further investigates this argument about politicising homophobia, looking at the ideologies of actors from both political and civil society.

Level of ideologies

Catholic-inspired populism in political society

For two years until the snap elections of November 2007, the governing coalition consisted of the right-conservative PiS, the Catholic-nationalistic League of Polish Families (LPR) and the populist Self-Defence. The LPR came out of the post-Solidarity electoral alliance (AWS) and entered the political scene in 1995 under the leadership of Roman Giertych. In June 2006, the party leader Roman Giertych held the ministry of education. Giertych is the youngest descendant of a political dynasty with roots back to the pre-war nationalist movement of Roman Dmowski (Schmid 2006). Consequently, in the mid-1990s he revived the nationalistic pre-war youth movement, All-Polish Youth. Its members were well known for being opposed to the Equality Parades from 2004, while some held an office within the LPR (Blumberg-Stankiewicz 2008).

Significantly, in the 2004 European parliamentary election the LPR took second place, with ten deputies elected. In the Polish parliamentary elections, however, only about 8 per cent voted for the LPR.[32] With regard to the conflict about implementing gay rights, Giertych played a crucial role. As minister of education, his idea was of a Polish society that was based on traditional Catholic and nationalistic values. More elements of his politics included prohibition of sex education at public schools (in accordance with the Catholic Church), the censorship of schoolbooks concerning sexual issues, the introduction of school uniforms, and the promotion of traditional gender roles based on religious family values (Schmid 2006). Blaming teachers for promoting homosexuality in schools, he shifted the hitherto vague morality policy issue of homosexuality to the concrete field of education and created a policy of fear.[33]

Since polls showed that the support for the LPR had decreased dramatically, this anti-liberal policy agenda has also to be seen as a strategy to address the radical Catholic electorate, amounting to between 12 and 16 per cent of the population. However, in 2007 the LPR did not come to power again.[34]

Catholic fundamentalism in civil society

The last section concerns the relevance of ideology in civil society. In particular two Catholic organisations were able to mobilise people against the partnership law. Most striking was the Radio Maryja movement, founded in 1991. The Redeemer priest and charismatic leader Father Tadeusz Rydzyk created a radio station in Torn. Its programme consisted primarily of Bible-based lectures, Marian prayers and auditory discussions with xenophobic, anti-Semitic, homophobic, and Euro-critical tendencies (Mecke 2007). The auditorium, called the Radio Maryja Family, emerged within three years as a fundamentalist Catholic movement of about three million listeners. Furthermore, Rydzyk established the TV station Trwam with the same profile as Radio Maryja and a network of foundations and entrepreneurs. In this way, Radio Maryja became like the 'moral majority' movement in the United States in the 1980s (Burdziej 2005: 171). Its role in moral conflicts so far is twofold. Father Rydzyk was able to bring several thousand people on to the streets of Warsaw to demonstrate 'for life and family', and thus against abortion and homosexual partnerships. Second, the radio station offered a platform for politicians from the LPR and PiS to promote their world views (Mecke 2007). Rydzyk also did not hesitate to formulate voting recommendations, once for the LPR and once for PiS.

Although less visible, the Cracovian Association for Christian Culture, Piotr Skarga, was also active. Founded in 1999 and inspired by the American Society for the Defense of Tradition, Family, and Property (TFP),[35] it pursued the idea of fighting a counter-revolutionary 'crusade' against modern and 'anti-Polish' phenomena, such as homosexuality and abortion.[36] Piotr Skarga was tolerated by the Polish Catholic Church.

Participating in the above-mentioned pro-family demonstrations,[37] Piotr Skarga also addressed individuals. During the decision-making process in 2003 on equality partnership, it mobilised 300 registrars to encourage the government not to register homosexual partnerships, in case the law was approved. Furthermore, Piotr Skarga published and distributed several thousand leaflets to Cracowian households, which opposed the bill and promoted homosexuality as an 'illness' that had to be combated.[38]

This focus on the ideological level has shown to what extent populist and/or fundamentalist ideas could be converted into action. Looking at civil society, there were anti-liberal movements beyond the church with the capacity to mobilise people. These organisations served as allies for political actors with similar ideologies. To conclude, it is difficult to measure the direct impact of these movements on the political process. One can, however, assume that it impacted on public opinion to some extent (Anderson 2000).

Conclusion

The chapter sought to analyse the intertwining of religion and politics in the course of a moral conflict in Catholic Poland. The point of departure was the assumption that moral issues make a difference and can provoke public conflicts between liberal and Catholic world views. Understanding such conflicts as morality politics, the question was to what extent patterns of the relationship between religious and political actors constrained the success of social actors claiming to implement equal rights for gays and lesbians. In response, I suggested a tripartite analysis: the institutional, behavioural and ideological levels. I also proposed three public contexts where the interaction takes place: the state, political society and civil society.

We saw that gay rights activists were successful in terms of *agenda setting*, leading to slight but discernible changes in public opinion and with an impact on *policy formulation.* Attempts to encourage the state to implement a partnership law were, however, not successful. Overall, how can we evaluate the impact of the patterns of interaction between religious and political actors in Poland?

The conclusion for the institutional level is that the constitutional privileges of the Catholic Church, put in place after 1989, legitimised processes of privileged consultation between clerics and politicians on morally relevant issues. These formal and informal structures of communication were not only a tribute to the historical role of the Catholic Church in Poland but also depended to a great extent on the decisions of individual politicians (Grabowska 2006). With regard to the character of interaction, we conclude that, unlike Htun's argument regarding Latin America, in the Polish case the conflict concerning the question of Poland's integration into the EU did not offer a window of opportunity for liberalisation but instead encouraged interdependence between church and state. This resulted in co-operation which risked the implementation of liberal moral policies.

As to the behavioural level, it was important to examine various issues, including both parliamentary and presidential elections; traditionally low voting' turnout, and competition among small conservative parties in a fragmented party system. Overall, politicians decided to instrumentalise the issue of homosexuality in order to try to win the votes of the small ultra-Catholic electorate. The final rejection of the formulated partnership bill may be explained in this context, as a decision informed by intense political competition.

The ideological level serves as a complementary perspective, shedding light on political and religious populism in moral politics in Poland. With regard to the political context, the homophobic agenda, mainly driven by Roman Giertych and Lech Kaszyński, helped develop a 'politics of fear', particularly among school teachers. At the same time, homophobic politics served to strengthen bonds within the still weak gay and lesbian movement, while the image of homosexuals in the mass media changed somewhat for the better. In civil society, we saw that the ultra-Catholic movements were able to mobilise a conservative part of society, while also building alliances with influential actors from political society.

As a general conclusion, this threefold perspective sheds doubt on the assumption that the Polish Catholic Church is the only driving force in moral politics. Instead, we can conclude that while 'the Church remains a bastion of conservatism, at least where sex is concerned' (Ramet 2006: 146), various political actors are also influential in deciding the degree of co-operation with the church and other Catholic actors (Bruce 2003).

In other words, in order to analyse the church's influence on this issue, it is necessary to focus on three factors: political opportunity structures, political leadership, and connections to conservative Catholic organisations.

Regarding the future, there are two plausible scenarios. First, assuming liberalising effects over time of changing values, civil education, generational changes and growing diversity of lifestyles, we may see an increasingly liberal attitude towards homosexuality and gay rights in Poland. The second scenario is that the politics of equal rights, coupled with increasing secularisation, contextualised by growing social insecurities, may serve to encourage increased mobilisation of anti-liberal (both religious and nationalistic) counter-movements (Inglehart and Welzel 2005), which in turn might lead to more Catholic defence of the moral authority of the Roman Catholic Church in Poland.

Notes

1 Starting points were, in 1994, the resolution on equal rights for gays and lesbians in the European Community, and in 1996 on the fight against discrimination of homosexuals as part of §84 concerning the respect of human rights. Available at http://europa.eu.int/scadplus/printversion/en/lvb/l33113.htm (accessed 7 June 2006).
2 Jelen and Wilcox call the Catholic impact in Poland a 'transcendent basis for regime transformation' (Jelen and Wilcox 2002: 15).
3 Other examples of morality policies concern controversies about the legalisation of abortion, pornography and divorce.
4 Casanova (1994) refers to the three levels of a polity formulated by Stepan (1988).
5 There are four different legal regulations: unregistered and registered cohabitation, unregistered cohabitation (same rights for homosexual couples as for not-married heterosexual couples), registered partnerships (similar rights as for heterosexual couples but only for homosexuals), and marriage (same rights and duties as for heterosexual couples despite the right to adopt children). Available at www.ilga-europe.org/europe/issues/marriage_and_partnership (accessed 22 April 2006).
6 In an interview, Biedroń told me that in 2006 these three priests resigned from their appointments because of the increasing pressure of the Catholic Church; 28 October 2006, Warsaw.
7 The Polish sociologist Mandes emphasised the phenomenon that the moral authority of John Paul II after his death is increasing. Interview with Sławomir Mandes, 16 March 2007, Warsaw.
8 Marriage is allowed in Belgium, Spain and the Netherlands. EU countries without any regulation are Bulgaria, Estonia, Greece, Italy, Latvia, Lithuania, Malta, Poland, Romania and Slovakia; see www.ilga-europe.org/europe/issues/marriage_and_partnership (accessed 12 October 2008).
9 Founded in 2000, the KPH is one of the two most important Polish NGOs advocating lesbian, gay, bi- and trans-sexual (LGBT) rights. Their activities concentrate on education in the wider field of anti-discrimination and civil rights. More information is available at www.kampania.org.pl (accessed 24 October 2008).
10 Lambda, founded in 1990, was the first LGBT umbrella organisation in Poland and marks the beginning of the institutionalisation of the homosexual movement in Poland. More information is available at http://warszawa.lambda.org.pl (accessed 24 October 2008).
11 More information is available at www.paradarownosci.pl/index.php?&lang=en (accessed 24 October 2008).
12 The pictures are available at http://niechnaszobacza.queers.pl/strony/galeria.htm (accessed 24 October 2008).
13 Interview with Marta Abramowicz, 20 October 2007, and Robert Biedroń, 28 October 2007, Warsaw.
14 More information available at www.porozumienie.lesbijek.org/LaendariumLestesmy-Polska.htm
15 Document available at: www.szyszkowska.strefa.pl (accessed 24 October 2008). Biedroń argued that it would have been too early to include the abortion issue as well.
16 The full title is 'The Position of the Representatives of the Bishops' Conference

within the Common Commission between the Government and the Episcopate Concerning the Legislative Initiative of Registered Partnership'; available at www.episkopat.pl/?a=dokumentyKEP&doc=2004223_0 (accessed 5 June 2006).

17 Interview with Maria Szyszkowska, 22 March 2007, Warsaw.

18 Available at www.mojeprawa.info/ (accessed 12 October 2006).

19 Right after the elections representatives from feminist and homosexual groups pleaded for a meeting with Donald Tusk in order to discuss the possibilities for a new political agenda that would address issues of equality. According to Robert Biedroń, the request was refused, with the argument that other issues were more crucial at the moment. Interview with Robert Biedroń, 19 December 2007, Warsaw.

20 Available at www.europarl.europa.eu/sides/getDoc.do?pubRef=-//EP//TEXT+TA+20 060118+ITEMS+DOC+XML+V0//EN&language=EN#sdocta9 (accessed 22 April 2007).

21 Available at www.episkopat.pl/?a=dokumentyKEP&doc=2006131_1 (accessed 6 May 2006).

22 The organisers – Marta Abramowicz and Robert Biedroń from KPH (interviews 20 March 2007 and 28 March 2007, Warsaw) and Yga Kostrzewa from Lambda (interview 18 March 2007, Warsaw) – strongly emphasised this point.

23 This results from the annual report on homophobia published by KPH. Every fourth assault happens at school. Available at www.kampania.org.pl/cms/data/upimages/ raport_sytuacja_bi_homo_2007.pdf (accessed 22 April 2007).

24 Other figures indicate increasing public support of the gay parades precisely during the time when they were a matter of conflict in 2005. While in July 2005 about 20 per cent were in favour, in December this had already risen to 33 per cent (CBOS 2005).

25 Based on indicators of church–state relations by Chaves and Cann (1992) and Minkenberg (2002).

26 Anderson, however, shows that minority denominations lack the same status (Anderson 2003).

27 In March 2003, 73 per cent of the people who wanted to take part in the accession referendum declared themselves to be in favour of Poland's EU accession; see www. gallup-europe.be/epm/epm_POL_030323.htm (accessed 6 December 2008).

28 Pro-choice activists were already claiming in 2002 that the government and the Catholic Church had silently agreed to stop the project of liberalising the abortion law in the change of a pro-European position of the Catholic Church. In February 2002 they wrote a public 'Letter of a Hundred Women' to the European Parliament, complaining about the 'abortion deal'; available at: http://pl.wikisource.org/wiki/List_Stu_ Kobiet (accessed 20 October 2008).

29 The notion of 'new evil' implies the observation, shared also by Polish Jews, that anti-Semitism has been to a certain extent replaced by homophobia (Graff 2006: 444–5).

30 At the parliamentary elections in 2001, only 46 per cent participated. In 2005, this fell to only 40.57 per cent (Grabowska 2004: 308).

31 Interview with Maria Szyszkowska, 22 March 2007, Warsaw.

32 PiS won with 27 per cent, while PO was second with 24 per cent (Markowski 2006: 822).

33 A striking example was the dismissal of Sielatycki right after Giertych came to power. As director of the educational centre, he had arranged the publication of the teachers' guidebook *Compass* in Polish, distributed by the Council of Europe, which encouraged teachers to discuss, among other things, the issue of homosexuality as part of civil society education and to invite representatives from gay and lesbian organisations for that purpose. *Compass* is available at http://serwisy.gazeta.pl/wyborcza/2029 020,34513,34512,3407781.htm (accessed 11 June 2007).

34 In October 2006 the LPR had only 3 per cent, which increased in December to 6 per cent. In March 2007 the support was only 2 per cent. However, PiS continuously held about 25 per cent, while most support (around 30 per cent) went to the opposition party OP, which won the election in November 2007 (CBOS 2007).

35 More information is available at www.tfp.org (accessed 12 October 2008).
36 More information is available at www.piotrskarga.pl/ps,0,8,0,0,I,informacje.html (accessed 12 October 2008).
37 From 2006 on, Piotr Skarga together with Foundation Pro imported from Washington the idea of putting such pro-family demonstrations on an annual basis.
38 The association also published and translated the book from the American TFP titled *In Defence of All Rights. Why We Do Have to Oppose the Legalisation of Homosexual Partnerships*. More information is available at www.ksiegarnia.piotrskarga.pl/product_info.php?products_id=28 (accessed 12 October 2008).

Bibliography

Almond, G. A. and Verba, S. (1965) *The Civic Culture*, Boston: Little, Brown.

Anderson, J. (2000) *Public Policymaking. An Introduction*, Boston: Houghton Mifflin.

Anderson, J. (2003) *Religious Liberty in Transitional Societies. The Politics of Religion*, Cambridge: Cambridge University Press.

Bachmann, K. (2006) 'Die List der Vernunft. Populismus und Modernisierung in Polen', *Osteuropa*, 56, 11–12, pp. 13–31.

Biedroń, R. (2004) '"Nieerotyczny dotyk". O hypokryzji i homofobii Kościoła Katolickiego w Polsce', in Z. Sypniewskiand B. Warkocki (eds), *Homofobia po Polsku*, Warsaw: Sic, pp. 201–24.

Blumberg-Stankiewicz, K. (2008) 'Rechtsradikale (Re-)Formulierungen eines nationalen Selbstbildes in Polen', in R. Fritz, C. Sachse and E. Wolfrum (eds), *Nationen und ihre Selbstbilder. Postdiktatorische Gesellschaften in Europa*, Göttingen: Wallstein Verlag, pp. 280–305.

Bruce, S. (2003) *Politics and Religion*, Oxford: Polity.

Burdziej, S. (2005) 'Religion and Politics: Religious Values in the Polish Public Square since 1989', *Religion, State and Society*, 33, 2, pp. 167–74.

Calvo, K., Martinez, A. and Ramon Montero, J. (2006) '*Eadem Sed Aliter*: Religious Voting in Portugal and Spain', paper presented at the Forum de Recerca, Dept. de Ciences Politiques i Socials, Universitat Pompeu Fabra, Barcelona.

Casanova, J. (1994) *Public Religion in the Modern World*, Chicago and London: Chicago University Press.

Casanova, J. (2003) 'Catholic Poland in Post-Christian Europe', *Transit Europäische Revue*, 25; available at www.iwm.at/index.php?option=com_content&task=view&id=2 39&Itemid=415 (accessed 6 December 2008).

Casanova, J. (2008) 'Public Religion Revisited', in H. de Vries (ed.), *Religion: Beyond the Concept*, New York: Fordham University Press, pp. 101–19.

Castles, F. G. (1994) 'On Religion and Public Policy: Does Catholicism Make a Difference?', *European Journal of Political Research*, 25, pp. 19–40.

CBOS (Public Opinion Research Centre) (2005) 'Preferencje partyjne w styczniu', CBOS, BS/7/2005.

CBOS (Public Opinion Research Centre) (2007) 'Preferencje Partyjne w Marcu', CBOS, BS/42/2007.

CBOS (Public Opinion Research Centre) (2008) 'Prawa Gejów i Lesbijek. Komunikat Badan', CBOS, BS/88/2008.

Chan, K. K.-L. (2000) 'The Religious Base of Politics in Post-Communist Poland', in D. Broughton and H.-M. ten Napel (eds), *Religion and Mass Electoral Behaviour in Europe*, London: Routledge, pp. 176–97.

Chaves, M. and Cann, D. E. (1992) 'Regulation, Pluralism, and Religious Market Structure', *Rationality and Society*, 4, 3, pp. 272–90.

Czeładko, R. (2007) 'To mnie nazwał zboczonym. Rozmowa z nauczycielem gejem', *Gazeta Wyborcza Stołeczna*, 2 (19 March).

Drzonek, M. (2006) *Między Integracją a Europeizacją. Kościoł katolicki w Polce wobec Unii Europeijskiej w latach 1997–2003*, Cracow: Societas.

Eberts, M. (2003) 'The Blessed Union? The Roman Catholic Church and Poland's Accession to the EU'; available at www.inter-disciplinary.net/AUD/Eberts%20paper.pdf (accessed 6 December 2008).

Gowin, J. (1999) *Kościoł w Czasach Wolności 1989–1999*, Cracow: Wydawnictwo ZNAK.

Grabowska, M. (2004) *Podział postkomunistyczny. Społeczne podstawy polityki w Polsce po 1989 roku*, Warsaw: Wyd. Naukowe Scholar.

Grabowska, M. (2006) 'Kościół i polityka', *Tygodnik Powszechny*, 17 February; available at http://tygodnik.onet.pl/1547,1311109,0,407143,dzial.html (accessed 24 October 2008).

Graff, A. (2006) 'We Are (Not All) Homophobes: A Report from Poland', *Feminist Studies*, 32, 2, pp. 434–49.

Graff, A. (2007) 'The Return of the Real Men and Real Women: Gender and EU Accession in Three Polish Weeklies', in Carolyn Elliott (ed.), *Global Empowerment of Women: Responses to Globalization. Politiczed Religions and Gender Violence*, London: Routledge, pp. 191–212.

Gutmann, A. and Thompson, D. (1997) *Democracy and Disagreement: Why Moral Conflict Cannot Be Avoided in Politics, and What Should Be Done about It*, Cambridge, MA: Belknap Press of Harvard University Press.

Haider-Markel, D. P. and Meier, K. J. (1996) 'The Politics of Gay and Lesbian Rights: Expanding the Scope of Conflict', *Journal of Politics*, 58, pp. 332–50.

Heclo, H. (2001) 'Religion and Public Policy', *Journal of Policy History*, 13, 1, pp. 1–18.

Hierlemann, D. (2005) *Lobbying der katholischen Kirche: das Einflussnetz des Klerus in Polen*, Wiesbaden: VS Verlag für Sozialwissenschaft.

Htun, M. (2003) *Sex and the State: Abortion, Divorce, and Family under Latin American Dictatorship and Democracies*, Cambridge: Cambridge University Press.

Inglehart, R. and Welzel, C. (2005) *Modernization, Cultural Change, and Democracy: The Human Development Sequence*, Cambridge: Cambridge University Press.

Jackowska, N. (2003) 'Polens katholische Kirche und die Europäische Integration', *Welt-Trends*, 39, 2, pp. 120–32.

Jelen, Ted G. and Wilcox, Clyde (2002) *Religion and Politics in Comparative Perspective. The One, the Few, and the Many*, Cambridge: Cambridge University Press.

Kalbian, A. H. (2005) *Sexing the Church. Gender, Power, and Ethics in Contemporary Catholicism*, Bloomington: Indiana University Press.

Kollman, K. (2007) 'Same-Sex Unions: The Globalization of an Idea', *International Studies Quarterly*, 51, pp. 329–57.

Lochon, T. R. and Mazmanian, D. A. (1993) 'Social Movements and the Policy Process', *Annals of the American Academy*, 528, 7, pp. 75–87.

Lowi, T. (1964) 'American Business, Public Policy, Case-Studies, and Political Theory', *World Politics*, 16, 4, pp. 677–715.

Majka-Rostek, D. (2002) *Mniejszośc kulturowa w warunkach pluralizacji. Socjologiczna analiza sytuacji homoseksualistów polskich*, Wrocław: Wyd. Wrocławskiego.

Markowski, R. (2006) 'The Polish Elections of 2005: Pure Chaos or a Restructuring of the Party System?', *West European Politics*, 29, 4, pp. 814–32.

Martin, D. (1978) *A General Theory of Secularization*, Oxford: Blackwell.

Mecke, B.-D. (2007) ' "Im Apostolat der Medien" – Radio Maryja', *Polen-Analysen*, 16, pp. 2–8.

Mieżelińska, J. (2001) ' "The Rest is Silence ..." Polish Nationalism and the Question of Lesbian Existence', *European Journal of Woman Studies*, 8, 3, pp. 281–97.

Minkenberg, M. (2002) 'Religion and Public Policy: Institutional, Cultural, and Political Impact on the Shaping of Abortion Policies in Western Democracies', *Comparative Political Studies*, 35, 2, pp. 221–47.

Mooney, C. Z. (2001) 'The Public Clash of Private Values: The Politics of Morality Policy', in C. Z. Mooney (ed.), *The Public Clash of Private Values: The Politics of Morality Policy*, New York, London, Catham House Publishers, pp. 3–31.

Mooney, C. Z. and Schuldt, R. G. (2006) 'Does Morality Policy Exist? Testing a Basic Assumption', paper presented at the annual meeting of the American Political Science Association, Marriott, Loews Philadelphia, and the Pennsylvania Convention Center, Philadelphia, PA, 31 August.

Norris, P. and Inglehart, R. (2004) *Sacred and Secular. Religion and Politics Worldwide*, Cambridge: Cambridge University Press.

Pater Kozuch, M. (2005) 'Homoseksualizm: niedojrzałośc, nie choroba', *Gazeta Wyborcza*, 10 June.

Ramet, S. P. (2006) 'Thy Will Be Done: The Catholic Church and Politics in Poland since 1989', in T. A. Byrnes. and P. J. Katzenstein (eds), *Religion in an Expanding Europe*, New York: Cambridge University Press, pp. 117–47.

Ratzinger, J. K. and Amato, A. S. D. B. (2003) 'Erwägungen zu den Entwürfen einer rechtlichen Anerkennung der Lebensgemeinschaften zwischen homosexuellen Personen', *Dokument der Kongregation für die Glaubenslehre*.

Rynkowski, M. (2005) 'Staat und Kirche in Polen', in G. Robbers (ed.), *Staat und Kirche in der Europäischen Union, 2. Auflage*, Baden-Baden: Nomos, pp. 455–76.

Schmid, U. (2006) 'Eine glückliche Familie. Die Giertychs und ihre Ideologie', *Osteuropa*, 56, 11–12, pp. 69–80.

Semka, P. (2003) 'Wolność na wyłączność?' *Rzeczpospolita*, 28 April.

Smith, A. T. and Tatalovich, R. (2003) *Cultures at War. Moral Conflicts in Western Democracies*, Toronto: Broadview Press.

Steger, P. (2001) *Abschied vom katholischen Land? Polens Kirche nach dem Kommunismus*, Wien: Studien zur politischen Wirklichkeit.

Stepan, A. (1988) *Rethinking Military Politics*, Princeton: Princeton University Press.

Stepan, A. (2000) 'Religion, Democracy, and the "Twin Tolerations" ', *Journal of Democracy*, 11, 4, pp. 37–57.

Teitel, R. (1999) 'Partial Establishment of Religion in Post-Communist Transitions', in A. Sajo and S. Avineri (eds), *The Law of Religious Identity: Models for Post-Communism*, The Hague: Kluwer Law International, pp. 103–16.

Twiston Davies, B. (2005) 'Spain's Struggle between Church and State', *Times Online*; available at: www.timesonline.co.uk/article/0,,3933–1531746_1,00.html (accessed 25 January 2008).

Warkocki, B. (2006) 'Die Branche schweigt nicht mehr', *Freitag*, 25 (23 July); available at: www.freitag.de/2006/25/06251701.php (accessed 24 October 2008).

Interviews

Robert Biedroń (KPH), 28 March 2007, Warsaw.
Marta Abramowicz (KPH), 20 March 2007, Warsaw.
Yga Kostrzewa (Lambda), 19 March, 2007, Warsaw.
Sławomir Mandes (Warsaw University), 16 March 2007, Warsaw.
Mirosława Grabowska (Warsaw University), 29 March 2007, Warsaw.
Maria Szyszkowsla (Warsaw University), 22 March 2007, Warsaw.

Websites of NGOs referred to in the chapter

www.kampania.org.pl (Campaign against Homophobia, gay and lesbian NGO)
http://niechnaszobacza.queers.pl/strony/galeria.htm (pictures from the exhibition 'Let Them See Us', as described in this chapter)
www.warszawa.lambda.org.pl (Lambda, gay and lesbian NGO)
www.ilga-europe.org (The International Gay and Lesbian Association)
www.piotrskarga.pl (Association for Christian Culture Piotr Skargi, Catholic NGO)
www.tfp.org (American Society for the Defense of Tradition, Family and Property)

Conclusion

Jeffrey Haynes

Religion and Politics in Europe, the Middle East and North Africa is one of the few books that has an explicitly comparative focus on the relationship between religion and politics in Europe, the Middle East and North Africa. Consequently, the book has a defensible claim to uniqueness. The book's overarching theme is the attempts by various religious actors – Christian, Muslim and Jewish – to try to assert their values and pursue their goals in both domestic and international contexts. We have seen that they seek to do this in a context that is not only one of secularisation and political changes, some of which emanate from within countries, while others come from outside, often a consequence of globalisation.

The regions upon which we focus in this book are not, of course, unique in this regard. For example, in officially secular India, there have been numerous examples of militant Hinduism in recent years, with the storming and destruction of the Babri Masjid mosque by Hindu militants at Ayodhya in 1992 an emblematic event in this regard. This event was instrumental in transforming the country's political landscape, to the extent that a Hindu nationalist political party, the Bharatiya Janata Party (BJP), grew in the 1990s to swift political prominence. From the mid-1990s, the BJP served in several coalition governments and until 2004 was the leading party in government.[1] In addition, in Israel Jewish religious parties regularly serve in government, the religious right has been a consistent political presence in the USA, the Muslim world is heavily influenced by political Islamism, and the Roman Catholic Church played a leading role in recent turns to democracy in, *inter alia*, Spain, Poland and numerous Latin American and African countries. Overall, it is absolutely clear that there are numerous examples of recent religious involvement in politics in various parts of the world, in both domestic and international contexts.

In recent years, scholars have identified a range of religious actors with a variety of political goals. This book has examined political activities of selected religious actors in primarily Christian, Muslim and Jewish contexts, in Europe (Greece, Italy, Poland and Spain) and the Middle East and North Africa (Israel, Morocco and Turkey). The basic hypothesis of the contributors was that various religious actors – including Islamist groups, and the Roman Catholic and the Orthodox churches – pose assorted challenges for issues of citizenship, democracy and secularisation in these countries and regions of Europe, the Middle East and North Africa (MENA).

Contributors also worked from an understanding that in recent years, around the world, numerous religious actors of various kinds demonstrably do affect a range of political outcomes in various ways. However, despite this recognition, there is still a relative lack of clear understanding regarding what they *do*, of importance in enabling us to understand clearly *why*, *how* and *when* religious actors act politically. To conceptualise these issues we sought to answer a key question in the book: *Why, how and when do religious actors seek to influence political outcomes, in particular in relation to citizenship, secularisation and democracy in Europe, the Middle East and North Africa?* This question did not, of course, arise in a vacuum. It followed three decades of religion's 'reintroduction' into politics.

The background is that prior to the eighteenth century and the subsequent formation and development of the modern (secular) international state system, religion was a key ideology that often stimulated political conflict between societal groups both within and between countries. Following the Peace of Westphalia in 1648 and subsequent development of centralised states first in Western Europe and then via European colonisation to most of the rest of the world, the political importance of religion declined around the world, including as an organising ideology both domestically and internationally.

In the early twenty-first century, however, there is clear resurgence of political involvement involving a range of religious entities. This has been especially noticeable in the post-Cold War era (that is, since 1989) in all regions of the world, including among the so-called 'world religions' (Buddhism, Christianity, Confucianism, Hinduism, Islam and Judaism). Although what started this development is open to question, many scholars would agree on the importance of the Islamist Iranian revolution of 1978–9 as a key event that definitively marked the 'reappearance' of political religion in global politics. This was such an epochal event because the government of putatively 'modern' and 'secular' Iran decided to remove religion from the public realm in the interests of 'progress' and 'development', like Turkey decades before, and to pursue a consciously Western-derived, secular development model.

But that was not all. Over the last three decades, scholars have sought to explain numerous examples of religious actors acting politically around the world, including in Europe, that most apparently secular of regions. While in Europe it was long believed that religion was increasingly marginal in terms of its public role, in recent years political controversies have raged over issues such as the wearing of headscarves in schools in France and elsewhere and the mention of Christianity in the putative European Constitution. More generally, as several of the contributions to this book have made clear, religious issues are of growing importance in many European polities and in an overall European context. A recent book edited by Byrnes and Katzenstein (2006) focuses on effects that the recent enlargement of the European Union (EU) – to include countries with different and stronger religious traditions – may have on the

Union as a whole, especially on its presumed homogeneity and assumed secular nature. When examined through the focal point of the region's main trans-national religious communities – Catholicism, Orthodoxy and Islam – it is clear that various religious factors are not stepping stones but stumbling blocks towards Europe's further integration. This is because each of the religious tradi-tions is putting forward concepts of European identity and European union that differ substantially from how the European integration process is generally understood by political leaders and scholars. Rapid and drastic secularisation in Western Europe over the last few decades has not, however, substantially dimin-ished the continuing unease with which many non-Muslim Europeans consider the presence of Islam and European Muslims in their midst. Exacerbated by 11 September 2001, the subsequent American and British involvement in Afghani-stan and Iraq and the London bombs of 7 July 2005, societal unease has centred on several concerns. Both secular European elites and Europe's religious Muslim citizens have been concerned with the issue of how to assimilate and incorporate different cultural backgrounds into the societal and political fabric of their coun-tries and, by extension, Europe overall. There is also, however, another factor: a fundamental division between the 'secular' – regarded by many Europeans as 'normal', 'progressive' and 'enlightened' – and the 'religious' – widely regarded as 'backward' and 'reactionary'.

Clearly, the issue of the role and position of Muslims in relation to issues of citizenship, secularisation and democracy is central to our understanding more generally of the nature of the relationship between religion and politics in Europe. However, among religious actors not only Muslims seek to pursue polit-ical and societal goals. Davie (2000) reminds us that it is not only Islam which falls into this context in Europe. She underlines that there is a particular empha-sis in the region on (1) currents of religion outside the mainstream churches, (2) the significance of the religious factor more generally in European societies and (3) how Europe fits in overall parameters of faith around the world. Davie is particularly interested in what she calls 'European exceptionalism'. This is a ref-erence to patterns of religion in Europe that are not prototypical of global religi-osity, but peculiar to the European continent. It follows that the relatively low levels of religious activity in modern Europe are not simply the result of early modernisation; they are part of what it means to be European and need to be understood in these terms. In a later book, Davie (2002) examines Europe from the outside, asking what forms of religion are widespread in the modern world but do not occur in most parts of Europe. One important example she notes is Pentecostalism.

This is not, then, to claim that the public role and position of religion is only a European issue. Take the example of the United States, where Pentecostalism is an important, albeit minority, religious tradition. There is much scholarly and popular agreement that secularisation is less well advanced than in Europe. In the USA, for example, more than half Americans claim to attend religious ser-vices regularly, which is three to four times the European norm. In addition, eight words – 'In God We Trust' and 'United States of America' – appear symbiotically linked, appearing on all US currency, both coins and notes. The continuing popular significance of religion in the USA is, however, a historical issue with cultural roots, deriving from the original European settlers in the seventeenth and eighteenth centuries, many of whom shared an Anglo-Protestant culture. This has stayed an important cultural factor until the present time.

Yet America is by no means an exception that 'proves' the 'modernisation equals secularisation' hypothesis. Around the world, especially over the last three decades we have seen increased political involvement of religious actors in many countries, as well as internationally. Since 11 September 2001, in particular, much journalistic and scholarly attention has been focused upon Islamism[2] (pejoratively, 'Islamic fundamentalism'), particularly in the MENA, to the extent that a casual observer might assume that the entire region is polarised religiously and politically between, on the one hand, Jews and Muslims and, on the other, various strands of pro-status quo and anti-status quo Islam. This perception is perhaps understandable in the light of the fact that both Jews and Muslims claim 'ownership' of various holy places, including the city of Jerusalem, with its numerous religious buildings, many of which have fundamental importance to various religions, including Christianity, Islam and Judaism. Consequential conflict has also been a result of the plight of the continuing struggle for power between (mainly Jewish) Israel and the (mostly Muslim) Palestinians. In addition, throughout the MENA region, other political issues – notably what to do about a large number of non-democratic regional regimes and the role of Islam in relation to any fundamental political changes – also help focus attention on different perceptions of what is or is not desirable in relation to the interaction between religion and politics.

Overall, it is abundantly clear that political Islam is a significant political force, not only in the MENA but also further afield in, *inter alia*, Africa, Asia and Europe. In each of these regions, social and political movements inspired by Islam have recently grown in influence while in many cases emergence of new institutions and the opening of new places of worship have brought greater attention to religious observance. Only a few decades ago, Muslims were virtually invisible in Europe. Today, however, increased immigration has changed the situation, sometimes dramatically. Most obviously this is the case in terms of symbolic representation of 'Muslim-ness', reflected in burgeoning numbers of Mosques and Islamic centres, now found in numerous European population centres. In addition, in relation to both society and politics, Muslims are consistently visible throughout all aspects of social and political life. The consequence for our understanding of Islam and its political and societal ramifications is profound. No longer can we speak easily and unthinkingly about one 'traditional' Islamic world and one 'modern' Europe. Now, we need to think about, discuss and analyse the significance of Islam in Europe. At the same time, Islam has also engaged in a process of modernisation, seeking to come to terms with its status as a minority religion in some parts of the world and a majority one in others.

In the European context, as already noted, the key question is Islam's regional and country-specific institutionalisation. There, secularisation represents much more than the legal separation of politics and religion: it has become the cultural norm for increasing numbers of Europeans. A consequence is that Muslim communities and their claims for the public recognition of Islam are perceived by some Europeans as a threat. The important issue then is the nature and consequences of societal and political interactions between Muslims and the more or less secularised public spaces of European countries, with the aim of assessing challenges which such interactions necessarily imply both for European Muslims and for the societies where they live.

Ramadan (2003) argues that Islam can and should feel at home in Europe and elsewhere in the West. He focuses on Islamic law (*shari'a*) and tradition in order to analyse whether Islam is in conflict with Western ideals. According to Ramadan, there is no contradiction between them. He also identifies several key areas where Islam's universal principles can be 'engaged' in the West, including education, inter-religious dialogue, economic resistance and spirituality. As the number of Muslims living in the West grows, the question of what it means to be a Western Muslim becomes increasingly important to the futures of both Islam and the West. While the media are focused on – some would say obsessed with – radical political Islam, Ramadan claims a 'silent revolution' is sweeping Islamic communities in the West, as Muslims actively seek ways to live in harmony with their faith within a Western context. 'Western' Muslims, both women and men – living, *inter alia*, in Denmark, France, Germany, the Netherlands, Spain, the United Kingdom and the United States – are now in many cases reshaping their religion into one that is faithful to the principles of Islam, albeit increasingly contoured by European and American cultures, and definitively rooted in Western societies. Roy (2004) also examines the issue of Muslims in the West. He is interested in the prejudices and simplifications used in much popular culture and media in the West regarding Muslims. Like Ramadan, Roy explores how individual Muslims are reacting to (not necessarily against) globalisation and Westernisation, informed by various political and social issues.

Captured in the title the book has a general focus – religion and politics in Europe, the Middle East and North Africa. It also has a specific one: challenges to citizenship, secularisation and democracy in these regions. The first section of the book focuses upon the topic of citizenship in various political contexts, including that of post-Second-World War European integration. We saw that over the last sixty years the politics surrounding the project of European integration have provided a clear context and focus whereby various religious actors – including, individuals, groups and institutions – have all played important roles. Various roles have been adopted which have spanned a range of reactions to the project of Europe: on the one hand, there are the esteemed founding fathers of the original European idea and ideal, while, on the other, there are the determined and implacable critics and enemies. There are also, in addition, peacemakers and reconcilers, as well as those who cry loudly and consistently: 'no surrender'. Finally, there are scheming power-seekers and upholders of popular accountability. In the context of Europe's regional development, religious actors have rarely if ever been the most important personnel, although in some cases, like Northern Ireland's Ian Paisley, they have often been both the most colourful and those with the loudest voices. Overall, we saw that attempts to account for the changing and variable roles played by religious actors tested hypotheses which purport to make sense of them, on the one hand, by reference to their backgrounds in different confessional traditions and, on the other, by reference to the principal varieties of religion (observable across all traditions) to which they appear to conform.

We also saw that, despite such developments, neither transnational Islamic citizenship (the *umma*) nor regional citizenship (the EU) nor any other forms of what might be called post-national citizenship have replaced *national* citizenship; nor is there any indication that such a development might occur in the near future. In other words, *individual* rights and *nation*-states are the typical fundaments of membership rules and citizenship in individual countries in Europe. In Safran's (2002) recent edited book, contributors examine the place of religion in various countries and regions, focusing on Western and East–Central Europe, North America, the Middle East and South Asia. The indications are that many countries in these regions are comparable in three main ways: (1) they are committed to constitutional rule; (2) they embrace a more or less secular culture; and (3) they feature formal guarantees of freedom of religion. Yet in all the cases examined in the book, religion affects the political system in some form of legal establishment, semi-legitimation, subvention and/or selective institutional arrangements. In addition, its role is also reflected both societally and politically in other ways, including in relation to cultural norms, electoral behaviour and public policies. The overall finding is that while relationships between religion and politics come in many varieties in different countries, all are faced with three major challenges: modernity, democracy and the increasingly multi-ethnic and multi-religious nature of their societies.

One of the contributions to the present book focuses on this set of issues in relation to the Basque struggle for autonomy or independence. The Basque struggle is an anomaly: one of the last violent ethno-territorial struggles in Western Europe. The political process initiated by a recent ceasefire by the leading Basque nationalist group, ETA, in March 2006 raised hopes for a peaceful and permanent solution – but this optimism came to an abrupt end with ETA bomb attacks in Madrid on 30 December 2006. Before this, from the late 1980s, pro-peace associations from civil society had joined forces and fought against persistent violence, both in the Spanish and, to a lesser extent, in the French Basque Country. Over time, the Roman Catholic Church played a prominent role in these new forms of pro-peace action.

In the Basque context, the church's activism can be seen in relation to three complementary perspectives. First, the Catholic Church has specific features that differentiate it from other civil society actors. The church has long buttressed its actions by a theological and ideological principle of subsidiarity conducive to popular mediation and peace-keeping initiatives. Even in the secularised Basque society, or perhaps because of this secularisation, the Catholic Church is still favourably thought of by a large majority of the population. This is because many Basques see the church as both deeply involved in local realities and yet able to step aside from often ferocious and polarised political debates. This context enables the church to play a unique role as a mediator both within the Basque society and between the Basques as a people and the Spanish and French states.

Two of our contributors focus on the political role of the Roman Catholic Church, respectively in Poland and Italy. In relation to Poland, the main issue was the political role of the Catholic Church in relation to moral and ethical issues, with particular emphasis on gender-related issues. As already noted in relation to Israel, many European societies, including those of Poland and Italy, are now increasingly beset by what might be called 'moral conflicts': that is, where secular and religious world views collide; in Israel, the issue has perhaps reached the stage of a 'culture war'. What this leads to is that, despite continuing processes of individual detachment from traditional religion, both the secular state and 'non-religious' parts of society are obliged to accept the involvement of often resurgent religious communities in the public realm, involving in many cases a focus on often controversial issues of relevance to religion, covering local, national and sometimes international concerns. For example, under current conditions of swift and significant biotechnological developments and corresponding European efforts to harmonise policy regulations, national policies in all European countries are increasingly influenced by moral questions. Note, however, that this does not mean that religion necessarily gains the upper hand in such debates or that it is able to achieve the results it would prefer.

While concerns towards the legalisation of genetic engineering or euthanasia pose ethical problems to all liberal democracies, including that of Italy as we saw in the book, the quests for a liberal abortion regime and an agreed legal status for homosexual partnerships are also particularly salient issues, especially in predominantly Catholic or Orthodox Christian societies in Europe. In predominantly Catholic Poland, for example, this was not the outcome that was necessarily expected following the decline of communist rule and subsequent democratisation. Nevertheless, because the theme of societal values – especially those concerning family life and sexual ethics – are fundamental to the Catholic Church's teaching and societal position, it is hardly surprising that these concerns have become increasingly significant.

Casanova noted nearly twenty years ago that 'religion continues to have and will likely continue to have a public dimension' (Casanova 1994: 66). All the contributions to this book abundantly support Casanova's perceptive observation, while taking the basic observation further, furnishing both nuance and detail. In relation to Poland, for example, religious deprivatisation post-communism has influenced how the Catholic Church has seen its societal and religious position: resolutely to defend what it sees as its corporate interests, as well as those of its 'flock', in the public sphere. The post-communist era of democratic transition and eventual democratic consolidation has also impacted upon the wider relationships between society, public religion and politics in the context of a 'moral conflict', an issue of key importance to the wider issues of both democratisation and secularisation in the society.

We saw that Poles are increasingly unwilling to accept unthinkingly the view of the Catholic Church on a variety of both societal and political issues. Around 50 per cent of Poles now believe that that the church should in general be less influential on life in Poland. Within this context, gay, lesbian and feminist interest groups have become increasingly high-profile, demanding equal rights while opposing the position of the Catholic Church and its value-based political position. One of our contributions analysed the political engagement of homosexual and left-wing liberal actors and the church's response since the early 2000s, during a time of often dynamic democratisation. We saw that there were important areas in this context, including: agenda setting, policy implementation and policy output in the wider context of secularisation and democratisation.

The contemporary involvement of the Roman Catholic Church in moral issues in another European country was the focus of another of our contributions, this time in relation to Italy.

We saw that, as in Poland, the church in Italy now plays a different role in the political system compared to the past. For over fifty years, from soon after the Second World War, the church was represented in the political scene by the Christian Democratic Party (DC). Over time, however, notably in relation to the demise of the First Republic and the collapse of the DC, the church embarked on a new strategy to bolster its public presence, involving a revised political representation strategy. As a result, the church became an 'extra-parliamentarian' actor. More recently, key representatives of the church in Italy, including the Italian Episcopal Conference and its president, Cardinal Ruini, have performed a leading role in relation to the church's current strategy of continuation of its political and societal influence, especially on moral questions. Consequently, the Catholic Church has sought to distance itself from all political parties and political alliances. Instead, it has worked primarily as a lobby group, directly, without any intermediary. In other words, its political representation has moved 'from the party to the pulpit'.

Over the last few years, however, in a shift reminiscent of what we saw in relation to both Israel and Poland, the political scene in Italy has been complicated by the introduction into the public debate of ethical and moral issues. In Italy, the focus is mainly on *biopolitics* – that is, 'life as moral value' – and it is now at the heart of the political agenda, a new frontier in relation to social and moral questions. Specific issues – including, stem cell research, medically assisted fertilisation, abortion, non-surgical abortions using the RU486 pill, the 'biological will',[3] euthanasia and cloning, together with other social issues, including the family first and foremost, have all become issues where politics – and Catholic parliamentarians – seek to influence public debate and personal beliefs. As a result, both ethical and political bipolarism have become interwoven in public debate, and the confrontation among political and religious actors is often very heated. In Italy, over the last few years, the Catholic Church has played a direct and resolute role, taking a public stand, trying to influence political decisions. It has acted in the socio-political scene as a *political entrepreneur*, mobilising resources and taking advantage of the context and the (open) windows of opportunity in the political structure.

When we turn in the book away from Europe, there is a continuation of involvement of religious entities in both moral and overtly political questions. We examined the issue of the relationship between citizenship, politics and religion in contemporary Israel, in a context informed by concerns about morality in modern circumstances of, *inter alia*, globalisation. We noted that, against the predictions of the secularisation paradigm that forecast the public demise of religion and consequent irrelevance for public life, religion actually has lost none of its social and political significance in Israel. Indeed, it consistently plays a central role in political and social life. Casanova (1994: 2006) has described a process of religious deprivatisation that refuses to be relegated to the margins of society and emerges instead as a political force to be reckoned with. Thus, religious movements of various types clash with secularising trends to protect their preferred religiously oriented way of life (Haynes 2006) in what is sometimes referred to as a 'culture war'. In Israel, the notion of culture war refers to a tense social and political context, characterised by a growing schism between two poles – the 'religious' and the 'secular' – polarised by different values and moving towards what some see as an 'inevitable' clash over the precise boundaries of state and society. While dramatic events and statement at times give credence to the thesis, overall the evidence of a culture war in Israel, waged both locally and globally, involving an advancing, confident secularism and an equally resilient, resurgent religion, is inconclusive. As a consequence, the issue becomes something different: not only how and in what contexts religion and secularism are advancing or withdrawing but also in what realms these dynamics are operating and how the issue affects conceptions of citizenship in Israeli. As a result, what we see is not a 'culture war' between two coherent groups of citizens with set agendas but, rather, different struggles waged in different realms, involving different constituencies and with different levels of political intensity.

Comparing the case of Israel with other countries enables us to conclude that the former is a highly volatile example of a world trend of increasing but varied secular-religious clashes with, on the one hand, a territorial debate strongly informed by religious dogma and, on the other hand, a secularising public sphere in the context of a societal religious resurgence. Two major developments underscore the concern of a culture war. The first is the overlap between religiosity/secularity and hawkish/dovish perceptions that turns the question of Israel's future borders into a religious debate. The second development is the erosion of status quo church–state arrangements, which once defined the role of religion in public life in Israel, from the regulation of marriage to the observation of the Sabbath as a day of rest.

Moving on from a focus on citizenship, which occupied the first section of the book, the second key theme of the book is the relationship between secularisation and religion. Among other relationships, the book focuses on the often-noted social and political resurgence of Islam in the Muslim world; our case studies in the book in this regard include both Turkey and Morocco. The findings of this book underscore an often-repeated point: there is a widespread rise of political Islam or 'Islamism', typically involving local, national, regional and/or international networks. The book presents some important findings about a relatively little-known phenomenon: connections between political Islam, so-called 'Islamic economics' and transnational Islamist business networks in Turkey. The relevant transnational networks are reflective of processes of globalisation and its pervasive forces that foster extensive, sometimes unexpected, linkages involving various actors and spheres. Religion-based networks are no exceptions in this overarching trend. What role do they play in processes of secularisation?

Our focus on Turkey includes a perusal of what is sometimes known as *homo Islamicus*, with reference to 'Islamic economics', epitomising what some have regarded as an ideational legitimacy which fits in well philosophically with current, dominant discourses of neoliberalism. Islamic finance institutions in Turkey facilitate the workings of Islamic economics. Turkey is a particular interesting example as it is a country which is often said to be 'looking West while moving East', a reference to the country's European aspirations albeit with roots in Muslim culture. Islamic business in Turkey has strong linkages with the recent upsurge of political Islam, not least involving serving members of the current government, under the control of the AKP (Justice and Development Party). Our concern is to understand the interaction of both transnational and national Islamic business networks; expansion of Islamic finance and ideational factors sometimes referred to as the so-called 'quiet Islamic Reformation' or 'Islamic Calvinism' said to be taking place in Turkey at the present time.

We saw that Islamic capital began to be an important factor in Turkey's economy from the 1980s, with connections to the recent unprecedented and emphatic rise of political Islam in the country. In short, we saw the development of intertwined processes: the rise of transnational Islamist networks of business which facilitated dispersion of new ideas; and connections between these networks and political Islam. We saw political outcomes linked to emergence, development and expansion of expanding Islamic networks involving various economic actors.

The issue of secularisation and its impact on social and political processes is also the concern of our case study on Morocco. It gave further evidence for the highly controversial nature of the role of Islamist parties in the Middle East and North Africa (MENA). In many cases, for example Hamas in Palestine and Hezbullah in Lebanon, Islamist movements have decided to take part in conventional politics, often with considerable electoral success. Nevertheless, and here the examples of Hamas and Hezbullah are again notable, such attempts to play the 'game' of political participation are typically treated with considerable suspicion by domestic governments, domestic political opponents and international actors, including the United States and the European Union. On the other hand, there is a quandary, especially for the external actors. It is this: not to recognise the political clout of Islamists in a political system seeking regeneration is to make democratisation very difficult or impossible to achieve. Thus, some scholars and policy-makers see Islamism as a potential pro-democracy resource, while others see Islamists as enemies of democracy and potentially authoritarian. Such polarising attitudes are generally the product of an attempt to establish what can be considered the true nature of such movements, particularly with respect to their democratic credentials and commitment. Central to this question is the relationship between democracy and secularisation: what should the relationship be between them? Our case study on Morocco provides no clear answer.

One of our contributions seeks to bridge the gap between Europe and the MENA by looking at interactions between Greek and Turkish religious and political actors. The focus is on the role of the Greek Orthodox Church in the development of Greek–Turkish relations; a sub-theme is the role of religion in both countries' processes of democratisation over time. While both countries have democratised in recent years, Greek–Turkish relations are still highlighted by enduring political disputes, with various foci. In the related contexts of Greek nationalism and democratisation, the Orthodox Church has played an ambiguous role. Over time, it can be argued, the church has played an increasingly bifurcated role, illustrated during recent rapprochement efforts between Greece and Turkey. The key to understanding the political role of the church in Greece–Turkey relations is to understand that while one branch of the church – the Church of Greece – generally takes positions which do not contribute to the peaceful resolution of Greek–Turkish disputes and instead appears to embed existing prejudices, the Istanbul-based Ecumenical Patriarchate has a different, more conciliatory, position. Despite the fact that the latter has been undermined as a consequence of anti-minority policies enacted by successive governments in Turkey, it actively promotes Greek–Turkish cooperation and the peaceful resolution of existing disputes, and has earned the respect of international political and religious leaders. In particular, the Istanbul-based Ecumenical Patriarchate supports the use of democratic mechanisms to try to resolve the long-running disputes between Greece and Turkey. The overall conclusion is that the differing views of the two branches of the church have their roots in processes of democratisation – in Greece since the mid-1970s, in Turkey since the mid-1980s. To understand the overall picture, we need to bear in mind the status of state–church relations in Greece, the role of leadership, and socio-political conditions in both Greece and Turkey over time. This uncovers an interactive relationship between religion, nationalism and democracy in both countries.

Overall, our book has shown that the interaction of religion and politics in Europe and the MENA is rich, multifaceted and complex. We have seen in the book that, not only in Turkey but also more generally in the MENA, it is now common for religious political actors to be heavily involved in questions of citizenship, secularisation and democratisation, albeit with variable outcomes. We observed in relation to Europe that religious actors of various kinds can also influence political outcomes in countries that are already democratic and secular.

Notes

1 The secular Congress Party emerged as the largest party following the elections of April/May 2004. The breakdown of seats in the 542-seat Lok Sabha was: Congress and allies 220, BJP and allies 185 and 'Others' 137.

2 An Islamist is a believer in or follower of Islam, someone who may be willing to use various political means to achieve religiously derived objectives.

3

> The Biological Will is a written statement made by a person who is sound of mind, specifying the limits he deems appropriate to establish for medical treatment, should he be incapacitated to decide about his health due to the onset of a condition of disablement arising from a disease, with no reasonable hope of recovering intellectual integrity.
>
> (www.leadershipmedica.com/sommari/2007/numero_04/Intervista_Marino/ GeninaIacobone/GeninaIacoboneUK.htm last accessed 5 March 2009)

Bibliography

Byrnes, T. and Katzenstein, P. (eds) (2006) *Religion in an Expanding Europe*, Cambridge: Cambridge University Press.

Casanova, J. (1994) *Public Religions in the Modern World*, Chicago: University of Chicago Press.

Casanova, J. (2006) 'Religion, Secular Identities and European Integration', in T. Byrnes and P. Katzenstein (eds), *Religion in an Expanding Europe*, Cambridge: Cambridge University Press.

Davie, G. (2000) *Religions in Modern Europe: A Memory Mutates*, Oxford: Oxford University Press.

Davie, G. (2002) *Europe: The Exceptional Case. Parameters of Faith in the Modern World*, London: Darton, Longman and Todd.

Haynes, J. (ed.) (2006) *The Politics of Religion*, London: Routledge.

Ramadan, T. (2003) *Western Muslims and the Future of Islam*, Oxford: Oxford University Press.

Roy, O. (2004) *Globalised Islam. The Search for a New Ummah*, London: Hurst.

Safran, W. (ed.) (2002) *The Secular and the Sacred: Nation, Religion and Politics*, London: Frank Cass.

Index